Thinking Through Material Culture

ARCHAEOLOGY, CULTURE, AND SOCIETY

Ian Hodder and Robert Preucel, Series Editors

A complete list of books in the series is available from the publisher.

Thinking Through Material Culture

An Interdisciplinary Perspective

Carl Knappett

PENN

University of Pennsylvania Press
Philadelphia

10 9 8 7 6 5 4 3 2 1

Published by
University of Pennsylvania Press
Philadelphia, Pennsylvania 19104-4011

Library of Congress Cataloging-in-Publication Data

Knappett, Carl.
   Thinking throuch material culture : an interdisciplinary perspective / Carl Knappett.
     p.   cm.—(Archaeology, culture, and society)
   ISBN 0-8122-3788-9 (cloth : alk. paper)
   Includes bibliographical references (p.   ) and index.
   1. Material culture.   I. Title.   II. Series.
GN406 . K59   2005
930.1—dc22   2004055473

Contents

Preface

This book has arisen out of my continuing engagement with archaeological artifacts from the Aegean Bronze Age. Faced with such artifacts there is a constant urge to understand what they may have meant in their original social contexts. Yet archaeologists are surprisingly ill-equipped when it comes to tackling the meaningfulness of the objects they unearth. There are many reasons for this state of affairs, not least a rather rigid understanding of what objects are and how it is that humans interact with them. What I have sought to do here is explore these basic theoretical issues—the status of objects and of the humans producing and using them—by looking at developments in a range of fields that confront such questions in relation to objects in the contemporary world. The disciplines in question include cognitive science, psychology, anthropology, sociology, and art history. I have also attempted to create a network of connections between some of these fields, and as such this volume endeavors to open up new paths for investigation. It seems important, however, that theoretical discussion should eventually be steered back toward archaeology; hence a deliberate effort is made to put the theory into practice. My concern is with material culture in both the present and the past.

An interdisciplinary venture of this kind entails a certain number of risks. Inevitably, much of the reading matter lies beyond orthodox academic boundaries. Although the rigidity of such boundaries is often decried, one quickly begins to see the logic of their existence—the implicit research agendas and hidden academic battles make for tricky terrain. Progress can be slow as one seeks to digest texts written with different vocabulary and accumulated assumptions. Mistakes and misunderstandings will surely be more common than one would have hoped. The hope is that these shortcomings may be forgiven, for the sake of seeing the value of new connections, if only roughly drawn.

One resource that is indispensable in such a project is time—time to head off along blind alleys and find a way back again. I have been fortunate enough to have been granted this luxury in the form of a Junior Research

Fellowship held at Christ's College, University of Cambridge. The vast majority of this book has been researched and written during the fellowship, and I would like to offer my thanks to the Master and Fellows of the College for this opportunity. I can only hope that the present contribution goes some way toward repaying their trust in leaving me to my own devices.

I owe an additional debt of gratitude to the series editors: to Ian Hodder, for his early enthusiasm and continued support, and to Bob Preucel, for his invaluable input. My thanks also go to Nic David for his careful reading and positive criticism. Others who have read sections and provided helpful remarks include Sander van der Leeuw, Clive Gamble, Sofia Voutsaki, Jane Hiddleston, Kostalena Michelaki, and Lambros Malafouris. To Lambros I am particularly grateful for a whole series of stimulating discussions over the course of the last couple of years.

As well as reading an earlier draft, Sander van der Leeuw was instrumental in organizing a two-month stint for me in Paris, during which time I was able to access bibliography unavailable in the UK. The Bibliothèque Nationale de France was an excellent environment in which to work, as was the office space in the Maison de l'Archéologie et de l'Ethnologie at Nanterre, kindly arranged by Serge Cleuziou.

I should also mention my involvement in a recently launched EU project entitled The Information Society as a Complex System (ISCOM), codirected by David Lane, Sander van der Leeuw, and Geoffrey West. Although the project is only in its early stages, I have already gained much from discussions with the various collaborators, not least Tim Evans, Ray Rivers, and Ole Peters of Imperial College, London, and Andrea Ginzburg, David Lane, Margherita Russo, Roberto Serra, and Federica Rossi of Università di Modena e Reggio Emilia.

For many useful discussions on a range of archaeological issues I should like to thank the following: John Bennet, Andy Bevan, Nicky Boivin, Neil Brodie, Cyprian Broodbank, James Conolly, Tim Cunningham, Jan Driessen, Véronique Durey, Donald Haggis, Yannis Hamilakis, Tim Ingold, Valasia Isaakidou, Vedia Izzet, Andy Jones, Vangelio Kiriatzi, Colin Macdonald, Sandy MacGillivray, Sophie Méry, Kostalena Michelaki, Nicoletta Momigliano, Irene Nikolakopoulou, Nicholas Postgate, Jean-Claude Poursat, Colin Renfrew, Valentine Roux, Hugh Sackett, Ilse Schoep, Peter Tomkins, Metaxia Tsipopoulou, Sofia Voutsaki, Peter Warren, and last, but very far from least, Todd Whitelaw.

For granting permission to reproduce figures and photographs my thanks go to the following people and institutions: Thierry Bonnot and the

Écomusée du Creusot-Montceau; David Kirsh; Lynn Margulis; Donald Norman and the Sandra Dijkstra Literary Agency; Alan Rayner; Duncan Watts; John Younger and Paul Rehak; Jean-Claude Poursat and l'École Française d'Athènes; Gerald Cadogan, Sandy MacGillivray, Colin Macdonald and the British School at Athens; DACS/ADAGP; MIT Press; Nike Inc.; Routledge and Thomson Publishing Services; The Library Company of Philadelphia; and the Library of the American Museum of Natural History. Olivier Gosselain has been especially helpful in providing material for figures 7.14 and 7.15. Antony Gormley has most generously allowed me to reproduce an image of his sculpture *Quantum Cloud VII* for the cover of this book, for which I am very grateful. I am also indebted to Seán Goddard of the Department of Archaeology at the University of Exeter for expertly redrawing a number of the figures and for help with formatting much of the artwork.

Finally, I would like to thank the team at Penn Press for all their good work—Jo Joslyn, Ted Mann, George Lang, and Alison Anderson.

Chapter 1

Introduction: Thinking Through Material Culture

A fire hydrant, a taxi cab, a rush of steam pouring up from the pavement—they were deeply familiar to me, and I felt I knew them by heart. But that did not take into account the mutability of those things, the way they changed according to the force and angle of the light, the way their aspect could be altered by what was happening around them: a person walking by, a sudden gust of wind, an odd reflection. Everything was constantly in flux, and though two bricks in a wall might strongly resemble each other, they could never be construed as identical. More to the point, the same brick was never really the same. It was wearing out, imperceptibly crumbling under the effects of the atmosphere, the cold, the heat, the storms that attacked it, and eventually, if one could watch it over the course of centuries, it would no longer be there. All inanimate things were disintegrating, all living things were dying. My head would start to throb whenever I thought of this, imagining the furious and hectic motions of molecules, the unceasing explosions of matter, the collisions, the chaos boiling under the surface of all things.

—Paul Auster, Moon Palace

This book advocates a full theoretical reappraisal of material culture and offers some initial steps toward this larger goal. Evidently it is written by an archaeologist and uses archaeological case studies. Indeed, of all disciplines it is archaeology that needs material culture most. It is perhaps surprising then that archaeology, while developing ever more sophisticated methodologies for artifact study, has not yet constructed similarly sophisticated theoretical models for understanding the roles of artifacts in human societies. So complex and daunting is such a task that it must inevitably be interdisciplinary in its scope, drawing upon cognitive science, psychology, sociology, anthropology, and history. And yet here's the rub. Many of these disciplines have only relatively recently begun to focus on material culture as a field worthy of serious attention. And rather than rue that this should have taken so long, we may see this as an exciting time to be thinking through material culture and its central yet ambiguous role in human societies. There seems to be real potential for building a more broadly based understanding of material culture, relevant to the past, the present and the future.

So a serious challenge lies before us: how are we to research material culture in an interdisciplinary fashion? Given the increasingly specialized nature of academic research, how is it possible to create an integrated body of theory that draws upon a wide range of disciplines? Does it not make the tag "jack of all trades, master of none" almost unavoidable? This book certainly runs this risk, but in the firm belief that it is a risk well worth taking. There are inevitable dangers in working with relatively unfamiliar areas such as cognitive science and psychology. But to my mind, the advances in these fields simply cannot be ignored by archaeologists truly interested in the role of material culture within human societies.

This interdisciplinary venture demands a process of hybridization, whereby connections are created between two seemingly different fields to form a common ground. Although rather daunting at first, it gradually becomes apparent, in a rather surprising fashion, how readily some areas lend themselves to such interbreeding. Interdisciplinarity is of course nothing new. Archaeologists have long looked to social anthropology (much more than anthropologists have looked to archaeology), and with the growth of cognitive archaeology more and more attention is being paid to some areas of psychology, notably evolutionary psychology (e.g., Mithen 1996; Renfrew and Scarre 1998). However, some deep fault lines that have existed for some time are only now being mended, such as between anthropology and psychology/cognitive science (cf. Hutchins 1995, 371), and anthropology and biology (Ingold 2000). Some of the various interdisciplinary connections that make up cognitive science are usefully summarized in diagram form by Bechtel et al. (1998, 94)—although archaeology is not explicitly included, it can easily be integrated, within what they term "sociocultural studies." Using the network diagram of Bechtel et al. as an analogy, the objective of this book is to explore some of the interconnections between disciplines as a means of moving us towards an integrated theory of material culture. I aim to create a new "network" in which previously separate entities and ideas are interwoven. Within this network, archaeology is considered to be a full and equal partner, able to make its own unique contribution to the interdisciplinary study of material culture.

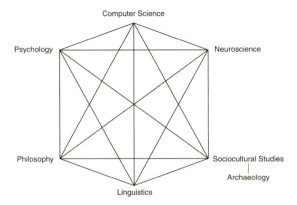

Figure 1.1. Diagram showing role of archaeology in relation to cognitive science.

To cut to the chase, I believe that to expand material culture theory we need to review the relationship between mind and matter, between agent and artifact. Given that the entire archaeological project of understanding past societies relies on these fundamental relationships it is surprising how little theorized they have remained.

Mind, Thought, Cognition

The "default" archaeological approach to recovering mind and thought is probably best encapsulated in the following lines from Childe's "Piecing Together the Past":

The archaeological record is constituted of the fossilized results of human *behaviour*, and it is the archaeologist's business to reconstitute that behaviour as far as he can and so to recapture the *thoughts* that behaviour expressed. (1956, 1; my emphasis)

There are a couple of important assumptions within this viewpoint that demand our attention. First, there is a clear hierarchy: thought is primary, behavior is secondary, and material expression is at the bottom of the chain. The archaeologist, of course, must work back and up from the material remains. Second, given that thoughts are separated from objects by behavior, it follows that the internal mind is buffered from the external world via the medium of action. We shall see in due course that this perspective is a classic expression of the Cartesian dualism that pervades not just archaeology but much social science.

Childe apparently believed such a progression, from materials to be-havior to thoughts, to be well within the realm of possibility for the archae-ologist. It is a hierarchical progression of this sort that was dubbed by Hawkes (1954) the "ladder of inference," though he was of the opinion that the ideational realm was all but inaccessible. To go no further than recon-structing past behavior from the archaeological record seems also to have been a tenet of New Archaeology, with attempts at recovering past thoughts dismissed as "palaeopsychology" (e.g., Binford 1965, discussed in Hodder 1984). There are, however, various ways Binford's perspective involves an almost willful misunderstanding of what "thought" might imply. First, it is hard to fathom exactly how Binford sees fit to isolate behavior from thought; as succinctly stated by Hodder, "the idea that archaeologists can get away without reconstructing ideas in the heads of prehistoric peoples is pure false consciousness and self-delusion" (1992, 18). Second, Binford insinuates that the archaeologists he accuses of engaging in "palaeopsychol-ogy" are chasing the conscious thoughts of individual people.[1] Returning to the Childe quote above, although no distinction is explicitly drawn between individual and collective thought, Childe certainly seems to imply the latter. This is understandable; after all, is not archaeology intrinsically better suited to commenting on the collective rather than the individual? The idea of "collective thought," of individuals somehow tuning into each other's minds, might sound a little odd when thus phrased. But it is meant in a sense more or less equivalent to "collective understandings" or "social atti-tudes." Thus Binford's fear that archaeologists might seek to recapture con-scious individual thought rather than tacit shared understandings is a rather peculiar one. Of course it is impossible for the mental processes of past in-dividuals not to form a part of a cognitive approach, but it is only a very limited part in relation to the collective (Hodder 1993, 254).

There is a third way in which Binford's views on the archaeological reconstruction of past thoughts are problematic: he assumes that thoughts occupy an internal domain, separated from the external world (following an essentially Cartesian logic). In this, however, he is not alone—Hodder too, as seen in the above quote, talks of the "ideas in the heads of prehis-toric peoples." It is apparent that, as far as Hodder is concerned, "thoughts" occupy the domain of the internal mind and are not to be found in the external world, that is to say, the domain of material culture. One of the main arguments of this book is that this dualistic conception, almost universal in archaeological thinking, hinders the full development of a satisfactory theory of material culture. Indeed, it is even found in some of the attempts that are made to define the scope of a "cognitive archaeology" (e.g., Flannery and Marcus 1993). Here the mind is conceived almost solely in terms of conscious mental operations, such as are assumed to be at work in the use of language. It is the mind's capacity for the mastery of symbolic systems that lies behind language, and indeed other forms of communication. It appears that Renfrew, for example, considers "cognitive" to be largely equivalent with "symbolic" (1993, 249; cf. also 1994, 1998), referring to those aspects of meaning that operate in a language-like fashion, notably in their ability to "communicate" a consciously encoded message (a theme to which we shall return below). However, some cognitive perspectives within archaeology barely concern themselves with symbolism at all—the *chaîne opératoire* approach depicts technological processes such as flintknapping or pottery manufacture as cognitive activities. Schlanger (1994), for example, states that such activities are related to the "doing mind" rather than the "thinking mind"—in other words, his focus is on the practical rather than the symbolic facets of cognition.

This distinction is echoed in the work of Hodder, who identifies two types of socially situated cognition (1992, 205; 1993, 255; 1999, 76). His proposed scheme of "linguistic knowledge" on the one hand and "practical knowledge" on the other is largely based on a distinction made by Bloch (1991), an anthropologist rather than a psychologist. One way of understanding the difference is through an example—riding a bicycle. It is possible for someone to be told how to ride a bicycle, to understand the principles involved in the activity, without actually being able to perform those activities. It is argued that the cognitive processes through which we acquire explicit understandings of phenomena (linguistic knowledge, or "connaissance") are quite different from those involved in the acquisition and embodiment of motor skills (practical knowledge, or "savoir-faire"). The first type of knowledge is held in the mind, the second in the body; the first is explicit, is based on formal symbolic codes, and is focused on communication, whereas the second is implicit, nonsymbolic, and noncommunicative. Given that the model for the first type of knowledge is clearly language, the difference between the two seems essentially to be that of "saying" versus "doing" (Hodder 1993, 255), and tallies with the distinction made by Schlanger between the "thinking mind" and the "doing mind."

Therefore, one assumption would be that any communication in material culture operates in a language-like fashion, that is, through symbolism. But then we also find contradictory statements, such as those that emerge when the distinction between linguistic and practical knowledge is likened to that between "connaissance" (knowing that) and "savoir-faire" (knowing how). Hodder elsewhere (1992, 205) chooses to subdivide "connaissance" into discursive and nondiscursive knowledge—the former is explicit and linguistic, the latter is implicit and nonverbal.[2] If "connaissance" is at the same time equivalent to "linguistic knowledge," we then find ourselves discussing explicit vs. nonverbal linguistic knowledge. Clearly this latter category does not make a great deal of sense. One might, of course, alter this to speak of verbal as opposed to nonverbal communication, and adapt Bloch's "linguistic knowledge" so that it becomes "communicative knowledge." But a plethora of problems remains nonetheless. For example, how is nonverbal communicative knowledge organized—according to symbolic codes (i.e., like verbal knowledge), or through nonsymbolic cognitive processes? And how do these communicative forms of knowledge connect, if at all, with practical knowledge?[3]

Hodder's version of "cognition" is clearly problematic, in many of the same ways as Renfrew's version—particularly in terms of the connections made between cognition, symbolism, language, and communication. Thus both cognitive-processual and post-processual approaches run into difficulties because of their adherence to a set of assumptions, based on a Cartesian worldview, that situate mind, cognition, language, and thought in a different domain from body, perception, practice, and action. Renfrew's equation between cognition and symbolism (1993, 1994), particularly as taken up by Flannery and Marcus (1993), results in the exclusion of many practical, "nonsymbolic" domains from the remit of cognitive archaeology (as we shall see below). On the other hand, the *chaîne opératoire* approach chooses these very nonsymbolic domains as its focus, and it too can be seen as a version of cognitive archaeology. Hodder's version does allow for the existence of nonsymbolic cognitive processes, and their relevance to a cognitive archaeology. The issue of how to arrive at a nondualistic theory of cognition is crucial—we shall be exploring this constantly through the chapters that follow, particularly in Chapter 3. But another major sticking point for both cognitive-processual and post-processual approaches is the confusion over symbolism and communication in material culture. We will now discuss this confusion, particularly as it brings us around to the issue of *meaning* in material culture too.

Symbolism and Meaning

Within cognitive-processual approaches, cognition and symbolism are, as we have seen, very much interwoven and inseparable issues. Thus, logically, "cognitive" applies only to those areas of communication that are organized on a symbolic basis, that is, in a language-like way, using formal conventions. Flannery and Marcus express this quite perfectly when they recommend restricting the scope of cognitive archaeology to the areas of cosmology, religion, ideology, and iconography.

Flannery and Marcus do acknowledge that "such common subsistence-settlement behaviours as hunting, fishing, farming, plant-collecting, tool-making, and so on" actually involve the deployment of intelligence. Nonetheless, such activities and their material correlates are deemed to lie beyond the scope of cognitive archaeology. This is presumably because such activities are not considered "symbolic"—fishing does not communicate a message (and thus a "belief") in the way a religious inscription or funerary depiction can. The problem here seems to lie in the narrow equivalence drawn between "symbolism" and meaning. Yet there are many ways in which objects and actions can be meaningful without necessarily being in the least bit symbolic. Fishing may not be symbolic in the strictest sense, but can we then say that the activity has no meaning? Of course not. Quite simply, we need to recast the equivalence drawn by Renfrew between "cognitive" and "symbolic." But let us first see how others have approached the connections between symbolism, communication, and meaning.

Just as Flannery and Marcus use an essentially linguistic model in implicitly equating "communicative" with "symbolic," so we see a parallel tendency in the post-processual literature, albeit far more explicit: "Given the long tradition which considers the symbolic in terms of signs in a language (Hodder 1989), the challenge of a symbolic archaeology is to explore the relationship between material culture and language" (Hodder 1992, 201). Here we see the idea that objects are to material culture as words are to language: they are elements within a symbolic code (Hodder 1989; Buchli 1995). Just as one needs to understand a language as a symbolic system to understand properly an individual word within it, so the symbolic meanings of objects can only be understood with a knowledge of a culture's symbolic codes. This is very much an idealist approach, a criticism that can be leveled at both processual and post-processual camps. Yet in the post-processual scheme (as epitomized by Hodder at least), this is not the only way in which meaning occurs. Hodder acknowledges the existence too of "functional meanings," which accrue through practice rather than through representational codes (e.g., Hodder 1992, 1993, 1999). Although he is keen to stress that symbolic and functional meanings are very much interdependent, in effect, the two do tend to remain rather separate in archaeological analysis.

Thus it emerges that the boundary between two domains, the practical/functional on the one hand and the symbolic/communicative on the other, is drawn in different ways. Flannery and Marcus assume that the practical cannot be meaningful, symbolic, or communicative; presumably they would also maintain that the reverse is true, that the symbolic cannot really be treated on the same terms as the practical (hence for them only the symbolic domain becomes the subject of cognitive archaeology). Hodder too constructs a boundary between functional and symbolic domains; in contrast, however, he contends that meaning *can* inhere in the functional domain. In his earlier work, he also says the reverse is true, that the symbolic domain can be treated from a functional perspective. In *Symbols in Action* (1982), for example, he takes on broad aspects of the "symbolic functionalist" approach, in which it is argued that the functional meanings of artifacts may sometimes lie in their capacity for communicating information, presumably through "symbolic" processes (cf. Wobst 1977; Wiessner 1983; and more recently Wattenmaker 1998). Aspects of material culture, notably "adjunct" features such as decoration, are invested with energy because they have a communicative role. Thus the symbolic is brought within the realm of the functional; but it does not seem as if this approach allows for the functional to be treated from a symbolic perspective. There are a number of problematic assumptions, such as the idea that a producer knowingly encodes information in an artifact so that it may be interpreted by the consumer, not to mention the uncritical borrowing of a linguistic model for material culture (for further criticisms see Dietler and Herbich 1998).

What we can certainly say for all of the above approaches is that they confuse the difficult concepts of "communication" and "signification" (see Dietler and Herbich 1998, 244). They fail to acknowledge that an entity may be seen as a sign without necessarily being part of a communicative act. For example, smoke usually indicates the presence of fire, and as such is a sign. However, this is not the same as saying that smoke communicates a message. If a forest fire ignites spontaneously, the smoke seen in the distance is understood to have meaning, but is not communicating a message. However, if a forest fire is interpreted as an act of arson, with the arsonists responsible known to be using this means of conveying a political message, then the smoke seen from a distance may well be understood to be communicative. The point to draw from this example is that, although signification and communication may very often overlap, they need not do so at all.

Archaeologists and anthropologists have tended to think of both signification and communication in narrow linguistic terms; in other words, symbolism is thought to be fundamental to both. Yet we need to realize that communication is about pragmatic action as much as it is about signification; and, moreover, that signification involves much more than just symbolism. There are many different ways in which entities can have meaning without being symbols—after all, smoke is not a *symbol* for fire, but is rather an *index* of fire (for more on this, see Chapter 5). This means, of course, that taking on the subject of cognition requires an engagement not just with symbolism, but with the much broader topic of signification. This can incorporate many forms of association and reference, besides those that are language-like. And, most important, all those everyday activities dismissed by Flannery and Marcus come right back onto the agenda. Acknowledging that the domain of the pragmatic and the everyday may be meaningful is just one step among many. We also need to work hard at overcoming a series of deep-seated dualisms between practical and linguistic, between doing and thinking, between functional and symbolic. Thankfully, this appears to be happening already, with dialectical perspectives on human-thing relations just emerging in archaeological theory (Thomas 1998b, 2000a; Kus 2000; Hodder 2001, 9). Nonetheless, the difficulties we face in this task are considerable, as expressed by Jean-Pierre Warnier in his book *Construire la culture matérielle*, in which he says that although we know that an articulation between the pragmatic and significative domains exists, we do not know *how* it works.[4]

Understanding the nature of this articulation is crucial if we are to construct a theory of material culture that is at all adequate. But there are many steps we need to take to get even close. For instance, we only have an approximate grasp of the status of physical objects in relation to human subjects; thus in the chapter that follows we examine this relationship, developing the idea that the human subject must be understood simultaneously in terms of biological animacy, psychological agency and social personhood. We look at the extent to which physical objects are drawn into these roles. In Chapter 3 we introduce the topics of cognition, perception, and action in an attempt to throw some light on the processes through which mind, action, and matter hold together and coimplicate each other. In this we draw heavily upon work in cognitive science and ecological psychology, arriving at an approach to cognition that is appropriate to material culture, sailing between the extremes of idealism and materialism.

This allows us to move toward further theory-building in Chapter 4, through a discussion of various kinds of network models for understanding the connectivities that hold together humans and nonhumans in heterogeneous social groupings. Chapter 5 takes on this theme of connectivity, but with a more explicit focus on cultural meanings: we develop a semiotic approach to material culture, based on the fundamental work of Charles Sanders Peirce and more recent contributions by scholars such as Sonesson, Gottdiener, and Gell, rather than being derived from Saussurean linguistic models that are inadequate for understanding meaning in material culture. The overall approach thus constructed is then put into practice in Chapter 6, through a discussion of various categories of contemporary material culture; everyday objects, art objects, and magical objects are all investigated, with an emphasis on the fluidity between these different registers. Cases cited range from the everyday coffee cup to Trobriand canoe-boards, and from French stoneware to the ready-mades of Duchamp. In Chapter 7, in order to emphasize that our approach is readily applicable to ancient as well as modern contexts, we present archaeological case studies drawn from the Aegean Bronze Age. The focus is on certain categories of Minoan artifacts and techniques, and the ways in which they can be understood as meaningful within sociotechnical networks. Finally, Chapter 8 contains concluding remarks and some comments on future prospects: if cognitive archaeology is to be the archaeology of the future (Renfrew 2001, 33), it needs to be developed in new post-Cartesian and nondualistic directions. This is the aim of *Thinking Through Material Culture.*

Chapter 2
Animacy, Agency, and Personhood

Sauron was diminished, but not destroyed. His Ring was lost but not un-made. The Dark Tower was broken, but its foundations were not re-moved; for they were made with the power of the Ring, and while it re-mains they will endure.

—J. R. R. Tolkien, The Fellowship of the Ring

The piecing together of a theoretical framework for understanding material culture is a precarious process, as a number of key conceptual relationships are in need of review and adaptation. Here then we begin with a consideration of the status of objects in relation to the various guises taken by the human subject. Humans are organisms, like any another animal species, with biological animacy and corporeality. Yet humans also possess agency and personhood, which can be considered from psychological and social perspectives respectively. Durkheim saw the biological and the psychological together forming "the individual," a level of existence separated from "the social" (Gofman 1998, 66). Mauss, however, rather than adopt this dualistic formula, chose to elide these human dimensions in describing "l'homme total" as *bio-psycho-social* (Mauss 1936; Warnier 1999a, 18). He saw the psychological as a kind of cogwheel ("roue d'engrenage") between the biological and the social; and Warnier (1999b) suggests that where Mauss uses the term psychological we may replace it with "subject." Warnier's point is well taken, but I would argue that the term "subject" is too broad; what is required is a term that can be linked to the psychological dimension of "l'homme total." I propose the term "agent" as more workable. Thus in this chapter we are able to discuss the various aspects of the human being as ecological organism, as psychological agent and as social person.[1] This still leaves us the possibility of investigating the idea that the human as *agent* is somehow intermediary between the human as organism and as person.[2] And, of course, in none of these guises is the human subject neatly separated from the surrounding environment: the human organism-agent-person becomes inextricably enfolded with material culture. Exploring the processes whereby this coalescence of object and subject occurs is a crucial step in our attempts to build material culture theory.

The Nature of Life

How do we differentiate between a human subject and a material object? The most fundamental difference between them would appear to be that the former is animate while the latter is not. It seems to be nothing more than a matter of common sense that objects are inanimate; they occupy an entirely separate ontological category from living organisms. But what exactly is it that differentiates them? How do we go about defining a living system as opposed to an inanimate one? Of course characterizing the nature of *life* is an age-old problem, the roots of which lie at the dawn of Western philosophy and the debate over the relative importance of form versus substance.[3] Pythagoreans separated the two and considered form to be preeminent. In biological terms, this would mean understanding a living organism in terms of its overall pattern and form rather than its substance and composition. In other words, it is "form" that differentiates the animate human from the inanimate object. For Aristotle, however, matter and form were very much interdependent and neither could exist without the other: the two were brought together, biologically speaking, through development and growth. This perspective led to a worldview that portrayed the universe as a single organic living whole, and which was only really challenged in the sixteenth and seventeenth centuries with the growth of scientific enquiry and Cartesian philosophy. The idea that the operation of the whole could best be understood from the properties of its parts, a reductionist or mechanistic philosophy, not only overturned Aristotelian principles but also represented a reversal of the Pythagorean position. As an approach, it can also be identified with the search for the basic cellular building blocks of life that characterized nineteenth-century mechanism (stimulated by improvements to the microscope): identify the substance of life, the individual cells, and the understanding of organismal form will follow. In other words, it is "substance" or "composition" that differentiates the animate human from the inanimate object. This perspective could be said to continue in the molecular biology of the twentieth century, as scientific discoveries revealed molecules and not cells to be the fundamental building blocks of life.

The dominance of the essentially mechanistic approach of molecular biology (according to Capra 1996, 78) meant that very little attention was devoted to the role of pattern and form in living systems. Indeed, some critics argue that the overemphasis on DNA and molecules has weakened the capacity of modern biology to understand biological organisms as holistic systems (Hayles 1999, 150; Goodwin 1994; Lewontin 1993; Fox Keller 1995; Doyle 1997). Nonetheless, from the 1970s "systems thinking" did begin to have some impact on biology.[4] Systems thinking was already important in management and engineering, but only impinged upon biology with advances in the mathematics of complexity and theories of self-organizing systems. Some of the earliest attempts to model self-organizing systems were in relation to the simulation of neural networks by McCulloch and Pitts (1943). In the first instance, theories of self-organization were linked to first-wave cybernetics, which was geared toward understanding mind and computation more than the operation of biological systems (see Ashby 1952, 1956). As a model for understanding mind and computation, cybernetics was soon superseded by what was to become artificial intelligence (e.g., Newell and Simon 1956), and the idea of self-organizing systems seems to have receded with it.

However, in the 1960s and 1970s, Ilya Prigogine developed the notion of dissipative structures, perhaps one of the most influential descriptions of self-organizing systems (Prigogine 1967; Prigogine and Stengers 1984). One might also cite the work of Manfred Eigen and his theory of hypercycles (Eigen 1971a, b). Although both Prigogine and Eigen sought to understand the implications of their groundbreaking work for biological systems, their primary research was on physical and chemical systems, Prigogine having analyzed heat convection in terms of nonlinear thermodynamics, and Eigen self-organizing chemical reaction cycles. One scholar who dared look for similar self-organizing processes in living biological systems was Humberto Maturana, who with Francisco Varela elaborated the concept of autopoiesis (Maturana and Varela 1980). In contrast to the tenets of molecular biology, they worked from the basis that form and organization were key to living systems, and that they were independent not only of the properties of the system's components (i.e., composition), but of anything outside the system. That is to say, the behavior of the system was established by the system itself, and not imposed upon it by any "external" environmental conditions. Thus a key feature of a self-organizing system, or autopoietic network,[5] was its autonomy.

This notion of autonomy demands examination. What Maturana and

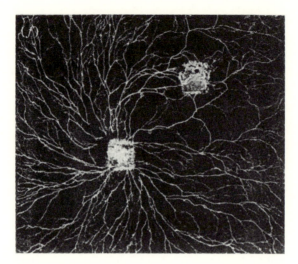

Figure 2.1. Mycelial fungi (after Rayner 1997, fig. 6.12f). Courtesy of A. D. M. Rayner.

Varela mean chiefly is organizational autonomy, such that a living system is organizationally closed. However, it is worth noting that Maturana and Varela based their ideas of autopoiesis and organizational closure largely on unicellular life forms and computer simulations. In such cases, defining organismal boundaries and autonomy may be a relatively clear-cut procedure. That such ideas have been readily extended to multicellular organisms may be in part attributable to the almost universal assumption in biology that all organisms can be delineated by formal boundaries. But Rayner (1997) stresses that difficulties can often arise in defining organismal and indeed cellular boundaries, citing the example of mycelial fungi which, in certain environmental conditions, form into tubes (hyphae) that branch out to create cellular networks (Figure 2.1).[6] There are indeed other examples that underline the difficulties of defining quite what "the" organism is in a given situation. What if an organism is in fact two or more beings? With hermatypic coral, for example, there are actually two different organisms involved, the coral polyps and their symbionts, zooxanthellae, a species of dinoflagellate protozoa (Turner 2000, 19–25). What sort of "organism" does coral then represent if it is in fact two organisms? Another key feature of hermatypic corals concerns their physiological process, a significant component of which occurs "outside" the coral, rendering their organismal boundaries rather difficult to specify. This would appear to be more than just a question of open structure, implying open organization too. These problems in pinpointing "the" organism are not sufficiently anticipated in Maturana and Varela's unicellular focus.

It thus appears that living systems, including humans for that matter, may actually be organizationally *fuzzy* rather than closed, despite the assertions of Maturana and Varela.[7] In developing autopoietic theory, Maturana and Varela were concerned with *information* rather than matter and energy;[8] to them, organizational closure was synonymous with informational closure (Hayles 1999, 10). We shall deal with the themes of information and cognition in the next chapter, arguing that living systems do not operate through organizational or informational closure, and do not operate within the boundaries of an organization that closes in on itself and leaves the world on the outside (Hayles 1999, 136).

In this chapter information and cognition are not our principal concerns. Nevertheless, it is our intention to demonstrate how information is fully articulated with energy and matter, and to show how ultimately all three are implicated in "l'homme total," as biological organism, psychological agent, and social person. This kind of articulation was resisted in autopoietic theory, and indeed in first-wave and second-wave cybernetics generally, because of the absolute distinction that was maintained between "structure" (composition, or matter) and "organization" (information). If we are to understand the flows of matter, energy, and information, then we need to overcome this dichotomy between structure and organization, between composition and form, and between mind and matter. And, crucially, the means to ensure this are highlighted by Capra, who identifies "process" as the key reconciliatory concept.[9] An inanimate object like a bicycle can be described as having both organization (interrelated components) and structure (metal, rubber, etc.). And yet both form and composition are fixed once the object is designed and produced. With a living organism, however, that which maintains the articulation of form and substance is "process." There is a constant flux—a movement of matter through the system. Capra is keen to stress the interdependence between form, substance and process, positing that "the process of life is the activity involved in the continual embodiment of the system's pattern of organization" (1996, 159). This inclusion of "process" as a criterion for defining living systems is very important, and effectively brings us full circle back to the Aristotelean position (Capra 1996). It is a point we shall now explore farther.

Fuzzy Objects, Extended Organisms

It seems most appropriate to think about organisms less in terms of form and substance and more in terms of "process." Goodwin (1988), for example, states that "it is not composition that determines organismic form and transformation, but dynamic organization."[10] And as Ingold has observed, such a definition does tend to "dissolve the very boundaries of the animate" (1988, 2). The unit of analysis is no longer the isolated organism or species, but becomes the indivisible process of "organism plus environment" (Ingold 2000, 20). This allows one to see how *inanimate* objects may constitute part of a dynamic organismal system, as in the case of coral mentioned above, and encapsulated in the idea of "extended phenotypes" (Dawkins 1982). Other illustrative cases are forthcoming. Earthworms, for example, coopt the soil as an accessory organ of water balance (Turner 2000, 119)—this could then be taken to imply that the soil, as an organ, is an extension of the earthworm phenotype and should be included within a definition of the earthworm as an organism. Assigning a fixed boundary to an organism is certainly a difficult, and perhaps misguided endeavor. We may be better off thinking about the boundary between the organism and the environment, between the animate and the inanimate, as being decidedly fuzzy in terms of both structure (composition) and organization (form).

This is already quite a step when dealing with earthworms and coral, but becomes still more daunting and confusing when we turn to social insects such as bees or termites. A termite mound can be described as a heart-lung machine for a termite colony, and thus as an extension of the termite phenotype and indeed organism.[11] But it is an extension of the entire colony, not of an individual termite; with this in mind, it has been suggested that the mound and the colony together form a sort of "superorganism" (Turner 2000, 179).[12] Yet whether it be organism or superorganism, it is hard to answer anything but "yes" to the following question posed by Turner: "If an organism modifies its environment for adaptive purposes, is it fair to say that in so doing it confers a degree of livingness to its apparently inanimate surroundings?" (2000, 6).

Thus the termites' mound, the earthworms' soil, and the coral's calcite foundation are all inanimate objects that are coopted in such a way that they become part and parcel of the dynamic organization of biological organisms; presumably, therefore, it can be said that they partake of animacy.

The Human Organism

Even though Turner's focus is on invertebrate organisms, we can certainly extend the same logic to other forms of organism too, even humans. This is, of course, where we began this chapter, before it became apparent that we needed to discuss not just human life but life more fundamentally. Yet, as in biology more generally conceived, there is a strong tendency in Western culture and medicine to see the human body as a bounded entity, and indeed as the seat of the individual (Le Breton 2001). It is only by overcoming these deep-seated and peculiarly Western assumptions that it becomes possible to imagine that, as physiological organisms, humans may have fuzzy boundaries (both organizationally and structurally). A particularly striking example involves the image of a hospital patient connected to numerous tubes and machines (artificial respirators and the like). In this rather direct sense, humans too provide themselves with external organs. In such cases it may be difficult to circumscribe the physiological boundaries of the organism (patient). Moreover, one might very well argue that not only do the machinic objects operating as external organs confer life upon the organism (they are called life support machines after all), but that by the same token they have "livingness" conferred upon them by the patient.

Other examples than the hospital patient may also be considered. Rather more prosaically, the simple tools of everyday life can be portrayed as extensions of the body's physical boundaries. The following quote from James Gibson conveys the point with particular clarity:

When in use, a tool is a sort of extension of the hand, almost an attachment to it or a part of the user's own body, and thus is no longer a part of the environment of the user. But when not in use, the tool is simply a detached object of the environment, graspable and portable, to be sure, but nevertheless external to the observer. This *capacity to attach something to the body* suggests that the boundary between the animal and the environment is not fixed at the surface of the skin but can shift. (1979, 41; original emphasis)

As with the life support machine, tools not only constitute extensions of human animacy but also confer new possibilities for animacy on the human actor. One particular tool for which this is particularly true is the blind man's cane, an example that has been used by innumerable philosophers and theorists from Descartes to Merleau-Ponty to Harré. The connection between the cane and the blind man's body is not just physical but also deeply perceptual, psychological, and social. Although particularly pro-found in this case, it is true to say that all tools entail some degree of psy-chological and social connection with their users. This point has received relatively little attention, as we shall discuss in due course below.

The examples used thus far all involve objects that are just outside the surface of the body and in some form of contact with it. One might also mention in this respect clothing and cosmetics (Dant 1999), and indeed cars (Graves-Brown 2000) and houses (Blier 1987), all of which can be seen as "second skins" in contact with the body and extensions of it. But we can blur the boundary between animate and inanimate still farther by traveling in two separate directions. First, we can go *inside* the body—more and more inanimate objects are being incorporated within the human body to create "bionic" humans.[13] Second, we can extend far *beyond* the confines of the skin to incorporate inanimate objects that barely touch human flesh but which nonetheless form part of our "livingness"—for example, communi-cation devices and networks.

The Internalized Hybrid

Let us start then with those cases which involve some cybernetic compo-nent *internalized* within the organism. Inanimate objects such as prosthetic limbs, joint replacements and pacemakers are now as a matter of course incorporated into living human bodies, thereby creating partially artifact-ualized organisms. Ever more innovative technologies are being developed apace, with cochlear implants already benefiting the profoundly deaf (Spitzer 1999; Rauschecker and Shannon 2002; see also discussion in Chap-ter 3). Retinal implants have had promising results in animal experiments and are in the process of being perfected for implementation in human pa-tients (Zrenner 2002). One researcher has even had surgery to implant in his arm a microchip that can pick up discrete nerve signals relating to the movements of his arm. Kevin Warwick, of the University of Reading, is hoping that it will then be possible to replay some of these signals to the nerves in such a way that his arm will be triggered into moving involun-tarily (Warwick 2002). A similar kind of experiment has already been per-formed on an owl monkey by Miguel Nicolelis at Duke University, using microelectrodes implanted in the brain cortex.[14] The neural signals that were recorded when the monkey engaged in a particular activity (reaching for food) were subjected to computer analysis and relayed to a robotic arm, which in real time followed the same movements as the monkey when reaching for food.

Most of these examples involve the implantation of inorganic, artificial components into the human body. There is of course another class of implants, consisting of biological, "living" components: the surgical transplantation of live organs into living bodies is now a common occurrence, with about 2,000 patients with end-stage heart failure receiving heart transplants in the U.S. every year (McCarthy and Smith 2002, 998). However, Hogle (1995) questions whether transplant organs are properly "alive" or are to be commodified as objects. To what extent can a living human body that incorporates an organ from another human be considered a cyborg, given that the new "component" is noncybernetic? Such questions are rendered even more complex by the advent of biomaterials and tissue engineering. To take one example, bioartificial livers are now being designed through the bioengineering of hepatocytes, the most important cells found in the liver.[15] The very phrase "bioartificial" effectively conveys the hybridity of such devices, perched precariously between the organismal and the artifactual.[16] Thus, not only is the human body hybridized by technological implants, but the implants themselves are now becoming hybrids. Which does, of course, beg the question of how we are meant to describe the status of the resulting organism—as yet another form of cyborg, a biotechnologized organism? Whatever we decide are the effects of such alterations on the corporeality of the body, the question whether there will be any ramifications for the status of the body as a mindful, social being has remained something of a moot point (a topic addressed below).[17]

The Externalized Hybrid

The term cyborg can be extended to include other hybrid types. We need only think back to our earlier case of the hospital patient connected to tubes and machines. Even though the machinic component is external rather than internal, we can still consider the patient-machine system as a cyborg. More radically still, the external machinic component of a cyborg need not be directly connected to the organism in the obvious way that the patient is linked to an artificial respirator; even if the organism is only connected "indirectly" to seemingly distant external technologies, we may still cast the resulting amalgamation as a cyborg. Take the following familiar scenario:

A 32-year-old man, in excellent health, sits at his computer and "talks" with colleagues over the Internet. He logs off, hops on his bike, custom-built with the latest technology. He heads for the health club, where machines will grow his muscle mass and sense his body parameters. One could say he is an average modern-day cyborg, functioning with the help of everyday technologies. (Hogle 1995, 203)

But this kind of cyborg is different to the kind envisaged by Warwick and others. It is not so much a physical cyborg, more of a functional cyborg, or "fyborg" (Chislenko 1995; Stock 2002, 25). Chislenko defines a "fyborg" as a "biological organism functionally supplemented with technological extensions" (Chislenko 1995). As fyborgs, postmodern humans are perhaps all very widely distributed chimeras, bodies unbounded by skin. Although Donna Haraway uses the term cyborg, not fyborg, she is probably the most renowned and radical proponent of this perspective, claiming herself to be, as a cyborg, a quintessential technological body (Haraway 1991, 1995). But Haraway also maintains that this is very much a post-World War II phenomenon. Perhaps this is true with regard to the particular types of functional cyborgs we may now have become, intimately and systemically connected to our phones, faxes, and computers; but have humans not been quintessential technological bodies for at least two million years? If one considers even a basic stone tool as a kind of prosthetic extension of the body (Burkitt 1998, 63), then have humans not always been fyborgs of some sort?

There is no reason why we should a priori limit the term fyborg to humans; it could conceivably refer to any sort of organism that goes beneath or extends beyond its own skin and coopts inanimate elements of the environment for adaptive purposes. This of course brings us back to Turner's notion of the extended organism (e.g., earthworms and soil, termites and nest), and makes us see the conceptual overlap between the functional cyborg and the extended organism. However, humans are perhaps unique among organisms in their capacity for extending functionally both so far beyond and indeed within themselves. Do any other organisms ingest or take on board inanimate elements for adaptive purposes? Certain instances do spring to mind of organisms coopting other organisms, and it is ironic that a major proponent of cyborg theory has highlighted one of the most intriguing examples—Donna Haraway draws our attention to the case of the microorganism *Mixotricha paradoxa* (see Figure 2.2)—a nucleated microbe that inhabits the hindgut of a South Australian termite (Haraway 1995, xvii; cf. also Margulis and McMenamin 1997, 42–43; Rayner 1997, 64).

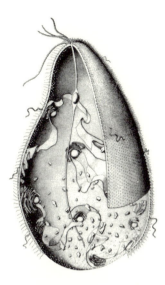

Figure 2.2. Microbe *Mixotricha paradoxa*, found in the hindgut of a wood-eating termite from Australia. Two kinds of spirochetes are permanently attached to the microbe (after Margulis 1997, fig. 4, drawing by Christie Lyons). Courtesy of Lynn Margulis.

It is one of a number of organisms that ingests crumbs of wood and thereby produces compounds that the termite is able to digest. But the symbiosis goes much further: the *Mixotricha* microbe itself carries thousands of spirochetes, spiral-shaped bacteria that actually allow the microbe to swim (Margulis 1997, 120, fig. 9.4). The symbiosis is in fact more complicated still, as there are two different species of spirochete involved, and three other kinds of symbiont; each *Mixotricha* host supports and is supported by about one million of the five kinds of symbionts (all prokaryotes). Dubbing this "a kind of obligate confederacy" (Haraway 1995, xviii), Haraway shows how fraught an exercise defining the boundaries between organism and nonorganism really is, unless one accepts that such boundaries are necessarily fuzzy. But, of course, this example differs from most of those employed by Turner in that all of the components are animate. As such we can hardly describe this confederacy as a cybernetic organism (*cyb*org) hybrid.

Thus far we have only discussed the merging of the inanimate and the animate, of technology and the human body, as a physical and functional amalgamation. But what are the psychological and social correlates, or ramifications, of this process? In terms of humans at least, should we not expect the physical differences between internalized cyborgs and externalized fyborgs to carry with them some fundamental psychological and social differences too? Such questions are difficult to answer, not least because the psychological and social implications of hybridity are rarely tackled. Some scholars (such as the psychologist Serge Tisseron) have made the rather general point that we enter into social and psychological relations with everyday objects, much as we might with humans. We shall therefore make an attempt here to open this topic up, to see if the fuzzy boundary between humans and nonhumans exists not only physically but also psychologically and socially.[18] Perhaps it is difficult to really treat these three dimensions separately.

Psychological Agency and Social Personhood

If we have thus far used the term "animacy" to convey the sense of an organism being biologically alive, how are we to describe the sense of an organism, the human organism in particular, being psychologically and socially alive? The term "agency" springs to mind. Agency is often taken to imply some kind of intentionality, of a capacity for causing events to happen (Gell 1998, 16). When such an equivalence is drawn between agency and intentionality, the idea that agency is a uniquely human trait seems a strong one. However, agency and intentionality are not necessarily quite so coterminous as we may often assume. Artifacts such as traffic lights, sleeping policemen, or catflaps might be described as possessing a kind of agency; yet it would be much harder to argue that they manifest intentionality. In addition, it should be noted that not all human agency necessarily involves intentionality (Searle 1983). Thus separating agency from intentionality reveals that, whereas agency may be either human or material, intentionality is a human trait that "appears to have no counterpart in the material realm" (Pickering 1995, 17–18). That said, the human plans and goals that constitute intentionality are not formulated as pure internal mental representations that are then simply executed in the exterior world; intentionality is "predisciplined" by the cultural environment in which the human agent is located (Pickering 1995, 19).

Thus we cannot simply define agency as a human property; we need to acknowledge the existence of both material and human agency. Although agency in and of itself is not strictly speaking a psychological capacity, human agency, incorporating intentionality—the formulation of conscious intentions prior to and in the course of acting—may well be described as such. The importance of this is that, in this chapter, we are seeking to define the various aspects of the bio-psycho-social human condition. Therefore, if we are able tentatively to link intentional agency with the psychological dimension, where does this leave the social? In that a human protagonist invariably formulates intentionality within a milieu of not just material but also social relationships, human agency is perhaps inescapably a social as well as a psychological phenomenon; and indeed the term "social agency" has been commonly employed of late (Gell 1998; Dobres 2000). However, in an attempt to achieve some kind of analytical separation between the psychological and the social (cf. Mauss 1936), and at the risk of meeting with the disapproval of some readers, we shall here use the term "person-hood" to cover the social dimension, reserving human "agency" for the psychological.[19] Most of the following discussion will focus on agency rather than personhood.

We have already used the life support machine example as a demonstration of the fuzzy boundary between organism and environment, and hence of the *distributed* character of biological animacy. Can we stretch this example still farther to show how the idea of a fuzzy boundary applies to the human not only as physiological organism but also as psychological agent? In what ways is agency, like animacy, also a *distributed* phenomenon, in which not only humans but also nonhumans are implicated? It seems that an added twist to the tale is supplied by Serge Tisseron, who in *Comment l'esprit vient aux objets* (1999, 19) tells of hearing a hospital patient yelp in pain when a nurse squeezed the patient's feeding tube, even though the nurse's action should have been perfectly painless. Although obviously aware of the physical, physiological connection between feeding tube and patient, the nurse saw the former as a technological object separate from the organismal patient. For the patient, however, the division between internal subject and external object was blurred, albeit subconsciously, such that an apparently external object was integrated not just physically but also perceptually so that a painful *touch* could be perceived. One might try extending the implications still further; if human corporeality and perception can be so tightly bound up, then it is presumably not only the sense of touch that is affected. Might it not also be the case that an individual attached to a feeding tube could start to *see* and *hear* the world differently too?

So the human and the life support machine, when conjoined, can form not only a physiological symbiosis but also a psychological/perceptual one (with social personhood perhaps playing only a minor role?). However, it is very difficult to pursue such an example farther because of the special circumstances involved, in which the human is static and incapacitated in a fixed environment. This is a crucial point, given extra weight by the fact that both James Gibson and Maurice Merleau-Ponty (two of the principal contributors to theories of perception, see Ingold 2000, 260–66) are at great pains to emphasize the importance to human perception of *movement* in an *environment*. A more instructive case of a perceptual system that indivisibly conjoins human and nonhuman elements might then be the blind man with his cane, an example used above. Here, too, human and object achieve a close physical connection (although one might hesitate to call it physiological) that is at the same time a highly integrated psychological/perceptual system (as well as raising the question where the organism ends and the object begins). The stick becomes an integral part of the blind man's corporeal presence in the world as much as it does a part of his perceptual presence. Indeed, with such an example it is hard to imagine separating the corporeal from the perceptual at all.[20]

Nonetheless, separating animacy from agency is not altogether impossible—it occurs when a patient is in a coma. It can also be achieved through the artificial means of anaesthesia: agency is taken away from the still animate patient. One might consider too the case of phantom limbs, which, although physically absent, may be very much present perceptually and psychologically (see Spitzer 1999, 148–63, for elaboration). And then there is the question whether agency can continue without corporeal animacy, as is considered the case in many religions.

These caveats notwithstanding, the picture that develops is of a thorough intertwining of animacy and agency. This is entirely compatible with a point made forcefully by Ingold: that it makes little sense to treat the human being as two separate phenomena, biological organism and social person. These splits between the biological, the psychological, and social—between animacy, agency, and personhood—may have been created for us by the divisions between the disciplines of biology, psychology and anthropology, but Ingold stresses that the challenge before us is to reconcile all three so that we may recognise how it is that the organism and the person come into being inseparably (Ingold 2000, 2–3).

Humanized Artifacts?

Thus we see that the bio-psycho-social human is impure, hybridized by the artifactual. But what if we turn the tables and focus upon the artifactual—is it in turn hybridized by the human? This is perhaps an even tougher pill to swallow, to imagine that objects might partake of "human" properties. Yet if we are prepared to accept that technologized human agents exist, surely we should be able to do the same for the flip side of the coin—humanized technological artifacts (J. Pickering 1997). What "humanized" means here, of course, is open to question: we should examine its implications in terms of animacy, agency, and personhood.

Starting with animacy, it does at first seem difficult to grasp that objects might be corporeally animate. Can the physicality of objects somehow be reconfigured as corporeality? As in the earlier discussion of technologized human organisms, the conceptual possibilities seem immediately limited by the hierarchical opposition between people and things pervading modern Western thought (Latour 2000). Yet, drawing on earlier discussion, we should perhaps not be seeking to delimit animacy within the boundaries of any particular entity. To what extent can we say that the earthworm has animacy while the earth surrounding it does not? Or that the termite is animate but the termite mound is inanimate? And what status are we to assign to transplanted organs? Earlier we also emphasized the importance of understanding organisms not just as form and substance but also as *process*. Thus, if a transplanted organ comes to be an integral part of the organism's biological process, then it must surely partake of animacy itself. This is perhaps easier to accept for artifacts that are "internalized" in an organismal system, but what of those that are "externalized"? A life-support machine may be external, an extreme form of fyborg, but nonetheless it is integrated within the organism's process. As such, it too can be said to partake of animacy.

But what of the possible psychological and social correlates of animacy? We might be able to suggest that artifacts are in some senses animate as a function of their integration within biological systems, but surely it is going too far to say that they may also have agency and personhood? In our earlier discussion of technologized human agents, organisms with cochlear implants and bioartificial livers, it seemed that there were often problems in raising the possibly troubling psychological and social ramifications of hybridity. Even thinking about the uncertain corporeal status of such hybrids was enough, without considering their status as agents and persons.[21] As far as the converse is concerned—humanized technological artifacts—we are little better at getting to grips with their psychological and social character. Bruno Latour's confession that "we cannot even define precisely what makes some human and others technical" (2000, 20) has not prompted very much serious scientific consideration of the matter.

It seems we prefer only to confront such issues within the controlled environments of fairytales, science fiction, and laboratories. Science fiction is a realm densely populated with ambiguous human-technical hybrids: the replicants of Ridley Scott's *Blade Runner*, the Terminator, Robocop, and the Mechas of Spielberg's *AI*. Yet despite inhabiting fictional worlds, most of these hybrids are "created" by human protagonists. In the slightly more real world of artificial intelligence, researchers are striving to make ever more "humanized" robots (Brooks 2002), but this is for the moment not too unsettling within the controlled confines of the laboratory. Machines that appear to have a life of their own are not, however, a purely modern phenomenon, and it may be interesting here to turn to a recent work that discusses the "ancient history" of artificial life, of technological artifacts that have been explicitly and deliberately humanized. The case in point is particularly interesting: not only does it explore the question of artifactual *agency*, it also raises the issue of the unexpected psychological impact of these machines on their human counterparts.

Artifacts as Agents

Gaby Wood in her book *Living Dolls* (2002) takes us back to the eighteenth and nineteenth centuries to show us some early attempts at creating humanized technological artifacts. Of particular interest is a chess-playing automaton dubbed the "Automatic Turk," built in 1769 by a Hungarian named Wolfgang von Kempelen (see also Standage 2002). It was a life-sized carved wooden figure (with the appearance and clothing of a Turk) seated at and connected to a large chest on which a chessboard sat (see Figure 2.3). Mechanically, the doll was indeed impressive, able to pick up and move the pieces by way of some rather complicated machinery. But of course the real illusion lay in the machine's apparent ability not only to choose its own moves but to do so with consummate skill: the machine invariably won, with a number of notable players among its victims.

Naturally, many observers thought there must have been a human chess-player concealed within, and quite probably a dwarf, judging by the machine's size. Yet von Kempelen went to considerable lengths to convince the public of the mechanical credentials of his automaton, having designed it in such a way that its various internal mechanisms could be revealed. He

Der Schachspieler im Spiele begriffen · Le Joueur d'Echecs tel qu'on le voit pendant le jeu

Figure 2.3. "The Turk with the cabinet closed," from Charles Gottlieb de Windisch, *Briefe über den Schachspieler des Herrn von Kempelen* (1783). Courtesy of The Library Company of Philadelphia.

was also incredibly artful in convincing his audience that it was physically impossible for a man to fit within the automaton. The deception seems to have worked remarkably well, with all manner of contemporary commentators attempting and failing to explain its operation. Von Kempelen frequently stated that his goal was the creation of a playful illusion, but, as Wood points out, the sense of magic and marvel was often accompanied by a fear that this creation represented something rather more sinister (Wood 2002, 59). Wood suggests that this response, provoked by many forms of automata and androids, "arises when there is an "intellectual uncertainty" about the borderline between the lifeless and the living" (Wood 2002, xiv). In other words, hybridity seems to have a particular psychological impact.

But this is as nothing compared to the psychological effects apparently experienced by the chess-player secretly concealed within the Automatic

Turk. There is no particular need to go into the details here (for which see Wood 2002; Standage 2002); suffice it to say that a human (preferably one skilled at chess) concealed within the chest was able through a series of rather ingenious and complicated arrangements to operate the supposed automaton. Over the years a number of different players were pressed into service, including some tall men, such as six-foot Wilhelm Schlumberger, for whom life inside the machine must have been particularly cramped: it is known that he acquired a pronounced stoop (Wood 2002, 90). If there were indeed accompanying psychological effects upon Schlumberger they appear not to be known, but Wood does tell us of another player, Charles Schmidt, who apparently blamed the machine for ruining his life. Another of the machine's operators, a certain Jacques-François Mouret, also seems to have suffered considerably at its hands. At the very least, the Automatic Turk could be said "to have set a psychological problem for those who in-habited it"—at worst it was "at times a kind of parasite" (Wood 2002, 93). One is reminded of Andrew Pickering's observation, in a quite different context, that "around machines, we act like machines" (1995, 16), or indeed of Hayles who says "the computer moulds the human even as the human builds the computer" (Hayles 1999, 47).

The Automatic Turk can perhaps be thought of as a marionette with a difference: its "strings" (or levers) are on the inside and hence concealed from view. Given that this invisibility is the principal source of its deceptive power, it might be argued that it has a much more powerful psychological effect than a canonical marionette, with its more visible strings and more obvious connection to the human agency directing its movements.[22] This may well be the case, and helps to explain the pronounced psychological effects reported. However, this does not deny that a *two-way* psychological bond nonetheless exists between human and puppet, and indeed between human and nonhuman more generally. We tend generally to think of arti-facts and machines rather like puppets, as things we manipulate and con-trol; however, the Automatic Turk, although a rather extreme and explicit example of a humanized artifact, testifies to the ability of objects to "act back" and affect human psychology. Agency is not something we confer on objects in a one-way relationship; it emerges reciprocally as humans and nonhumans merge.[23]

Artifacts and Personhood

We have seen with the above example of the Automatic Turk the way a humanized artifact can "technologize" the human so that the person is quite literally made part of the artifact. The physical connection between human and nonhuman may only be temporary, but the psychological relationship may be more enduring (one might say the same too of fyborgs). Having discussed the psychological, can we do the same for the social? Is it feasible to talk of artifacts not only as agents but as persons too?

A deep-seated assumption became apparent in the above discussion of agency: if an artifact holds any kind of psychological presence, it is only a secondary effect of its connection with human protagonists, the "real" and primary agents. A similar assumption emerges in relation to artifacts and personhood: being obviously inert and passive, an artifact is not really socially alive, but it may sometimes appear to be active by virtue of its close association with living agents. This assumption, that the social life of objects is very much secondary to that of humans, is present even in work aimed at breaking down the distinction between a universe of animate people and one of inanimate objects: for example the idea, promulgated in both the anthropological and archaeological literature relatively recently, that objects, not unlike people, can have cultural biographies (Kopytoff 1986; Appadurai 1986; Riggins 1994a, b).

Subsequent work has focused less on ascribing social lives or personhood to objects per se, and more on understanding the critical role of objects in the constitution and negotiation of personhood. This has, on the whole, involved a shift of perspective away from dualism and toward relationality. In particular, the notion that personhood is a distributed phenomenon, implicating both human and nonhuman entities, has come to the fore. The work of Marilyn Strathern in elaborating the concept of the "dividual" person has been a key force in this process (Strathern 1988). Subsequent anthropological discussions have continued with Strathern's Melanesian perspective (Wagner 1991; LiPuma 1998; Gell 1998), although important contributions have also come through work on personhood in South Asian contexts (Busby 1997; Bird-David 1999). Furthermore, the theme of personhood has received considerable recent attention in archaeological circles (e.g., Chapman 2000; Thomas 2000b; Fowler 2001, 2002). However, I intend here to pursue discussion further through the use of a simple example presented by Latour (1999a). This case is instructive not so much for questions of personhood, which is not my primary concern in this chapter, but for the issues of symmetry and equivalence which are raised, and with which I shall conclude this chapter.

Latour (1999a) in particular emphasizes how hybrid social forms emerge as humans and nonhumans are "folded" into each other. One example he uses to demonstrate this enfolding is the gun (note that this kind of artifact is much less explicitly humanized than the living dolls discussed above). While the anti-gun lobby argues that guns kill people, the pro-gun lobby maintains that *people* kill people, with the gun as nothing more than a neutral tool. The dualism here is between *materialist* and *sociological* explanations (Latour 1999a, 176–77)—the former portrays the gun as responsible, the latter puts all responsibility in human hands.

Latour seeks to avoid the stalemate that arises from this dualistic posturing by adopting a radical relational perspective. He argues that it is in the very coming together of the human and the gun that the real sociological interest lies. When human and gun come together, neither one nor the other alone is the "actor." A new actor is created, a hybrid composed of both human and gun. It is this very "conjunction," Latour argues, that is insufficiently problematized within dualistic approaches. It is analytically harmful to separate the "technical" from the "social," because these never exist as pure forms; the "physics" of the gun cannot be simply isolated as objective, asocial facts.

Latour is concerned primarily with the social rather than the psychological implications; hence he refers to the change to the citizen with gun in hand—"a good citizen becomes a criminal, a bad guy becomes a worse guy" (1999a, 180). Moreover, Latour looks beyond the individual to the collective as a whole, which, like the individual citizen, is described as a hybrid, composed of humans and nonhumans. An object such as a gun embroils itself in the fate not only of an individual citizen but of entire institutions (different gun lobbies, manufacturers, etc.). The bodies we inhabit are internally and externally bioartificial; agency, which cannot be described as either a human or nonhuman property, is distributed across bodies, artifacts and environments; and we live not in societies but in sociotechnical collectives. Animacy, agency and personhood are all an enfolding of the human and the nonhuman.

Symmetry and Equivalence

The man-with-gun example shows not only that the relationship between humans and nonhumans is frequently cast in dualistic terms, but that the relationship is also invariably asymmetrical. Either humans intrinsically always have the upper hand, as in the *sociological* perspective, or they are at the mercy of technology, as in the *materialist* perspective. For Latour, however, agency is neither a quality that humans choose to bestow upon objects, nor something that nonhumans independently possess; it is instead conceived as a relational property, distributed across hybridized human-nonhuman networks. As a distributed phenomenon, it resides neither in humans nor in objects but in their "intra-actions" (Suchman 2000, 7). Latour's perspective is thus both symmetrical and nondualistic (Latour 1994, 1996, 1999a, 2000). At times, he is radical in venting his frustration with dualism:

Consider things, and you will have humans. Consider humans, and you are by that very act interested in things. Bring your attention to bear on hard things, and see them become gentle, soft or human. Turn your attention to humans and see them become electric circuits, automatic gears or softwares. We cannot even define precisely what makes some human and others technical, whereas we are able to document precisely their modifications and replacements, their rearrangements and their alliances, their delegations and representations. (Latour 2000, 20)

This emphasis on documenting the character of the connections between entities, rather than struggling to fix them as human or nonhuman, reminds one of the observation made by William Burroughs that "human . . . is an adjective and its use as a noun is in itself regrettable."[24] One might even argue that the use of the word "human" as a noun to refer to a bounded individual entity is an invention of modernity. The notion of a bounded human body, of a physical entity somehow separable from man's metaphysical existence, can be traced back to Descartes and beyond (Le Breton 2001). Indeed, Le Breton links the origins of the conception of a bounded human body with the development of anatomy in the sixteenth century. Before this time, he claims, a human being was more a node in a web of social relations rather than an individual as such. In order to emphasize that this conception might be the rule rather than the exception (with modern Western notions being the exception), Le Breton refers us to Melanesian conceptions of the person: the body does not exist as a bounded entity, a locus for the individual person, but is permeable, in a state of flux with its surroundings (Le Breton 2001, 18; see also Strathern 1988). Given that this resonates with the idea of a fuzzy boundary between organism and environment described by Turner, and, in particular, the notion of boundary as a *process* rather than an entity (2000, 5), this non-Western perspective is very much in keeping with the overall spirit of this chapter.

Yet Latour's radical relational perspective has not gone unchallenged in the social sciences. While a number of scholars in socio-anthropology seek to develop a nondualistic approach to the study of technology and material culture, they do not necessarily espouse Latour's "symmetrical anthropology" (cf. Semprini 1995; Lemonnier 1996; Segalen and Bromberger 1996; Löfgren 1996; Warnier 1999a). Indeed, it is confronted head-on in a fascinating debate between Latour (1996) and Pierre Lemonnier (1996). The latter criticizes Latour's "symmetrical" approach for its tendency, in treating everything as sociological, to overlook material constraints. In the context of the man-with-gun example, Lemonnier would say that Latour does not do sufficient justice to the physical characteristics of the gun. His approach instead would be to analyze these material traits in detail, then consider the social context of the human agent, and only subsequently combine the two to create an interconnected entity. Latour retorts by saying this represents a dualist approach, dubbing Lemonnier's methodology "purification/conjunction." He essentially agrees with Lemonnier's criticism that pure, asocial, material constraints do not exist within his scheme, but sees this as a strength rather than a weakness.

Although one feels inclined to agree with elements of Latour's position, Lemonnier's point, although not conveyed particularly effectively, is a strong one. It is perhaps better taken up, albeit briefly, by Jean-Claude Kaufmann (1997, 41–42). He suggests that while Latour's idea of symmetry may be effective in encouraging us to do away with the hierarchical opposition between people and things, and to admit that things may be just as important as people in social interactions, beyond this it is rather limited; things and people do not play the same role in such interactions—they have different properties and thus contribute differently to the hybrid forms that result. Kaufmann speaks of the three virtues of objects being immobility, patience, and silence. This formulation is underdeveloped, but it goes some way toward showing that we may need different tools for assessing humans and nonhumans.

Similar points are raised by Pickering (1995) in his discussion of the relationship between human and material agency: while acknowledging that they may display a significant degree of symmetry and interconnection, he adds that they should not be regarded as equivalent or interchangeable (Pickering 1995, 16). It is important to be alert to the different properties that the human and the nonhuman contribute to the hybridized form. While Latour, Kaufmann, and Pickering might all agree that in their coming together both human agency and material agency are transformed, Latour's position is that one cannot possibly isolate either as a "pure" form before their conjunction.[25] Pickering and Kaufmann, though, assume that one can at some level differentiate between the human and the nonhuman; however much they may intertwine, the human and the nonhuman are nevertheless seen as separable entities. That their positions retain the scope for assessing the human and the nonhuman independently as well as relationally is perhaps an advantage. Considerable difficulties do seem to arise when either an independent or a relational perspective is taken; an approach combining the two would seem to have much to recommend it.

Recap

In this chapter we began with a consideration of the relationship between human subject and material object. Given that the main criterion separating them would appear to be *animacy*, there followed a discussion of this phenomenon and the merits of defining it in terms of form, substance and/or process. The argument that living systems (unicellular or multicellular) might be described as structurally open yet organizationally closed was also entertained, and rejected in favor of the idea that living systems are both structurally and organizationally fuzzy. The question of animacy is clearly relevant to other entities besides humans, and so a range of examples was used, from coral to earthworms to termites. Then consideration was given to the particular capacity of humans (although exhibited by other animals too) to coopt inanimate objects into their physical and physiological operation; this is achieved both internally and externally in relation to the human body. In modern times, such hybridization is becoming more intensive internally (e.g., bioartificial implants) and more extensive externally (e.g., communication networks). Expanding from this initial emphasis on the physical and the biological, we then turned to the psychological and social dimensions of human livingness, namely agency and personhood. The important point was made, following Mauss, that "l'homme total" is a *bio-psycho-social* entity—simultaneously and indivisibly a biological organism, psychological agent, and social person.

Up to now, however, it has largely been from the perspective of the body that we have focused on the bio-psycho-social human. In doing so, we have used the examples of the patient with feeding tube, the blind man with cane, and various other forms of internalized and externalized hybridity. But there is a rather crucial dimension to which we have yet to give adequate consideration: that in all of these body-object conjunctions cognition and information are also implicated. It is not just an interdependence of body and object that we observe, but a coalescence of mind, body and object. And if we wish to understand how agency and personhood inhere in objects, we need also to understand how mind inheres in objects. And thus, to tackle this issue we must turn, in the following chapter, to the realms of psychology and cognitive science, which have only very recently seen the development of embodied and distributed perspectives on cognition that are of great relevance to our current concerns. Indeed, this perspective essentially depicts a fuzzy boundary between mind and matter, compatible with our previous discussion on the fuzzy boundary between body and object.

Chapter 3
Cognition, Perception, and Action

Rethinking Cognition

It was apparent in the last chapter that biologists have tended to focus on individual organisms independently of their physical environment; much the same can be said of cognitive scientists, in their propensity for isolating internal mental states in explaining cognitive phenomena (Clark 1997, 46). The upshot is that "mind" is still very commonly treated as a domain separate from the body and the world, not only in cognitive science but also in much psychology and in cognitive anthropology. In the pages that follow we shall critique this tendency, and propose an alternative perspective that links together cognition, perception and action much more fluidly. It is an approach that depicts cognition as a distributed, situated, and embodied process.

The common view to which we are reacting portrays the human body as the passive receptor of an array of stimuli from the environment, stimuli that are detected through various sensory modes (perception). The rather jumbled information embodied in these stimuli is then channeled through to the brain, imagined to operate as a kind of central processing unit. The information reaching the brain is duly processed and internalized; this operation allows for the information to be interpreted and given meaning. In interpreting this information, the mind creates a set of representations that allow for the formulation of an appropriate behavioral response, which is then conveyed to the body and enacted in the external environment. The feedback between external world and internal mind may be rapid and continuous, but world and mind nonetheless remain separate. Some key tenets of this perspective are that the cognitive processes of the mind are of a higher order; that cognition is an internal process, separate from the external world of perception and behavior; and that perception is somewhat "dumb," unguided, and passively responsive to stimuli.

This "internalist" perspective, essentially Cartesian in its separation of action and perception on the one hand and cognition on the other, conceives of mind as a computational unit. It is as if the information being processed is nothing more than a set of patterns (e.g., sequences of bits and bytes), disembodied and disassociated from any material presence (Hayles 1999). Within this very powerful computational perspective, there are two quite different threads: the symbolist and the connectionist. The former sees cognition as a process that operates through rule-based symbol manipulation (Bechtel and Abrahamsen 2002, 9; Kosslyn and Koenig 1992, 18). It can be partially explained by likening the brain to a computer, although originally it was the other way round: most computers derive from a design (by John von Neumann in the 1940s) that deliberately sought to mimic the operation of the brain, or at least as far as its operation was understood in the 1940s and 1950s. The development of the digital computer served to strengthen this general model and provide it with sophistication. Ironically, it was by developing artificial neural networks on such computers that some scientists put themselves in a position to argue for a radically different model of brain function—the model described above as connectionism.[1] Although some key aspects of this model have been around since at least the 1940s, for example in the concept of neural networks (McCulloch and Pitts 1943), it is really only in the last twenty years that it has come to the fore in discussions of brain function. In the intervening years, and especially the 1960s and 1970s, it was the symbolist model that dominated our understanding of the internal workings of the brain. However, the computer hardware that was supposed to be brain-like has helped to show how very unlike the brain it actually is.[2] Besides these artificial simulations, advances in neuroscience mean that much more is known about the inner workings of the brain; and this additional knowledge has itself encouraged the development of more "brain-like" computational models.

The fundamental idea of the neural network models that form the basis of the burgeoning connectionist paradigm is that the individual units that process information are akin to neurons (of course, in the brain they actually are neurons!). These neurons, be they real or simulated, are interconnected in such a way that they work in tandem in information processing—hence the term "parallel distributed processing." In the human brain a single neuron may receive signals from up to ten thousand other neurons. Modeling this kind of complexity is rather daunting to say the least, but some of the essential features of neural networks can nonetheless be illustrated with some simplified examples.

A refreshingly straightforward explanatory account can be found in

Goldblum (2001). She contrasts connectionist networks with semantic networks, and it may be worthwhile to start here. How is a concept registered in the brain? Let us take the concept of "bird." With semantic networks, popular within what we have referred to above as the symbolist approach, the concept "bird" would be represented by a single node in a network. It would find itself connected with other concepts, for example fish (another animal), feathers (a feature it has), and flying (something it does). There are all sorts of problems with this kind of network (see Goldblum for more on this). Goldblum suggests that whereas in semantic networks the concepts reside in the nodes, in a connectionist network they reside in the connections: "the nodes and the links change roles." All the different elements that constitute the concept "bird" intersect and connect at various points; it is in the space of these intersections and connections that the concept resides. Each individual concept is thus represented by a whole network. Crucially though, it also appears that a whole set of concepts of a particular type is located in a single network. As Goldblum emphasizes, this raises an interesting and critical question: how can a single network "know" which concept it is using at any given moment? If "cat" and "dog" are mapped on the same network, what distinguishes them?

It appears that the answer to this lies in the patterns of neuron activation, which differ according to what is being represented. Let us imagine that a certain sector of a network is composed of a series of interconnected neurons that fire in a particular way when stimulated by the sensory input corresponding to the output "cat." Because these neurons have developed connections of differential strength, and because they possess variable activation threshold values, the network sector in question will, topographically speaking, consist of a particular pattern of peaks and valleys. In short, the output "cat" consists of a certain kind of topographical map. Its topography will differ a little from that of the map correlating to the output "dog." This system of topographic recognition is essentially based on parallel distributed processing, a kind of processing to which a network is well suited. The conventional computer, however, would have to tackle the same task of differentiating cat from dog using algorithms to process the information sequentially (Spitzer 1999, 25–26). This may work for relatively simple tasks, but, once the patterns get a little more complex, the sequence becomes very long and the operation is jeopardized by even a single small error. Conventional computers have shown themselves to be rather poorly adapted to the solution of pattern-recognition problems (recognition of faces, handwriting, etc.).

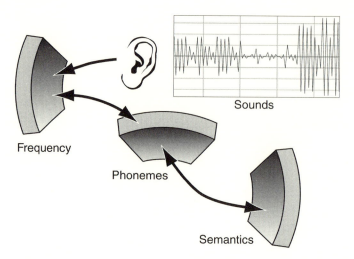

Figure 3.1. Diagram of auditory perception (after Spitzer 1999, 139). Copyright ©
MIT Press. Courtesy of MIT Press.

Such network-based topographical maps are apparently crucial to
brain function at a number of levels. The question of registering "cat" or
"dog" is in fact the most interpretive level, the "semantic." There are more
basic perceptual levels in operation—in terms of listening to language these
are the phonemic and the phonetic. To hear and interpret a sound as the
word "dog" or "cat," the phonemic, phonetic, and semantic must interact.
A critical example concerns the neurological changes that occur when patients suffering from hearing loss receive cochlear implants (Spitzer 1999,
137–38; Rauschecker and Shannon 2002). At first, the implants are no help
at all to the patients—the signals being sent to the brain by the artificial
inner ear are quite different in frequency from those that were previously
provided by the natural cochlea. These signals simply cannot be decoded.
But, about a year after the operation, the patients are able to understand
spoken language: the brain gradually adapts to the new auditory input patterns it receives. Yet the reconfiguration of tonotopic maps, remarkable
though it may be, is in itself insufficient. For the patients to hear, the new
frequencies can only be made sense of as speech when they are contextual-
ized in terms of both phonetics and semantics (see Figure 3.1). The reconfiguration at one level must be carried through to other levels too. Given
that all these levels are involved synthetically in auditory perception, it may

well be that semantic maps are themselves affected by changes in input patterns.

The notion that not only simple features but also more complex, semantic features may be represented on topographical feature maps does not initially seem unreasonable. If simple features like sound pitch, graphemes, or phonemes can be topographically represented, then why not also the meanings of ideas, actions and objects (Spitzer 1999, 224–27)? The idea is that semantic feature maps could self-organize in such a way that similar concepts would be arranged relatively close together. Thus white and black may be found close together, as may hoofed animals (e.g., zebra, horse, and cow). When "white" is registered as an input, "black" may also be partially activated. Thus by seeing "white" our brains are primed for "black" too, and if the latter concept does subsequently arise we recognize it more quickly than we might otherwise have done. A single idea in this way has a *spreading activation* effect (Spitzer 1999, 225).

Spitzer's introduction of the idea of semantic networks in connection with neural networks may at first seem rather confusing, because any mention of semantic networks creates links with the symbolist rather than the connectionist approach (Goldblum 2001; Bechtel and Abrahamsen 2002). These have generally been portrayed in the literature as competing paradigms. The symbolist (or representational) perspective considers that, in a semantic network, concepts are represented by nodes; these are connected to other nodes by various forms of association (Goldblum 2001, 35–39). The connectionist viewpoint, increasingly dominant in recent years, maintains that a single concept is not represented by an individual node but by a whole interconnected set of nodes. For Spitzer to merge what Goldblum would have us believe to be two irreconcilable positions might appear contradictory. Yet Spitzer's objective is to develop a hybrid position that says concepts are neither widely distributed through a network, nor confined to a single node. He uses Kohonen feature maps to show how certain concepts may occupy relatively restricted topographical areas, consisting of a limited number of neurons.

Related concepts may come to be located topographically close to one another on a feature map—their proximity means that when one concept is activated, this activation may very well spread to the neighboring concept and partially activate that one, too. This differs from connectionist networks, in which related concepts might be distributed over precisely the same set of neurons (Goldblum 2001). Noting "symbol-based semantic networks with spreading activation" as an example of a hybrid model, Bechtel and Abrahamsen tentatively suggest that it might be possible to achieve more of such reconciliation between symbolist and connectionist approaches (2002, 15).[3]

A rather more radical suggestion, however, is that symbolists and connectionists, far from representing quite different positions, are not in fact all that far apart. Timothy van Gelder and Robert Port (1995) argue strongly that both approaches are guilty of ignoring the environment and constructing static models of its inputs. They instead advocate a *dynamicist* perspective, insisting upon the revolutionary consequences of Dynamical Systems Theory when introduced into cognitive science. They claim that "The cognitive system is not a computer, it is a dynamical system. It is not the brain, inner and encapsulated; rather, it is the whole system comprised of nervous system, body and environment" (van Gelder and Port 1995, 2–4).

Van Gelder and Port are rather skeptical of any computational model, be it symbolist or connectionist. Bechtel and Abrahamsen, however, feel that the dynamicists overplay their hand. Their impression is that, considering how the dynamicist perspective grows out of studies focusing on sensorimotor function,[4] such studies do not need to give much consideration to representations or symboling. But this does not mean that van Gelder and Port are justified in rejecting the entire symbolist project just because it plays little apparent role in their own specialist domain of sensorimotor function. Their dynamical approach, while appearing to hold much in common with the embodied/situated cognition perspective developed notably by Edwin Hutchins and Andy Clark (Bechtel and Abrahamsen 2002, 243), is actually somewhat more extreme. Clark has dubbed this extreme position that sees little or no role for "internal" representations or categorizations in either cognition or perception (e.g., Gibson 1979; Brooks 1991; van Gelder and Port 1995) the "Thesis of Radical Embodied Cognition" (Clark 1997, 148). He notes that historical precursors for this kind of scepticism over the role of internal representation include Heidegger (1927) and Merleau-Ponty (1942).

As will be seen below, Clark has been one of the principal proponents of a less computational and more distributed approach to cognition. And yet he realizes, nevertheless, that the representational approach is still hard to replace when it comes to the human capacity for reasoning about the distant, the non-existent or the highly abstract—such kinds of problem-solving tasks, entailing a degree of disembodiment and internalization, are "representation-hungry" (Clark 1997, 166). They cannot be accounted for within the *radical embodied cognition* standpoint. One cannot help but agree with Clark's "ecumenical" stance, that we cannot reject the symbolist approach outright: it may not be at the heart of everyday, procedural activities as we maneuver ourselves through our environments, but it is difficult to see how else to explain certain human reasoning capabilities (see also Strauss and Quinn 1997). If we embrace the optimism and spirit of compromise of Clark, and of Bechtel and Abrahamsen, then it may ultimately be possible to create links between the neuroscience approach of Spitzer, and the situated/distributed cognition approach of Clark and Hutchins. This would represent a marriage between two recent movements in cognitive science, one "vertically" or "downward" into the brain, and the other "horizontally" or "outward" into the environment (Bechtel, Abrahamsen, and Graham 1998, 77, 90). One would hope that these two approaches do prove compatible as each field develops, but, at the present time, this is still a vanguard development and so rather premature for us to take any further.[5]

Thus this is simply a cautionary note: while the embodied nature of cognition needs its case to be put strongly in the face of the long dominant representationalism, this does not mean we should swing to the other extreme, as van Gelder and Port have done, and deny representationalism altogether. The crucial point, somewhat marred by the overly radical nature of their exposition, concerns the idea that cognition is both a *dynamic* and a *distributed* process. Humans are purposeful agents, actively seeking out environmental features rather than passively awaiting cues and stimuli. Moreover, the separation between an internal mind and an external world is wrong-headed; "the skilled practitioner consults the world, rather than representations inside his or her head, for guidance on what to do next" (Ingold 2000, 164). Ingold implies that the whole of cognitive science persists with the opposition between mind and matter, and that only James Gibson's ecological psychology offers a way out (2000, 167–68). Yet Suchman (1987), Hutchins (1995), Kirsh (1995) and Clark (1997, 1998), among others, show clearly how cognitive science is itself rising to meet the challenge, through the emerging fields of artificial life and situated cognition. Usefully, some of these cognitive scientists draw upon Gibsonian ecological psychology.[6] The following discussion is drawn from such work.

Human cognitive processes are adapted to provide solutions to problems encountered in the course of everyday life. In the coarsest sense, the brain is just another organ adapted to perform a series of functions. This perspective in which brain, body, and world are integrated grows quite naturally from our attempts thus far to understand agent and object as mutually constitutive. And just as we have argued that agents and organisms extend beyond their own obvious boundaries, so we shall posit that "mind" is similarly unconfined.

How is it possible to believe that mind can exist anywhere but in the brain? Well, in many ways, most of our earlier comments on the fuzzy boundary between organism and environment apply equally well to the mind. This is stunningly encapsulated in recent cognitive science, particularly in the work of Hutchins and Clark. Describing the boundary between mind and world as "the plastic frontier," Clark suggests that "mind is a leaky organ, forever escaping its 'natural' confines and mingling shamelessly with body and with world" (1997, 53). This kind of perspective requires us to rethink many deeply entrenched assumptions, of the kind discussed above. Thanks to various examples supplied by Clark (1997), we can see that a mind/brain operating in such a way would not be particularly efficient. Imagine a brain that first seeks to solve a jigsaw puzzle through "pure" thought, without any direct manipulation of the pieces themselves. Or try playing Scrabble without shuffling the tiles around as a means of prompting the brain into thinking of new words (see also Maglio et al. 1999). This is how such a mind would operate, when we know from our own experience that this is not what happens. Instead, the search for cognitive solutions in these and indeed other circumstances seems to involve the constant manipulation of *external* structures and supports. When the world is its own best model, why bother wasting valuable on-line neural resources to store information that can be much more readily and reliably stored in the environment itself? Some of our actions, categorized by Kirsh and Maglio (1994) as "epistemic" actions, are aimed primarily at altering the nature of the mental tasks with which we are faced. To come back to the jigsaw puzzle, an epistemic action would be to sort through all the pieces and set aside those with a straight edge and a patch of blue sky. This serves to modify, and hopefully simplify, the mental task with which the mind is confronted.

By way of further exemplification of the embodied/distributed cognition approach, Clark (1997, 65–66) discusses the computer game Tetris, another example deriving from the research of Kirsh and Maglio (1994). This game involves placing different geometric shapes (zoids) into rows—each time a row is completed it disappears, allowing more space for new zoids (Figure 3.2). The zoids fall from the top of the screen and, as they do so, the player can rotate and flip the zoids before dropping them in such a way that they best fit into the already accumulating rows and columns.

One hypothetical means of playing this game would be to solve the

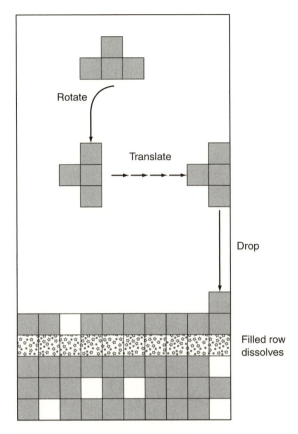

Figure 3.2. Tetris (after Kirsh and Maglio 1994). Courtesy of David Kirsh.

problem posed by each descending zoid through "pure thought" and then quickly implement the solution through the requisite actions on the screen. It was observed, however, that advanced players of Tetris manipulate the falling zoids as an active means of arriving at a solution. Such players are thus employing epistemic actions to reduce inner computational effort, and this strategy is the only way of coping once the speed of the game increases significantly (as it most certainly does at advanced levels). In such cases it seems as if the brain is completing patterns suggested to it by external structures in the world. Brain, body, and world complement each other, and one might even go so far as to dub this complementary system "mind," particularly when the mutualism runs as deep as it does in playing Tetris at an advanced level. Indeed, such a conclusion finds support in the work of

Jean Lave on the use of mathematics in everyday contexts—"cognition is seamlessly distributed across persons, activity and setting" (1988, 171).

Direct and Indirect Perception

This perspective thus portrays the mind as being a system heavily oriented toward action.[7] Cognition and perception are geared toward tracking possibilities for action in the world, and objects in that world are recognized and perceived in terms of the possible actions they might afford (Clark 1997; Glenberg 1997, 4; Kirsh 1995). Indeed, the Tetris zoids embody this point particularly well. In any context other than the game the form of the zoids is meaningless, yet within the game the possibilities each zoid offers can be "directly" perceived. This "direct" perception of the properties of objects holds true in many real-world situations—very often when we encounter objects within active contexts we are able to "directly" perceive their possible uses. When encountered in broadly appropriate contexts, the potential of a plate for eating from and a chair for sitting on announce themselves to the user in an unmediated fashion. This is highlighted in amusing fashion in the following quote from Georges Henri Luquet, one of the early students of child psychology:

One small girl I knew always described objects according to their role, not their name. A chair was "for sitting on," a plate "for eating on," and so on. One day, in the hope of catching her out, I showed her a slug and asked her what that was for. I was left feeling completely sheepish when she said that it was for squashing. (Luquet 1913, 134)

Costall (1997, 79) has also used this quote to illustrate what he calls "teleological reasoning"—the tendency, particularly noticeable among children, always to ask what an object is for.[8] This propensity for teleological reasoning is by no means the sole preserve of children—for humans, generally, an understanding of what an object *is* seems to be fundamentally linked to how that object is encountered in active situations.[9] Where solely physical characteristics are concerned, one can see that this argument makes a good deal of sense. But how far can this idea be extended? Is it possible that more abstract properties, such as the appropriateness of an object for eating or for ritual uses, may also be "directly" perceived? This is an area of considerable debate and controversy within the psychology of perception, the reasons for which we shall now explore.

The idea that the function of objects can be directly perceived runs counter to most psychological thought. It is generally held that humans are only able to understand the function of an object indirectly, through internal representations. That is to say, once we perceive the physical structure of an object (e.g., four legs, flat surface), the next step is to place it in a preexisting category within our memory ("chair"). Only then, once the category "chair" has been accessed, are we able to retrieve the potential function of the object ("for sitting on"). Thus, the human perception of function is believed to be indirect, mediated by cultural representations (a two-stage process of perception and conceptualization). Unsatisfied with this orthodoxy, the psychologist James Gibson developed the notion of "direct perception," in the course of his work on visual perception (1979). For Gibson, the potential of an object for sitting on, to continue the chair example, could be observed without first categorizing the object as "a chair." The potentialities held by an object for a particular set of actions was termed by Gibson its "affordances."

The perception of affordances has barely been studied, for various reasons: not only did Gibson die shortly after developing his theory, but his analysis was unclear in some crucial respects. Moreover, the indirect/mediated approach to perception has long been dominant (Palmer 1999, 409). Some scholars have pursued a Gibsonian ecological psychology since the early 1980s, but they have been in a definite minority.[10] Yet the approach appears to be attracting increasing attention, to the extent that Stephen Palmer (1999) describes the affordances concept as one of two major theoretical approaches to the visual perception of function (the other being the "categorization" approach). The concept has also been granted serious consideration in general works on visual perception by Gordon (1997, 180–220) and Bruce et al. (1996).[11] The general impression is that, although far too radical as developed by Gibson, the concepts of affordances and direct perception have much to offer. Perception of function, it would seem, is likely to rely both on affordances and categorization, on direct and indirect components.

Affordances

Having outlined the nature of the debate, let us now explore the affordances concept further, returning in particular to the question whether it can be stretched to encompass properties other than the purely physical. Gibson,

Figure 3.3. Mailbox and trash bin (after Palmer 1999). Copyright © MIT Press. Courtesy of MIT Press.

of course, considered that many kinds of objects, indeed perhaps all objects, could have their function directly perceived. This is a rather radical position that seems difficult to maintain; one example used by Gibson represents the way the idea is overextended. For Gibson, a mailbox can be said to afford letter-mailing (1979, 139). Indeed, the physical size and shape of the slot would seem to invite the deposit of a letter-sized object (see Figure 3.3). But, as is pointed out by Palmer (1999, 409), many kinds of trash bins also have slots of similar size and shape that could be taken to afford letter-mailing. The reason people use mailboxes rather than litter bins to mail letters is not solely to do with the physical form of the receptacle; the user possesses cultural information such that he/she knows the letters will be emptied from the box and eventually delivered (Noble 1991, 207–8). This understanding of the function of the mailbox is not accessible from its physical form alone, but derives from numerous associations and access to internal representations. Its function is thus in large part *indirectly* perceived.

The mailbox contravenes one of the two important conditions identified by Palmer (1999) as fundamental to direct perception: that the relation between an object's form and its affordance must be transparent. The other condition is that of observer relativity—it is in relation to a particular organism that an object can be said to have affordances. When the functional properties of an object conform to both of the above conditions, Palmer sees fit to talk of "physical affordances." Crucially, he goes on to say that "Physical affordances are the only ones for which a sensible case can be made that perception of function is direct in the sense of not requiring mediation by categorisation" (Palmer 1999, 412). Let us discuss further the two conditions described by Palmer, in relation to our previous example, the chair. As the arguments are relatively complex we shall deal with "relationality" and "transparency" in two separate sections.

The Relationality of Affordances

The function of the chair is relational in that it is codependent with the human body: although a chair may afford sitting to the majority of people, it may not to those of a particular size or shape (e.g., babies, the elderly). It may be, of course, that in certain circumstances the chair's affordance for sitting will not be recognized by the human actors present. Yet this does not mean that the chair stops affording sitting—its affordant properties are in a sense independent of the actors' perceptions. A chair does of course have other affordances too (see Figure 3.4), such as being used to prop open a door; this may be one of its affordances, but it is not its *canonical* affordance (Costall 1997, 79). Naturally, the chair's door-propping affordance persists regardless whether people actively recognize it or not.[12] As Gibson himself states:

> The observer may or may not perceive or attend to the affordance, according to his needs, but the affordance, being invariant, is always there to be perceived. An affordance is not bestowed upon an object by a need of an observer and his act of perceiving it. The object offers what it does because of what it is.[13]

Ingold suggests that Gibson shows himself to be somewhat inconsistent on the status of affordances, sometimes implying that they arise in the mutual relationship between object and agent, and sometimes, as here, that they inhere within the object. Noble (1993), too, is critical of what he sees as Gibson's tendency to describe affordances as existing independently of

Figure 3.4. Chair. Photograph by the author.

active subjects. But despite this particular quote, Gibson is not denying mutualism altogether in stating that a chair simply is a chair—the fact that he means this in relation solely to humans is surely implicit. This becomes clearer if we think of the matter at the species level—Gibson argues, for example, that grass *affords* eating insofar as there are grazing animals. Grass does not afford eating to humans, no more than chairs afford sitting to grazing animals. Whether or not an object's affordances are actually perceived, our bodies are constructed in such a way that a given object (e.g., a chair) affords certain activities to us that it does not afford to other animate bodies (e.g., grazing animals). To return to the example of the chair, it affords sitting to most human bodies, irrespective of whether a human body needs or perceives it. But this is not to deny that there is a mutualism between human agent and chair object. After all, if humans did not exist (along with any other being capable of sitting behavior), then chairs could hardly be said to afford sitting. Without grazing animals, grass ceases to afford eating.

Thus objects do not possess affordances that are truly independent and objective, and there has surely been some misunderstanding over this. There is only one sense in which one might say the affordances of objects are independent—affordances may be said to exist irrespective of whether they are perceived or not (which is precisely the point Gibson makes in the above quote). In other words, an agent may be physically capable of sitting on a chair, but may not need to sit and so may not perceive the chair as an object that affords sitting. The agent may in fact be looking for something to prop open a door, and sees the chair as an object that affords door-propping. Gibson's line is that affordances exist at the "ecological" level, as a relationship between an organism's body and its environment; these affordances remain even if the organism in question does not perceive or recognize them. Hence, from Gibson's viewpoint there is nothing necessarily mental or cognitive about affordances—the chair continues to afford sitting even if the agent does not have sitting in mind. Another way of avoiding the problem of perception is to focus on what the *situation* affords to an agent possessing a given *action repertoire* (Kirsh 1995).[14]

Harry Heft (1989), too, is keen to stress the relational quality of affordances; he suggests, however, that the body be considered not just as a physical entity but rather more broadly, as a conduit through which the individual expresses intentions and achieves goals. In saying that "an affordance is perceived in relation to some intentional act, not only in relation to the body's physical dimensions" (Heft 1989, 13), he seeks to introduce intentionality into the equation in a way that Gibson never did.[15] Yet Heft emphasizes that in so doing he is not breaking away from Gibson's legacy, but trying to clarify the nature of the tension between the "independent" and the "relational" properties of objects.

The Transparency of Affordances

Palmer's second key condition for an affordance is transparency—a chair affords sitting by virtue of the fact that its particular physical properties (shape, rigidity, etc.) render its function transparent and conspicuous. One might say that to understand the potential function of a chair requires no prior cultural knowledge and so may be perceived in a direct and unmediated fashion. But let us take the other example used by Gibson and cited above—grass. It seems quite "natural" that grass does not afford eating to humans, but is it a property that can be directly perceived, or one that has been learned? Surely its nonedibility is not a feature that is transparently knowable from its physical form alone? With an example that is a cultural artifact, such as the mailbox, it seems much clearer that its function lacks transparency and can only be ascertained through recourse to cultural knowledge. As for a noncultural object like grass, it is much less clear quite how we ascertain its affordances, directly or indirectly.[16] Indeed, as is noted by Palmer, the boundary between the two may be rather blurred.

Affordances and Meaning

So how does this excursion into "ecological" psychology help us with our overall focus in this book—the nature of meaning in material culture? Well, the concept of affordances does indeed provide the link, as we see in the following quote from Gibson himself:

Water causes the wetting of dry surfaces. It affords bathing and washing, to elephants as well as to humans. Streams of water can be dammed, by beavers as well as by children and hydraulic engineers. Ditches can be dug and aqueducts built. Pots can be made to contain water, and then it affords pouring and spilling. Water, in short, has many kinds of meaning. (Gibson 1979, 38)

Here we see a sort of conflation, such that the affordances of water essentially constitute its meaning too. Thus the tension we identified above between the independent and the relational properties of affordances carries over (in ecological psychology at least) into questions concerning the nature of meaning. A. M. Byers, for example, believes that Gibson's view depicts meaning as a property of things rather than as a mental property of intentional subjects; he takes exception to the implication that humans simply "pick up" the objective meanings that are "out there" (Byers 1994, 379). He rejects Gibson's objectification of meaning and relocates it in the active subject. Thus, as in the discussion of affordances, the issue of meaning residing independently within the object or as a property attached by intentional subjects comes to the fore, and Byers unfairly characterizes affordances in terms of a dualistic opposition between objects and subjects. William Noble (1993) also offers a strong critique of the Gibsonian perspective on meaning: "My thesis, contra Gibson, is that meanings are not properties of environmental entities awaiting discovery, any more than are affordances" (Noble 1993, 379).

Noble certainly hits the mark when he accuses Gibson's conception of meaning as being very limited—for Gibson, affordances and meanings seem to be largely equivalent. The idea that some elements of an object's meaning might inhere in its indirect associations rather than its direct affordances appears not to enter into his theory. Indeed Gibson's theory is particularly radical in its denial of any role for internal mental representation in the visual perception of function.[17] Yet Noble seems to fall into the same trap as Byers, that of adopting a dualistic line of reasoning. A much more fruitful approach would surely be to deradicalize Gibson's theory, as a means of reconciling it with the representational perspective. This is the line taken by Palmer (1999), Bruce et al. (1996), Clark (1997, 172), and indeed in some detail Heft (1989).[18] The latter makes a conscious (and cautious) effort to extend Gibson's predominantly "ecological" theory of meaning and affordances so as to cover cultural circumstances too. His idea is that the functional meanings of something like water may exist at a species-wide, transcultural level, but more often than not they will be to some extent culturally derived, too (Heft 1989, 17). Heft returns to the by now familiar example of the mailbox (itself taken from Gibson, of course). It was noted above that its physical form alone does not transparently announce its function; cultural information is required if one is to understand the mailbox's affordances. Heft stresses the importance of understanding the affordances of the mailbox in relation to the intentions of a knowledgeable actor (who seeks to mail a letter). And yet he cannot fail to admit that the intentional act of mailing a letter only finds a connection with the mailbox through cultural knowledge. The issue of direct versus indirect perception (and unmediated versus mediated access) is conveniently sidestepped by Heft. He is seeking, it would seem, to disassociate the concept of affordances from that of direct perception. Although the overall objective of seeking a compromise between extreme positions is sound, his means of achieving it devalues the potency of the affordances concept. The stance adopted by Palmer (1999) appears to have more going for it: limit the affordances concept to those physical properties that can be directly perceived (e.g. the capacity of water to wet, the ability of a flat rigid surface to bear weight), whilst recognizing that, in many cases, the human perception of an object incorporates not only affordances but also categorizations.

Another effort to adapt the Gibsonian model so that it might more readily incorporate cultural variables is also made by Norman (1998), albeit from a rather different starting point. The way Norman achieves this is interesting, so let us now focus briefly on his approach.

Affordances and Constraints

Donald Norman (1998, 9) uses the concept of affordances as a good base from which to explore the psychology of things, a psychology that is non-dualistic, neither mentalist nor materialist. He develops the concept in a number of ways, in particular, by coupling it with the notion of "constraints"—"whereas affordances suggest the range of possibilities, constraints limit the number of alternatives" (1998, 82). By devising experiments in which people were asked to construct simple composite objects from a series of parts, with no plan or specific knowledge of the finished product, Norman maintains that constraints fall into four broad categories: physical, semantic, cultural, and logical. One example of Norman's experiments involved the assembly of a toy motorcycle from a set of Lego pieces (Figure 3.5). There were thirteen parts, only two of which were alike. Through a combination of physical, semantic, cultural, and logical constraints, every person in the experiment was able to construct the motorcycle without instructions or help, even without ever having seen the process of assembly.

The physical constraints simply mean that large pegs cannot fit into small holes. The Lego motorcycle model was designed in such a way that the windshield, for example, only fits in one place. The semantic constraints, which "rely upon the meaning of the situation to control the set of possible actions" (Norman 1998, 85), dictate that the rider must be placed sitting forward. As this requires some knowledge of a socially constituted world, there might appear to be some overlap with cultural constraints. However, Norman posits that "some constraints rely upon accepted cultural conventions, even if they do not affect the physical or semantic operation of the device" (1998, 85). The three lights on the bike are red, yellow, and blue and, apart from their color they are indistinguishable and physically interchangeable. Yet red is a standard cultural convention for tail lights and yellow for headlights; thus cultural constraints solve the problem of

Figure 3.5. Lego motorbike (after Norman 1988, 83). Copyright © 1988 Donald Norman, published by Basic Books, reproduced by permission of the author and the Sandra Dijkstra Literary Agency.

where they should be positioned on the model. This does still leave the blue light, but, with only one place left to put it, logical constraints came into play. Logic also dictated that all the pieces should be used.

Affordances and Mediated Action

Norman's approach is interesting for its fluid approach to cognition, perception, and action, with seemingly no hard and fast boundaries drawn between them. His work emerges from within the distributed approach to cognition (allied closely to Kirsh and Hutchins), while also drawing upon Gibson's ecological psychology, with its relational approach to perception. Moreover, Norman demonstrates that the concept of affordances can have even broader relevance, notably to questions of action. Indeed, in the course of the above focus on perception, the question of *action* has emerged repeatedly. For example, Kirsh underlined the importance of understanding affordances in terms of the "action repertoires" of relevant human protagonists. In other words, to understand an artifact's affordances it needs to be situated within an active context. Norman proceeds to demonstrate this very point by examining the affordances and constraints of everyday objects in real-world, active settings. He selects objects that we frequently encounter in familiar situations, and which we tackle with straightforward action repertoires—such as various types of door, especially badly designed ones.

What emerges is a relational approach not only to cognition and perception but also to action. This emphasis on relationality with respect to action is found in the "mediated action" approach of James Wertsch and others, which derives ultimately from the work of the Soviet psychologist Lev Vygotsky.[19] Wertsch describes his perspective straightforwardly as a focus on how humans use "cultural tools" when engaging in action (Wertsch 1998). Although "cultural tools" here means not only artifacts, but also language, Vygotsky focused, in particular, on the latter and its instrumental role in action. Nonetheless, the concept clearly does have a much wider application, and can refer to any kind of "mediational means" employed in human action. In the way it is used by Wertsch, there are clear links with the distributed cognition approach within cognitive science.

A further interesting aspect of mediated action is that, according to Wertsch, mediational means are associated with both affordances and constraints (Wertsch 1998). This creates an extremely useful connection with Norman's work discussed above, for much of what Norman describes also makes good sense within the mediated action approach. For example, in his discussion of physical constraints, Norman uses the simple example of the door key—quite plainly, a vertical slot places a visible physical constraint upon how the door key can be inserted, yet there are still two possible orientations. Evidently, "a well-designed key will either work in both orientations or provide a clear physical sign for the correct one" (Norman 1998, 84). The key here can be understood as a "mediational means." Indeed, this sense that a cultural artifact such as a key may act as a mediator is wonderfully exemplified in a case study of a peculiar kind of door key described by the sociologist Bruno Latour (Latour 2000).

The key in question (Figure 3.6) is of a type used to lock and unlock the outer doors of apartment buildings in Berlin and its suburbs. The object resists interpretation, until, of course, it is encountered in its active context. Latour shows how, even to someone wholly unfamiliar with this particular technology, the material features of lock and key restrict possible patterns of action. In Norman's terms, there are clearly strong physical constraints in operation, dictating the ways the key can be inserted, turned, and removed. Logical constraints also come into play—one cannot just leave the key in the lock without retrieving it, and neither can one leave the door bolted but unlocked. Interestingly, this door key technology also incorporates strong semantic and cultural constraints—it inculcates the idea that the resident should unfailingly bolt the door at night and never during the day (the apartment block concierge only locks the door in this way after 10 P.M.). If an individual (an outsider) is unaware of this conceptual model, even given the strong physical constraints, it is hard to make sense of the technology and make it work (and thus Norman may consider it a case of poor design). Latour's point, however, is that this technology, through its very materiality, engenders a strong collective discipline among the residents (except for the resident who subverts it by doctoring his key). It is not as if the idea of collective discipline was constructed internally in the mind and then externalized in the form of the key—"the very notion of discipline is impracticable without steel, without the wood of the door, without the bolt of the locks" (Latour 2000, 19). The key is simultaneously and indivisibly material, agent and idea.[20] Latour's argument seems consistent with ideas on mediated action—the Berliner key is a cultural artifact that has a mediational role, acting as a kind of "pivot" between humans as they engage in action.

Although we may not realize it, objects are nearly always encountered in this way. It is what lies at the heart of what was described earlier as our

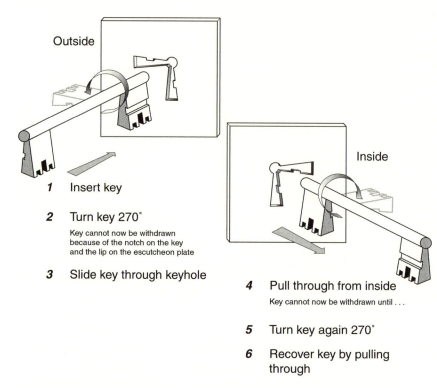

1   Insert key

2   Turn key 270°

Key cannot now be withdrawn
because of the notch on the key
and the lip on the escutcheon plate

3   Slide key through keyhole

4   Pull through from inside

Key cannot now be withdrawn until . . .

5   Turn key again 270°

6   Recover key by pulling
through

Figure 3.6. Berlin key (after Latour 2000, 15–16). Courtesy of Routledge and Thomson Publishing Services.

interpretative, teleological stance toward things—at the same time as we see the material, we unavoidably see the action and the conceptual model too. Analogous to this is the idea that an artifact "can be seen as an encapsulated 'theory of the task' and simultaneously a 'theory of the person' who fulfills the task" (Holland et al. 1998, 61). It is perhaps only in extreme cases that this does not hold true. The Berlin door key certainly threatened this for a moment. But the biggest challenge to our teleological attitude toward things comes from a series of fictional, invented objects put together by Jacques Carelman in his *Catalogue d'objets introuvables* (1994). There are dozens of fabulous and ludicrous cases, but we shall take just one—a "cafetière pour masochiste," sporting its spout and handle on the same side (Figure 3.7).

Figure 3.7. Carelman cafetière (after Carelman 1994, 63). Copyright © 2003 ADAGP, Paris, and DACS, London.

This object appears at first sight to obey semantic and cultural constraints, but with a second look it quickly becomes apparent that neither physical nor logical constraints are respected. Our intuitively teleological stance soon unravels, as we are thwarted in our efforts to project from the object any sort of meaningful intention or action; the Carelman cafetière reveals itself as a freakish, very unhuman artifact. It is thus perhaps one of those rare examples of an *isolated* object, albeit a fictional one (Carelman 1994).

To return to "affordances," the concept obviously does direct our attention firmly toward the properties of the object itself. Yet, at the same time, it forces us to see the object as a sort of nexus, where mind, agency and material meet and merge. With the Berlin door key we saw how an idea (collective discipline) requires materiality (the steel of the key, the wood of the door), and with Carelman's cafetière it was apparent that an object requires an idea. It has emerged that the dualistic perspective of Byers and others, whereby meaning must inhere either in the object or in the agent's intention, is misguided. In that ideas coopt objects, and objects coimplicate ideas, we can say that meaning is *distributed* between both.[21]

Sociality and Scaffolding

One point may have struck the reader through the course of the above discussion. The examples used by Gibson tend to be *natural* objects such as water or grass. Let us take another such natural object—a pebble on the beach. Some pebbles may be more suitable than others for what a person has in mind; if a hypothetical individual walking along the beach wishes to throw pebbles into the sea so that they skim over the surface, then presumably flat pebbles of a certain weight will be selected. Flat pebbles afford skimming, but they have not been *designed*. That is to say, other human agents are not implicated in the mutual coming together of agent and object.

A designed cultural object is different from a pebble because it means there is already a prior mutualism between producer and agent enduring within the object. As soon as design is involved, one can say that producers and consumers communicate with each other, however implicitly, through the nexus of the artifact. And this is, of course, the point that is made with the examples used above in connection with Norman's ideas on affordances and constraints, in particular the Lego model, but also the Berlin key. These cases encourage us to think of design as a social process that serves to focus the consuming agent toward the affordances of an object.[22] Therefore, a successfully designed artifact is one that announces its affordances and constraints. Through design, the producer is able to channel the impending mutualism between consuming agent and object along certain paths (although this is not to say that the design of an artifact is always fully respected and followed, for example when a chair is used as a door-stop). Whether or not the designer has intervened minimally or substantially, the resulting artifact is nevertheless a social nexus. What Gibson may have characterized as an ecological mutualism between agent and object turns out very often to involve a social relationship too.[23]

But let us return briefly to the pebble on the beach. Imagine that it is not an individual but a group (let's say a family) who are walking along the beach looking for pebbles to skim. The process of scanning the pebbles for good skimmers becomes a "joint practical activity" (Jackson 1989; Reed 1988a; Ingold 2000, 167), such that all the members of the family become attuned to what constitutes a good skimmer. One might also bear in mind that not all members of this beach-walking family will have the same bodily properties: a skimmable pebble for the father may be too large for the six-year-old to grasp and throw effectively. Nonetheless the point remains that a "natural" object like a pebble may through practical attention and use become a social object, a nexus through which a using group may come to communicate.[24]

This example of pebbles on the beach finds a fascinating ethnographic parallel in the work of Dietrich Stout (2002). His case study also serves to draw connections once again with the mediated action approach that is traced back to Vygotsky. Stout's research on the stone adze makers of the village of Langda in Indonesian Irian Jaya focuses on the skills required in stone adze manufacture and the means by which these skills are acquired. The first step in the production process, finding raw materials of sufficient quality, is also one of the most important. The search for suitable stone takes place at certain locales along the local river and is usually done in groups led by experienced knappers. Subsequent stages are also collective endeavors: during flake removal, for example, it is "common for knappers to observe and comment on the work of their neighbours . . . and even to give aid by taking over for a while from another individual who is having difficulties" (698). This kind of interaction, Stout explains, is most common between experts and apprentices. Indeed, it appears that almost all technical processes in adze production "are conducted as group activities, with a great deal of interaction among individuals" (702). The apprentice learns the craft within a context that is structured both physically and socially. The structure thus provided acts as a kind of "scaffolding" upon which the apprentice can hang new knowledge, allowing for a more rapid and effective acquisition of the requisite skills. With this opportunity to externalize at least some newly acquired information, the onus upon the apprentice to retain large chunks of new knowledge within the brain is much reduced. The notion of scaffolding derives from Vygotsky, and takes its place in developmental psychology. As is underlined by Holland et al., "individual skills originate in cooperative activity" (1998, 83).

Although the idea of scaffolding is particularly useful in understanding apprenticeship, it has a wider application to other learning contexts too.

There are many situations in which the meaning of an artifact or activity takes shape and is learnt within structured social settings. We discussed this point above in terms of "natural" objects such as stone and pebbles, but of course the same holds true for designed objects like chairs or keys. However, such objects do differ to some extent; in addition to the mutualism that develops between consumers in the course of use, there is an added mutualism between producer and consumer implicit within the design of the object.

Although for much of this chapter we have largely focused, and deliberately so, on the relationship between *individual* minds, agents, and objects, ultimately these relationships cannot be isolated from the social skein in which they are inevitably entangled. The fact that the human understanding of an artifact and its associated activity is very often a collective rather than an individual process finds further emphatic demonstration in the work of Edwin Hutchins (1995), briefly referred to earlier in this chapter. In his detailed study of the cognitive processes involved in complex navigational procedures at sea, he does indeed draw attention to the way in which producer and consumer communicate through the design of an artifact. The artifact in question is a nautical chart, the "key representational artifact" used to calculate position at sea. Hutchins describes the producers of the chart and those who ultimately use it as "joint participants in a computational event every time the chart is used" (1995, 64). But there are other social relationships involved in computation, not only between producer and user but also between different users within a navigation team. The cognitive task that is navigation is, more often than not, distributed among a number of individuals who must work together as a unit. The organization of these individuals' social interactions is as critical to the success of navigation computations as is the accuracy of charts and instruments or the level of skill of individual protagonists. Describing their solution to a particular navigational problem, Hutchins notes that "the team arrived at a division of cognitive labour in which the behavior of each of the participants provided the necessary elements in the information environment of the other just when they were needed" (1995, 345). Although most social groups may lack the formal organization of the navigation team, there is nonetheless a sense in which any individual's cognition is an unavoidably cultural process, coordinated within the framework of both material and social relations.

Isomorphy, Tuning, and Resonance

The examples of Carelman's cafetière and Latour's Berlin door key focused our attention on the codependency of idea, action, and material. These three dimensions coimplicate one another to the extent that it is difficult to conceptualize the material divorced from its associated action and idea. An object such as the Carelman cafetière that has no conceivable purpose or concept thwarts all our efforts at establishing the object's meaning. It would seem, therefore, that thought, action, and material form a "vertical" axis along which the meaning of the artifact is distributed. It is worth bearing in mind that this notion comes to us not only from distributed/embodied perspectives in cognitive science and psychology (e.g., Hutchins 1995; Clark 1997; Wertsch 1998), but also from anthropology, notably the work of Gell (1998). He uses the term "isomorphy of structure" to describe the links between "the cognitive processes we know (from inside) as 'consciousness' and the spatio-temporal structures of distributed objects in the artefactual realm" (Gell 1998, 222). The close correspondence between this and the arguments made above concerning both distributed cognition and indeed the notion of scaffolding, is uncanny. Moreover, comparisons can be made with Pickering's (1995) use of the term "tuning" to describe the interaction of human agency and material agency; we might equally well choose to use the term "resonance" instead of tuning. Gell's example of the circulation of Kula valuables in Melanesian society allows us to see how the resonances between the human and the material emerge:

> For success to accrue, the Kula operator must possess a superior capacity to engage in strategic action, which necessitates a comprehensive *internal model* of the external field within which Kula valuables move about. . . . The successful Kula operator controls the world of Kula because his mind has become coextensive with that world. He has internalised its causal texture as part of his being as a person and as an independent agent. "Internal" (mental processes) and "outside" (transactions in objectified personhood) have fused together. (Gell 1998, 231)

This application of the notion of structural isomorphy (or tuning, or resonance) to the world of Kula exchange is not only an excellent example of the potentially fruitful overlap between cognitive science and anthropology (and indeed archaeology, we hope), but is also an apt demonstration of what we mean by the vertical axis of cognition. Of course, Kula exchange involves whole networks of objects rather than single artifacts. This means that we are dealing not only with vertical but also horizontal networks, essentially a matter of "the significative networks in which all objects find themselves."

Recap

In this chapter, we have given consideration to the codependent nature of the connections between mind and object. Given that the received wisdom across much of the social sciences is that mind and object are clearly separable, we have had to rethink many of our common assumptions concerning the nature of cognition, perception and action. To this end, various novel perspectives being developed in the fields of psychology and cognitive science have been presented in this chapter; particular emphasis has been placed on the compatibility of these approaches with regard to cognition, perception and action. Not only is the idea of cognition as a situated and distributed phenomenon compatible with the relational approach to perception adopted within ecological psychology, but both are also compatible with Wertsch's approach to action that stresses mediation. Through an exploration of these various concepts we have moved toward an understanding of material culture meaning in which the codependency of mind, agent and object is fundamental.

The three examples discussed a little earlier, Norman's Lego motorcycle, Latour's Berlin door key and Carelman's cafetière, all served to illustrate the human teleological attitude toward objects, and the idea of objects having affordances and constraints. Perhaps more importantly still, they gently encouraged us to introduce the key social dimension into the equation— that to be human is to be not only a biological organism and a psychological agent but also a social person. In that all these dimensions feed into one another, objects are inevitably implicated in animacy, agency, and personhood (see previous chapter).

However, the properties of individual artifacts are just one part of the story. An exclusive focus on such characteristics runs the risk of dealing only with the *affordances* and not the *associations* of objects, when the very challenge before us is to understand the interaction of these two facets.[25] With this in mind, we should not treat objects as individual, isolated items; attention must be devoted to both their spatial and temporal situatedness. The former refers to the complex environment of human and non-human objects in which individual artifacts are enmeshed. The latter consists of an artifact's location within the flow of time, and how that artifact is experienced by agents over the course of a lifetime (cf. Riggins 1994a, 3). These patterns of associations are extremely significant in the constitution of an artifact's meaning; it is to such *networks* of association, and their role in the generation of meaning in material culture, that we turn in the chapters that follow.

Chapter 4
The Dynamics of Networks

In the previous two chapters we have seen how different phenomena come to be distributed through space and time. The phenomena
we discussed were cognition, agency and meaning. Cognition is distributed
in that it is not confined to the brain, but is invariably drawn into the body
and the external world.[1] Agency, although conventionally deemed to be in
the hands of human agents, is distributed among both humans and nonhumans in complex webs of interconnection. As for meaning, it is distributed
along both a "vertical" and a "horizontal" axis. The former refers to the
"vertical" connections that exist among brain, body, and object; meaning
does not reside primarily in any one of these, but is distributed among
them. This vertical axis was the focus of the last chapter. The focus of the
current chapter is what we have called the "horizontal" axis—that is to say,
the associations, physical or otherwise, that connect any given object with
innumerable others.

How might we characterize the organization of these associations? Assessing the organizational form structuring the interlinkages between objects is important because there are implications for the order of meaning.
If we consider objects as nodes (or vertices), and their associations as connections (or edges), then we can use the idea of the *network* to try to define
the overall structure of associations. However, there are many different
kinds of network, and the term is now almost omnipresent, thanks in no
small part to the telecommunications boom (Musso 1997; Lemieux 1999).
That the word *network* has become such a commonplace is due to its poly-
semic qualities. This is, of course, a double-edged sword—the concept's
flexibility renders it extremely useful but at the same time threatens its co-
herence. Employed in relation to so many different phenomena, the term
network risks losing any precision at all in its definition, whereupon its use
becomes counterproductive. A helpful step here is to give some thought to
the genesis of the term, for which we can turn to the insightful analyses of
Parrochia (1993, 2001) and Musso (1997, 2001).

Parrochia (1993) traces the meaning of the word "réseau," the French for "network," back to the old French word "réseuil," itself derived from the Latin "retiolus," a diminutive of "retis," meaning "net." This word is of relevance because it also lies behind the English term "reticular," another term describing network properties. "Retis" and "reticular" describe an ensemble of interwoven fibers or filaments. The term reticular is predominantly used in anatomical contexts. Indeed, the idea of networks has been closely linked to the human body since the birth of modern medicine with Hippocrates and Galen; the latter spoke of the brain as a network, the "rete mirabili" (Musso 2001). With the Enlightenment, and Descartes in particular, the human body began to be compared to a machine (Des Chene 2001); by implication, the network concept too was extended to include the machinic. And, ever since, one might argue, the symbolic charge of the term involves a double dynamic of body and machine, the organismal and the technical.[2]

Meanwhile, rational, formal approaches to networks were also being developed, initially at the beginning of the nineteenth century in crystallography. René-Just Haüy's work on crystals revealed the form taken by a solid network ("réseau solide"), leading to a science of networks influential upon both mathematics (e.g., graph theory) and astronomy (Parrochia 1993; Musso 2001). However, these solid networks were of a different kind from the more fluid type envisaged for the body in terms of the flow of blood through networks of veins. The French philosopher Claude-Henri Saint-Simon distinguished between these solid and liquid networks using the terms "corps brut" and "corps organisé" (Musso 2001). Significantly, Saint-Simon also envisaged a hybrid state midway between the solid and the liquid; thus it was considered that networks could take on different forms or aspects, the result being that the concept could be applied to a very wide range of spatial arrangements.

This distinction between solid and liquid networks has essentially continued in the physical sciences, with crystal lattices described as regular networks and gas molecules characterized as random networks (Figure 4.1). Interestingly, the hybrid state between the regular and the random that Saint-Simon hinted at has barely been explored (until recently that is—see below). This is an important point because (sociotechnical) networks in the real-world inevitably fall somewhere between the entirely regular and the random in their organization. Most of the networks I discuss in this chapter cannot be properly described as either solid or liquid. Such networks combine the structure of the crystal lattice and the flow of gas molecules. In-

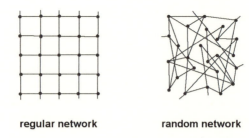

regular network   **random network**

Figure 4.1. Regular (crystal lattices) and random (gas molecules) networks.

deed, Henri Atlan has described the intermediary character of the network as "entre la rigidité du minéral et la décomposition de la fumée" (Atlan 1979, 5). He sees the network as the organizational form characteristic of living organisms, seemingly in much the same way as Capra, who, as we learned in Chapter 2, argues that "whenever we look at life, we look at networks" (Capra 1996, 82; cf. also 2002). And the same goes for other kinds of dynamic organizations such as sociotechnical networks, whether considered at the level of materials (e.g., the goods moved through a transport network), energy (e.g., electrical networks), or information (telecommunications networks).

This said, the idea that social networks are hybrid forms has been slow in coming to social scientists. It has commonly been assumed that "organization" more or less requires the rigidity and linearity of hierarchy. The opposite pole has long been thought to be anarchy, disorder and chaos—what possible order could there be without hierarchy? It is only relatively recently that the seemingly paradoxical ideas of nonlinear "chaotic" order, and of self-organizing nonhierarchical systems, have begun to take shape (Atlan 1979; Capra 1996; see also Chapter 2). The idea of the network has become central to this, as an organizational form that can easily be characterized as intermediate, incorporating both structure and flow, order and disorder.

Sociotechnical Networks

The idea that flow and structure might combine in a single organizational form makes sense of many sociotechnical networks in the real world. We mentioned above both transport and communication networks; each manifests a complex of interwoven lines, the intersections of which are its nodes. Flow is established by the connectivity of the nodes; it is the connections that are decisive in establishing the role and power of the nodes. And yet the flow is constrained by the rigidity of the structure; the locations of nodes, and indeed the connections between them, are not easily reconfigured. That both transport and communication networks exhibit flow within rigid structure is underlined by their often similar trajectories: for example, the establishment of the first national-level communication system in North America, the telegraph network, closely followed the creation of the first national-level transportation system, the railroad network. It is perhaps unsurprising that in each case a monopolistic situation soon emerged.

Of course, we no longer have just national-level telegraph and railroad networks, but also global aviation, radio, television, cellular phone, and computer networks, connected both visibly and invisibly. With the proliferation of such global networks, the interface between the local and the global becomes a major issue. Very often a global network is in fact a network of networks. In the worldwide aviation network, for example, it is not possible to access every node directly from a single position. Some carriers are global in their range, but in order to arrive at more out-of-the-way destinations itineraries may combine international with local (domestic) networks. Broadcasting networks may also be both local and global in their span—the global phenomenon of MTV, with its regional networks of MTV Asia, MTV Europe, MTV UK, MTV Latin America, MTV Japan, and MTV India, is one of the more far-reaching examples.[3] Another feature of such broadcasting networks, be they local or global, is that they are one-way, hierarchical, and tree-like. At first glance they would appear to differ from another form of network with both local and global properties, the Internet, which is essentially a global network that incorporates a whole series of local area networks, or LANS (Derfler and Freed 2000). It is often claimed that the Internet, unlike broadcasting networks, is a heterarchical structure (Chazal 2000), one that is intrinsically egalitarian. However, recent research suggests that both the Internet and the Web are actually hierarchical, with a limited number of sites serving as hubs through which the majority of all traffic passes (Buchanan 2002; Barabási 2002). Moreover, the Web has a unidirectional structure too, forming a "directed" network (Barabási 2002, 165–67).

In the telephonic networks upon which the Internet is based, the connections between nodes are quite variable: one key difference is that between *connected* and *connectionless* services within packet-switching networks (Stallings 1999, 312). The former possess many of the same characteristics as standard telephone networks—not only is a dedicated transmission path set up between nodes, but transmission is continuous, and the path is established for the entire "conversation." Such systems may be described as rigid in terms of their nodes and their connections, and indeed somewhat rigid in the nature of the flow too. However, connectionless networks are rather different—in not demanding continuous transmission, the sequential delivery of packets, or even a particular transmission route, they enjoy a degree of flexibility, fluidity, and self-organization that sets them apart.[4] Thus, although the flow through some network structures must follow rigid pathways, in others, the pathways themselves do possess a degree of plasticity.

Our principal aim in this chapter, then, is to investigate those networks that display a kind of hybrid topology, between the regular and the random, between structure and flow. It seems that most sociotechnical networks we observe in the world are hybrid forms. This is not to say, however, that other kinds of material and organismal networks might not also display similar properties. For example, in material science, hybrid substances can be engineered: the crystalline and the glassy are combined in alloys and other composite materials (Parrochia 1993). As for living entities, many different kinds of organism can be said to combine rigidity and fluidity—in order to demonstrate this, we shall look below at just a handful of examples, notably slime mold and ant colonies. We shall then also turn our attention to the organizational form taken by a single "organ" within an organism—the human brain. Then, finally, these same issues of rigidity and fluidity we shall also discuss with regard to human societies, with consideration given to some of the different sociological models that have been developed, such as actor-network theory.

Organismal Networks: Slime Mold and Ant Colonies

In Chapter 2 we stressed the importance of characterizing organisms in terms of not just form but also process. If we think about an organism as a dynamic process, then sometimes it is difficult to know where to draw the boundaries of the organism. Some organisms, such as mycelial fungi, are rather undefined in terms of form, composed of almost invisible networks spreading through the soil (Rayner 1997). Such an organismal network may be described as acentered and "deterritorialized."[5] Similar observations may be made about slime mold (*Dictyostelium discoideum*); it too is rather "slippery" in terms of form, but for different reasons. Much of the time, slime mold exists as thousands of separate single-celled units, but under certain environmental conditions (when the food supply is low) the individual cells coalesce to form a collective organism (Garfinkel 1987; Fox Keller 1995; Johnson 2001, 13). How this organizational feat occurs, though, has always been something of a mystery. It was assumed that some "elite" cells were "pacemakers," calling the shots to which the rank and file responded by aggregating. Yet the research of Fox Keller has shown that no such pacemaker cells exist. Rather, slime mold aggregation is organized from the bottom up. It is a nonhierarchical, collective, and self-organizing process. The individual cells are only able to "communicate" and form networks according to a set of rigid rules, yet the resultant multicellular structure exhibits plasticity.

Other organisms share this capacity for flexible self-organization; ant colonies in particular, with their capacity for sustaining a complex organization without management or central control, have formed the focus of a considerable amount of research by myrmecologists (e.g., Hölldobler and Wilson 1994; Gordon 1999).[6] Such properties are almost inconceivable to us humans, living as we do in a world in which organizational structures are invariably hierarchical. As Gordon emphasizes, no single ant is aware of what needs to be done to execute any colony task in its entirety (1999, vii). And yet despite the ignorance of any given individual ant, the larger entity of the colony functions successfully as an organism. How does this happen?

Individual ants are in almost constant interaction with their neighbors, forming highly connected networks; it is from these interactions between ants following simple low-level rules that the higher-level macrobehavior of the colony emerges. Most of the individual worker ants seen scurrying around the nest are sterile and are hence not reproductively viable units—the colony is the reproducing unit with the queen at its core.[7] And yet the queen is not an authority figure, controlling the workers' activities. Deborah Gordon's painstaking research on harvester ants in the Arizona desert has demonstrated that the allocation of tasks among the ants in a colony depends very much on ant interactions. The kinds of tasks ants perform include foraging, patrolling, nest maintenance, and midden work. If a single ant not engaged in any particular activity keeps on encountering other individuals performing midden duties, then the chances are that this ant will itself switch to midden work. How does this signaling occur? Gordon (1999, 161) has discovered that the fatty acids (cuticular hydrocarbons) with which ants coat themselves differ somewhat according to the task being performed—that is to say, an ant doing midden work has a certain odor that other ants can detect. It is thus through chemical signaling that ants communicate their tasks to one another.

The colony displays the emergent properties of a self-organizing system. It constitutes a functional structure in which any individual element (bar the queen) is superfluous, and contains no "obligatory points of passage."[8] It would appear that higher-level adaptive fluidity arises from lower-level rule-based rigidity; the ant colony may thus be characterized as a true network, a topological hybrid of structure and flow. It is not just collective organisms that we may characterize in this way: some organs, and notably the human brain, seem to share many such characteristics. Interestingly, the analogy between an ant colony and the human brain is used by Gordon herself. An ant is to the colony what a neuron is to the brain. Indeed, Gordon has devised with coworkers a neural network model to describe ant interactions in a colony. Let us now turn, then, to neural networks in order to explore further the properties of different topological forms.

Neural Networks

Due to the striking originality of his writing, it is probably Douglas Hofstadter who is best known for creating the analogy between ant colonies and neural networks (Hofstadter 1979; also Gordon 1999; Johnson 2001). Indeed, he refers to neurons as "the brain's ants" (Hofstadter 1979, 339).[9] There are many ways in which the analogy is a useful and thought-provoking one. One of the principal similarities, as we have noted, is that in each case higher-level behavioral adaptability arises from lower-level rule-following rigidity. Each individual neuron, like each ant, is dumb and follows set rules. But networks of neurons behave quite differently, achieving, through self-organization, not just remarkable processing power but also an impressive degree of fluidity and flexibility. How do neural networks manage this? What are their properties?

The topic of neural networks takes us back to territory covered in Chapter 3, in which we considered the role of the brain as a cognitive and computational device. Let us devote some attention to such computational activities from the perspective of flexibility and self-organization. We can

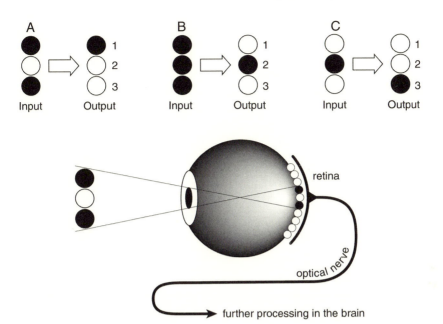

Figure 4.2. Simple input-output patterns (after Spitzer 1999, 25). Copyright © 1999 MIT Press. Courtesy of MIT Press.

start with a very simple network problem. Imagine that an organism receives three different inputs from its environment, patterns A, B, and C, to which it must respond with three different types of output behavior (Figure 4.2). One solution to the problem would involve a very simple neural network in which the three inputs form one layer of nodes and the three outputs another layer: each input node is connected to every output node (Figure 4.3; see also Spitzer 1999, 24–27).

The output nodes each have a threshold—only when the threshold is exceeded are the nodes activated. Given that every output node receives three inputs, its activation depends upon the combined strength of the connections from the inputs. And these connections between inputs and outputs are not equal in strength. As Manfred Spitzer emphasizes (1999, 27), "The differential strengths of the synaptic connections between the neurons of the input and the output layer are crucial to the effective functioning of the network." We can see in Figure 4.3 these differential strengths and how

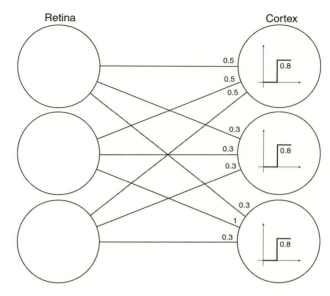

Figure 4.3. Simple neural network (after Spitzer 1999, 26). Copyright © 1999 MIT Press. Courtesy of MIT Press.

they are responsible for activating the output nodes and thereby forming a pattern recognition system of inputs and outputs. Of course this does raise the question how the connections come to have different weights in the first place. In artificial neural networks, the synaptic connections are tuned through "training"; one way this is achieved is through repeating inputs and outputs until they are mapped onto one another correctly. Such a supervisory process obviously requires an "external trainer" (Spitzer 1999, 49). This does not make much sense for neural networks within the brain, however. In the brain, a physiological process occurs whenever two neurons are simultaneously active, such that the connection between those two neurons is strengthened (the Hebbian learning rule). Discussion of the role of glutamate, NMDA receptors, long-term potentiation, and nitrogen monoxide in the biochemistry of synaptic change can be found in Spitzer (1999, 42–49). The point is that *real* neural networks must be self-organizing. Yet remarkably, this capacity for self-organization without supervision can also be displayed by *artificial* neural networks.

This capacity is seen in what are called "Kohonen networks," after the Finnish engineer Teuvo Kohonen, who devised them in the 1980s. These networks are akin to the simple network shown in Figure 4.3, but differ in an important respect: not only is each input node linked to every output node, but all output nodes are themselves interconnected. This layer of interconnected output neurons is called the Kohonen layer. One of its most interesting features is that every neuron stimulates the neurons that immediately surround it, while inhibiting the excitation of neurons that are farther away. Thus when input information is transmitted, it is not just one output neuron that is activated, but a group of them. This group will nonetheless form something of a spike, with one "winning neuron" at the center. If the input information is repeated, this structure in the output will tend to be fine-tuned and consolidated, until an accurate representation of the input pattern is formed. And as Spitzer aptly summarizes,

Because of this architecture, the neurons of the Kohonen layer can fine-tune their synaptic weights by self-organisation so that the representation of certain features of the input are located at specific points on the output layer. In short, the Kohonen layer forms a topographical map of the important features of the input. (1999, 95–96)

So not only do Kohonen networks extract regularities from the inputs, but they also create a structured, self-organized representation of these regularities in the output layer. The order that is produced takes the form of a topographical map, a landscape of peaks and valleys. However, the topography is dynamic and can be substantially redrawn.

As more data emerge from neuroscience, thanks in no small part to advances in neuro-imaging, so it is increasingly apparent that artificial neural networks really do reproduce many of the characteristics of human cognition. They are flexible, they can learn from experience, and they are self-organizing. One fascinating "real world" example of this "neuroplasticity" relates to cochlear implants, as discussed already in Chapter 3 (see Figure 3.1). The principal point of this example is that neuroplasticity is a pervasive phenomenon, affecting lower- and higher-order areas (i.e., both sensory and interpretive). There are a number of other possible examples, such as the increase in size of the cortical area representing the tip of the index finger that occurs when blind people learn to read Braille (Spitzer 1999, 11, 148). Not only can the local networks dealing with sensory stimuli reconfigure themselves, they can also exhibit flexibility in the way they are "wired" to other networks (e.g., phonetic and semantic ones). Remarkably, this fluidity is dynamic and self-organizing. Of course, we must not lead ourselves to believe that constant fluidity is the rule—these networks can, through learning and repeated experience, actually become rather rigid. Although sometimes the brain can cope with localized damage, with other areas taking up the functions previously performed by the damaged area, this is far from being the rule. It is this relationship, this precarious balance between rigidity and fluidity in networks, which we shall now explore further in a different context altogether—sociological studies of sociotechnical structures.

The Sociological: Actor-Network Theory, Arborescence, and Rhizomes

Actor-network theory emerged within a subfield of sociology dubbed "science and technology studies" (STS), which sought to understand the status of modern technologies within their sociopolitical settings.[10] STS was in itself something of a reaction against approaches to technological change that were rather unidirectional and deterministic, such as innovation studies and history of technology (Pinch and Bijker 1987, 21–22). The tendency in such perspectives to attribute the success of an artifact or technology to its technological superiority was something of a self-fulfilling prophecy, chiefly because the innovation in question only came to be an object of study once it had been successfully adopted by society. The reaction to this was to build multidirectional models: in the innovation process, technologies do not follow a linear route but may progress along a number of different avenues. Along this journey, some technologies die and some survive. Thus the survival of a technology is something that demands explanation in and of itself. For STS, the fact of survival or failure is assigned principally to social rather than technical causes—technology is deemed to be socially constructed. This approach was fine-tuned to create a model known as the "social construction of technology" or SCOT. Within this model, certain key notions were developed, such as "relevant social groups," "interpretative flexibility," and "closure" (cf. Pinch and Bijker 1987; Bijker 1995). One useful example comes from Wiebe Bijker's (1995) work on the invention of the bicycle during the 1880s. He identifies the coexistence of different *social groups* (male cyclists, female cyclists, anti-cyclists), each of which assign different meanings to the object in question. The negotiation of meaning that occurs as different types of bicycle are designed and used during this period of innovation is described by Bijker as *interpretative flexibility*. Eventually, flexibility gives way to *closure*, as meanings galvanize and fix onto one particular model, which then becomes "the" bicycle.

ANT came into being in the 1980s through the work of scholars such as Akrich, Callon, Law, and Latour. It evolved out of social constructivist approaches in that it sought a more satisfactory balance between the social and the technical than SCOT had managed. Although the achievement of SCOT in countering technological determinism was considerable, it may have veered too far in the other direction toward social determinism. SCOT also establishes a clear distinction between people and objects; even though they may interact in complex ways, John Law notes, they remain entirely different in kind (Law 2000, 3). With ANT, on the other hand, not only is equal emphasis placed on social and technical protagonists in examining technologies, but people and objects are not considered fixed entities (Law 2000, 3). To speak of "technical protagonists" or "nonhumans" as if they have agency may at first sound rather odd, but it belies one of the key tenets of ANT, and one of its main differences with SCOT: that there is a symmetry between the human and the nonhuman, with agency distributed equally between them. To return to the example of bicycle technology, ANT would maintain that it is not constructed solely by social groups; "nonhuman" technical features such as pedals and inflatable tires are as much agents as any of the human protagonists. In the two preceding chapters we emphasized the role of *agency* in the constitution of material culture meaning; as is clear from its very name, actor-network theory also places agency high on its agenda. Moreover, it does so in a way that acknowledges its distributed, hybrid character between humans and non-humans, a point also made earlier in this book. Thus, in this respect, ANT would seem to fit the bill well.

A further feature of ANT is its inbuilt tension between "networks" and "actors," mirroring the oft-cited sociological dyad of "structure" and "agency." This too can be perceived as an improvement upon SCOT, which did not manage to integrate the "network" or structural aspects particularly effectively. One can see this quite clearly in Bijker's later work (1995, 190; as opposed to Pinch and Bijker 1987), in which he strives to incorporate "structure" into his theoretical framework. In effect he criticizes SCOT for tending to limit its focus to one-to-one relationships between a social group and a particular artifact; usually a single social group will interact simultaneously with many different artifacts, and many different social groups may use a single artifact. Thus, the relationship between any given social group and a particular artifact occurs within a wider structure or network, or what Bijker calls a "technological frame." He describes it as follows:

A technological frame comprises all elements that influence the interactions within relevant social groups and lead to the attribution of meanings to technical artifacts—and thus to constituting technology. (Bijker 1995, 123)

The structural aspect Bijker combines with social interactionism to form the concept of "technological frame" is derived, he claims, from semiotics. Yet the "semiotics perspective" he adopts is based on a highly idiosyncratic understanding of semiotics. His approach stems principally from A. J. Greimas, a semiotician who can be criticized for a Saussurean failure to deal with materiality (cf. Gottdiener 1995). And it is perhaps because he is working from Greimas that Bijker's use of semiotics seems limited to language; for example, he argues that the process whereby an artifact comes to acquire a more stable cultural meaning "can generally be traced by analyzing the language actors use to describe the artefact" (1995, 194). To restrict the range of the semiotic process to language when one is dealing predominantly with material things seems rather odd, particularly when there is a substantial literature on the semiotics of objects; this point we shall deal with in some detail in Chapter 5.

ANT also draws upon semiotics as a means of elaborating its concept of network interconnections, but does so rather more successfully than Bijker. Indeed, it has been described by one of its protagonists as "a ruthless application of semiotics" (Law 1999, 3), such that entities take their attributes in large part according to their relations with other entities (in other words, entities do not have essences). But a purely semiotic approach is in itself not enough, as we have seen the way that many Saussurean-derived semiotic perspectives fail to get to grips with the materiality of the semiotic process (Bijker included). Thus in the chapter that follows we shall highlight the advantages of what has been called a "sociosemiotic" approach. Yet actor-network theory claims to meet this challenge, too, with Law describing it as a "semiotics of materiality" (1999, 4). So, conveniently and almost coincidentally, the principal tenets of ANT appear to tally well with many of the arguments that will be more fully formulated in Chapter 5—not only does it take semiotics on board, but it also seems to do so in a way that is consistent with sociosemiotics.

However, ANT is not quite as successful in some of its claims as it might be. For example, although it supposedly embraces semiotics and its materiality, there is little discussion of quite what this entails. It appears to be taken to mean that the properties of any object derive not only intrinsically from the object, but from its connections with a whole series of other objects. The semiotic process is understood to be little more than the associations that build up among various objects, thereby resulting in a kind of network (e.g., once you buy a car, you enter into the semiotic structure of highways, gasoline stations, traffic jams, etc.). The potential complexity and variability of these connections, the focus for discussion in Chapter 5, are barely credited. This may in part be because actor-network theory, as a sociological model, may be more focused on social interactions than on cultural meanings. As we shall see below, it is not just ANT but also other sociological models that come up short in this regard.

ANT has also been at the sharp end of criticism from some of its original protagonists, such as Latour and Law. Latour argues that the popularization of the network metaphor in relation to computers and the Internet means that its dynamic potential and freshness has been lost. Observing that in such contexts the term "network" refers to "transport without deformation, an instantaneous, unmediated access to every piece of information" (1999b, 15), Latour bemoans the rigidity and passivity that have come to be associated with networks. Yet, he claims, the idea of network does not necessarily bring with it these connotations; twenty years ago, in sociological studies of technology, the metaphor was a critical tool used to overcome rigid notions such as "institutions" and instead to focus attention on the series of dynamic transformations that were always occurring in fluid, flexible sociotechnical interactions. Indeed, Law has been striving to develop new forms of scrutiny that move beyond ANT in their capacity to cope with fluidity. He suggests that the network is just one kind of social space among many, and that "fluid space" is a topological form that has been overlooked (Mol and Law 1994). In contrast to network space, composed of nodes and lines, fluid space contains no "obligatory points of passage." Other proposals Law makes to try and focus our attention on the fragmented and the acentered dimensions of sociality include the ideas of *partiality* (Law and Mol 1994) and of *fractals* (Law 1999).

The limitations of ANT are further underlined by Lee and Brown (1994). They claim that ANT is not unlike conventional sociology insofar as it fails to focus on the spaces between the established nodes and lines of sociotechnical networks. While Lee and Brown acknowledge that the "fluid social topology" of Mol and Law is a step in the right direction, they go much further and draw upon the work of Deleuze and Guattari (1988) as an example of how to tackle network space and fluid space simultaneously. Deleuze and Guattari suggest that when searching for structure and order, scholars tend to seek out hierarchical, centered systems, which they term "arborescent" (the idea being that the tree is a metaphor fundamental to much of Western thought). If one considers a tree as a communication structure (or as an ordered system), then one branch can only communicate with another by following set paths. The structure of the tree also implies a genealogy, a temporal hierarchy—the tree builds from the bottom, so the oldest parts are at the bottom and the youngest parts at the top. The oldest part (the trunk) is indispensable, whereas a few young shoots are always somewhat expendable. However, focusing on arborescence ignores other kinds of structures that are nonhierarchical and acentered. Following their own organismal/plant logic, Deleuze and Guattari choose to call these "rhizomes." In contrast to an arborescent structure, any point within a rhizome can be connected to any other.[11] In that rhizomes consist only of lines and not nodes, there are no "obligatory points of passage." A further distinction is that the rhizome is antigenealogical.

Despite its very different genesis, this distinction between arborescent and rhizomatic networks exactly mirrors the dichotomy between regular and random networks discussed earlier in this chapter. This is further accentuated by the manner in which Deleuze and Guattari characterize the different kinds of space associated with arborescent and rhizomatic networks respectively. The terms they use are *striated* and *smooth* space. The former is punctuated by nodes and traversed by lines, with order following set channels; the latter is an open space through which order may flow. Pursuing this same topological theme, they note that an arborescent structure is territorialized, while a rhizomatic one is deterritorializing.[12] Lee and Brown (1994) make extensive use of these arguments of Deleuze and Guattari in criticizing ANT for dealing only with arborescent networks (and striated space), with little awareness of rhizomatic structures (and smooth space). Although Mol and Law talk of fluid social topology rather than rhizomes per se, they are making a very similar point. Yet for both sets of scholars it is not a question of rejecting arborescence and network space altogether in order to replace it with rhizomes and fluid space, nor is it a matter of creating a duality between them; as Deleuze and Guattari emphasize, "there are knots of arborescence in rhizomes, and rhizomatic offshoots in roots" (1988, 20). They are not two opposed models, but rather two topological tendencies or modes. Yet, ultimately, none of the above manages effectively to envisage a hybrid topology that combines the arborescent and the rhizomatic, the solid and the fluid, the striated and the smooth.

From the above it would seem that present attempts to characterize the topological configurations of sociotechnical networks are inadequate.

For all the complex theoretical discussion of arborescent and rhizomatic models, and indeed other kinds of spatial topology, we are left with the same dualism as before. If linear space is necessarily hierarchical, striated and genealogical, and fluid space is necessarily nonhierarchical and smooth, then what are the topologies of real-world networks falling in between these two theoretical extremes?

Small-World Networks

The work by Mol and Law (1994), and Lee and Brown (1994), seeks to revitalize ANT through the addition of randomness into otherwise regular networks. However, their theoretical approaches fail to reconcile the opposed tendencies of regular networks and random networks. Networks in the real world are, more often than not, characterized by this very intermediacy, somehow combining the regular and the random seamlessly. Some sociological research has succeeded in demonstrating this empirically, notably in the famous work by Stanley Milgram in the 1960s. In a groundbreaking experiment, Milgram selected a number of "sources" in Kansas and Nebraska, and asked them to mail a package to one of two "target" individuals in a distant state, Massachusetts (Milgram 1967; Watts 1999, 18–19). The sources were provided with some basic information on the status of their targets, but were prevented from trying to mail the packets to them directly. Instead, they were requested to send the packets directly to an individual with whom they were on first-name terms, in the hope that this individual might then be more closely connected to the target. One might imagine that none of the packages would have found the target, or that they would only have done so through a very large number of links. However, Milgram was able to show that on average only about five intermediaries were required for a package to arrive at its final destination. This would be infeasible if people were only connected to their nearest neighbors in regular networks; what it shows is the existence of "random" ties that drastically reduce the number of connections needed to cover a long distance. Milgram referred to this as the "small-world" phenomenon. A few years later, Mark Granovetter added a further important refinement, suggesting that even though it is such "random" connections that serve as the important bridges keeping together what would otherwise be isolated clusters, they are, nonetheless, often the weakest ties in the network, much weaker than the strong ties in local clusters (Granovetter 1973).

Yet, while both Milgram and Granovetter had gone some way toward documenting the "small-world" character of some social networks, they had not been able to explain their structural dynamics. The basic question remained—how does a social network manage to be both highly clustered and yet with such low levels of degrees of separation? Clustering is a property of regular ordered networks (e.g., a crystal lattice)—but it takes a very long time to travel across a highly clustered network, which can only be done step by step, from neighbor to nearest neighbor. In other words, a regular network displays many degrees of separation—given a global human population of six billion, and assuming each individual is connected with only 50 nearest neighbors, the number of degrees of separation would be around 60 million. This figure is clearly of an entirely different magnitude from the five degrees posited by Milgram, or indeed the six degrees postulated by John Guare in his *Six Degrees of Separation: A Play* (1990). Random networks (e.g., the interaction between gas molecules) *do* exhibit such low degrees of separation, but the flip side is that they are also very poorly clustered. As it happens, it is only very recently that satisfactory models have been formulated to account for this combination of clustering with low degrees of separation. In keeping with Milgram's initial terminology, these networks that fall "between order and randomness" have been dubbed "small-world" networks (Watts and Strogatz 1998; Watts 1999). One of the key features of such networks is that it only takes very few random connections in an otherwise regular network to bring down the degrees of separation drastically. So few, in fact, that the clustering is hardly affected. It only takes a handful of long-range "random" connections to transform a vast world of nodes and connections into a small world, as is seen in the intermediate graph in the center of Figure 4.4.

But the work of Watts and Strogatz has proven to be just the first, albeit critical step. Acknowledging the importance of their contribution, Barabási and Albert add an important critique, pointing out that the model makes two crucial assumptions: that the number of nodes in a network remains fixed, and that the probability that two nodes are connected is random and uniform (Barabási and Albert 1999; Albert and Barabási 2002; Barabási 2002). They emphasize that, on the contrary, networks are open systems that experience growth; and that most networks exhibit preferential connectivity—that there is a higher probability that a new node will connect to a node that already has a large number of connections. Thus they adapt Watts and Strogatz by adding the dimensions of growth and preferential attachment.

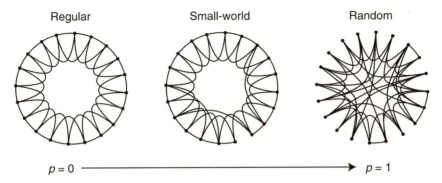

Figure 4.4. Small-world network (after Watts and Strogatz 1998, fig. 1). Courtesy of Duncan Watts.

Barabási and Albert argue that, following these principles, real-world networks will tend to take a certain form—they will consist of a large number of nodes with a small number of links, and a very small number of nodes with many links (what they call "hubs"). The pattern that emerges follows a power law. Moreover, Barabási and Albert also argue that as the scale of the network increases, its structure will not change—it can thus be said to be scale-invariant, or scale-free. Hence they proceed to coin the phrase "scale-free" network. Perhaps the best example of a scale-free network is the Internet. Scale-free networks look different from the small-world networks of Watts and Strogatz—indeed, as a means of differentiating between them, one observer has dubbed them "egalitarian" and "aristocratic" networks respectively (Buchanan 2002).

Amaral et al. (2000) offer a further modification that serves to narrow the gap between small-world and scale-free networks in a rather interesting way. They say that preferential attachment can be hindered by two classes of factors. First, nodes may undergo *aging*. For example, a highly connected node, let's say a famous actor in a network of actors, will at some stage stop receiving new links. Second, the addition of new links may have prohibitive *cost*, and nodes may have limited *capacity*. A good example is the aviation network—what emerged as hubs are now suffering congestion, as the physical costs of adding links and the limited capacity of a hub start to take their toll. Thus, although some small-world networks may have a hub structure and appear to be scale-invariant, others are in fact rather less reliant on hubs and are more "egalitarian." Buchanan (2002) adds, in relation to the aviation network example, that egalitarian networks may thus be seen to evolve out of aristocratic ones.

Whether aristocratic or egalitarian, hierarchical or heterarchical, these network models provide a powerful new means of understanding the topologies of intermediate social networks that are neither fully ordered nor entirely random. Their potency is in part demonstrated by their increasingly wide application within a range of disciplines, as Buchanan states:

Social networks turn out to be nearly identical in their architecture to the World Wide Web, the network of Web pages connected by hypertext links. Each of these networks shares deep structural properties with the food webs of any ecosystem and with the network of business links underlying any nation's economic activity. Incredibly, all these networks possess precisely the same organization as the network of connected neurons in the human brain and the network of interacting molecules that underlies the living cell. (2002, 15)

In such a perspective, the different areas of discussion within this chapter—organismal networks (slime mold, ant colonies), neural networks, and sociotechnical networks—can all be understood as various manifestations of a similar kind of organizational logic. The new science of networks has up to now been mostly applied to issues in biology (at various levels, from cells to ecosystems), economics, and computer science/Internet topology (Barabási 2002); that is to say, in the kinds of areas that are already accustomed to the mathematical modeling of complex systems. Indeed, the new science of networks is closely associated with the new science of complexity. However, despite some initial forays, there has not been much impact as yet on social science subjects such as sociology, anthropology, and archaeology. There is nonetheless considerable potential, particularly in the context of actor network theory outlined earlier. But a few notes of caution may need to be sounded. First, we need to think about the ways humans and nonhumans come together within sociotechnical networks that may be "scale-free" or "small-world" in character. Second, we need to consider the extent to which such network models have the capacity to cope with "meaning"—if the connections between human and nonhuman entities are frequently semiotic in character, what are the topological implications?

The conception of the network as an intermediate organizational form carries with it distinct advantages. The complex relationships between socially engaged humans and nonhumans may very well take the form of a heterogeneous network, composed of nodes and lines, more or less rigidly arranged, either hierarchically or nonhierarchically. But at the same time the notion that humans and nonhumans flow through one another and intermingle is a powerful one, as is the idea that, in the absence of obligatory points of passage, any part may connect with any other. This combination of perspectives shows the cooccurrence of structure and flow in the numerous associations through which objects interlink both with each other and with humans. As Mol and Law point out, rigid structures may crystallize out of a solution; nodes and lines can form, although there is always the chance that they may once again be reabsorbed. The territorialization (or crystallization) of a network achieves rigidity, but this rigidity is not absolute and permanent in that it is prone to deterritorialization (or reabsorption). This sense of a network's rigidity being one moment of crystallization among many moments can be carried over into other kinds of networks, indeed, of a type discussed earlier in this chapter—neural networks, both artificial and actual, are dynamic, flexible, and even self-organizing systems (e.g., Kohonen networks—see Kosslyn and Koenig 1992; Spitzer 1999; Llinas 2001). Connections are created that have both momentary rigidity and long-term plasticity.

Concluding Remarks

Organizational form is increasingly conceptualized, particularly given the nature of communication in the contemporary world, in terms of networks. Networks combine structure and flow and, as we have learnt from our wide-ranging exploration of ant colonies, neural networks, and sociotechnical systems, many organizational forms combine these two topological tendencies. This idea of organizational hybridity is one that we will encounter throughout this book. As we have seen above, it also lies at the heart of the notion, espoused particularly in actor-network theory, that networks are heterogeneous entities in which humans and nonhumans intermingle.

This understanding of the network as a metastable topological hybrid is indispensable to our overall attempt at building material culture theory.[13] It helps us grasp how agency and cognition are not only phenomena that are distributed, but that they are distributed according to certain organizational forms. Moreover, the concepts of structure and flow cast light on the nature of meaning in material culture. This we can attribute, at least in part, to the failure of most of the sociological models mentioned above to deal explicitly with the topological character of cultural meanings. This is not to say that they are fatally flawed, but it may be possible to develop them further by incorporating some points derived from semiotics. For instance, the associations between objects are variable, based upon different kinds of relationship, such as similarity, contiguity, factorality, causality, and convention. The operation of these different processes surely has implications for the essentially reticular quality of meaning. We shall attempt to illustrate this point in the course of our in depth discussion of semiotics in the next chapter.

Chapter 5
Networks of Meaning: A Sociosemiotics of Material Culture

Les objets sont en dehors de l'âme, bien sûr; pourtant, ils sont aussi notre plomb dans la tête.

—Francis Ponge

Previously, I have proposed that, since mind, agency, and matter are codependent and come together in the nexus of the object, neither materialist nor mentalist approaches to material culture are adequate. Minds, agents, and objects may appear to be bounded entities, but they are in fact rarely isolated, each spilling over into the other across "fuzzy" boundaries (as explored through a number of examples). This notion of mutualism was developed in Chapter 3 through the concept of affordances, which also allowed us to tackle the issue of meaning and how it comes to be distributed between object and subject. However, it was noted that the idea of affordances, while useful in focusing our attention on the relationship between material, action, and mind, brought with it two potential problems. One was the danger of isolating individual objects from their spatiotemporal associations with other objects. The other was the tendency to focus on functional meanings at the possible expense of symbolic meanings, thereby exacerbating the false split between the two that is implicit in most archaeological theory (see comments in introductory chapter). These two problems are interlinked, and both can be remedied through a concerted focus on reestablishing the significative networks in which all objects find themselves. Some scholars would go so far as to say that a theory of material culture cannot work unless it succeeds in articulating the evident links between the object as sign and the object as material (Warnier 1999a, 28).

So in this chapter the focus falls on the complex spatiotemporal associations of objects that are certainly key in the constitution of meaning in material culture. A crucial point of the argument is that these associations are inherently significative and referential, such that objects almost inevitably take on the quality of signs in a world of interminable reference. But, at this stage, we must develop our argument with great care, as it is here that a very significant shift tends to occur, a shift that lies behind the split that invariably opens up between functional and symbolic meanings. The problem is that the significative and referential content of objects is deemed to form a system in its own right, distinct from the "pragmatic" qualities of objects that we discussed in Chapter 3 through the prism of "affordances." There is a definite, albeit ill-informed logic at work behind this split, and it derives from certain domains within structuralism and post-structuralism.

Part of the problem lies in the adoption of a perspective on signification that derives from the work of Ferdinand de Saussure. His predominantly linguistic approach defines a sign as being constituted by the *signified* (e.g., the concept of "chair") and the *signifier* (the word "chair"), two parts together forming a "bifacial unity" (Gottdiener 1995, 6). These two parts are linked through a relationship grounded purely in convention; for Saussure the sign involves nothing akin to a referent or object possessing an "extra-mental" existence, out there in the world. This of course is not much of an issue for linguistic systems, in which signs are indeed based on formal, agreed-upon conventions, such that the relationship between signified and signifier can be largely arbitrary. However, problems arise when this non-grounded linguistic mode of analysis is applied to culture, and particularly to material culture, as Gottdiener (1995), Parmentier (1997), and Nellhaus (1998) have all cogently remarked. When material culture meaning is viewed from such a perspective, there is a temptation to see the sign properties of an object as being somehow quite separate from the materiality of that object. The object is caught up in a language-like system of reference and takes its meaning from its position within that quasi-linguistic system.[1] Thus the idea develops that the symbolic meaning attached to an object obeys fundamentally different logics from whatever pragmatic and functional meanings the object may have. This separation is akin to that made between linguistic knowledge on the one hand and practical knowledge on the other (Bloch 1991; Hodder 1992, 205). In implicitly following the Saussurean assumption that all signification is language-like, and hence communicative, it is evident that the domain of practical knowledge, being non-linguistic and nondiscursive in its cognitive organization, simply cannot possess a significative dimension. It is this very duality between the symbolic and the practical that this chapter seeks to confront.

Peircean Semiotics

The solution is not to abandon semiotics altogether. The Saussurean approach is by no means the only one; at about the same time, around the beginning of the twentieth century, an American philosopher, Charles Sanders Peirce, was developing a rather different perspective on signs and meaning. Peirce conceived of semiotics as a form of logic and hence as a branch of philosophy (Deledalle 2000). Being rather less predicated on language and rather more angled toward signification more broadly conceived, Peirce's approach represents a far more suitable basis for assessing the mechanisms by which meaningfulness in material culture is generated.

That Peircean semiotics is almost infinitely broad in its potential scope is demonstrated in the work of Thomas Sebeok, one of the most influential semioticians to work within a Peircean framework.[2] He has expanded semiotics far beyond the confines of human language to include all forms of animal communication; thus semiosis for Sebeok is not just anthroposemiosis but zoosemiosis. As such Sebeok identifies semiosis as one of the fundamental criteria of living systems. Although Sebeok has done much to develop Peircean semiotics, the nature of meaning in material culture has not been his overriding concern; therefore, his work does not figure greatly in this chapter.

As far as approaches to material culture are concerned, Peircean semiotics has actually been surprisingly underexploited. One notable exception is Parmentier's work in the field of semiotic anthropology (Parmentier 1994, 1997). While predominantly anthropological, Parmentier does turn his attention briefly to prehistoric archaeology to examine how Peircean semiotics might contribute to an understanding of artifactual style (Parmentier 1997, 44–52). This archaeological angle has in turn been developed further by Preucel and Bauer (2001). Although Parmentier confesses himself to be a "minimal Peircean," "unconvinced of the necessity of bringing to our cultural analysis the entire panoply of Peirce's semiotic distinctions" (Parmentier 1994, xiv), for the purposes of this chapter we are going to be even more minimalist. Parmentier explores Peirce's division of signs into three trichotomies: icon, index, and symbol; legisign, sinsign, and qualisign; and rheme, dicent, and argument (Parmentier 1994, 17). Of the 27 possible

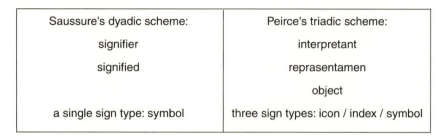

Saussure's dyadic scheme:	Peirce's triadic scheme:
signifier	interpretant
signified	reprasentamen
	object
a single sign type: symbol	three sign types: icon / index / symbol

Figure 5.1. Saussurean and Peircean schemes.

combinations, Peirce claimed that logically only ten are ever formed. Nonetheless, this hardly seems to represent minimalism on Parmentier's part; here we shall limit ourselves to Peirce's most basic semiotic categories: icon, index, and symbol.

For Peirce, the production of signs need not correspond to a motivated, language-like attempt to communicate a message; it may very often be a practical action occurring in the material world. The value of Peircean semiotics in this respect is conveyed very convincingly by a small but growing number of social scientists all eager to find a middle way between materialist and idealist standpoints (Sonesson 1989; Gottdiener 1995; Nellhaus 1998; Gell 1998). Moreover, the Peircean perspective is very much in keeping with the pragmatic, action-centered, material approach to meaning embodied in the notion of "affordances" (cf. previous chapter). Peirce's philosophy was indeed fundamentally based around what he called "pragmaticism"; it was also avowedly phenomenological or, to use Peirce's terminology, "phaneroscopic" (Deledalle 2000). Therefore Peirce's approach to signs (and recent work drawing upon that approach) puts us in a position to attempt an effective marriage between the often separated domains of meaning—the pragmatic and the significative.[3]

What, then, are the main characteristics of Peircean semiotics? A useful starting point is to draw a contrast with Saussure's system (see Figure 5.1). Whereas Saussure set up a dualism between signifier and signified, Peirce conceived of a triadic system composed of interpretant, representamen, and object.[4] In Saussure's scheme, devised primarily for linguistics, the association between signifier and signified is always one of formal convention; the absence of an "object" means that the sign system operates independently of any physical characteristics. The obvious examples of course come from language—the concept "chair" (the signified) is related in English to the word "chair" (the signifier). However, the English word "chair" has no particular physical characteristics that render it any more appropriate than words used in other languages to describe the same concept ("chaise," "καρέκλα").[5] Peirce too considered this to be an important mechanism through which signs are produced. Crucially, however, unlike Saussure, he did not think that this was the *only* way. He maintained that formal convention was one means through which an association between sign and referent might obtain, but that associations might alternatively be grounded in similarity or contiguity, that is to say, in certain physical, non-arbitrary properties of the object. Peirce's triadic schema renders this possible in a way that Saussure's dyadic one does not. Thus the proliferation of signs in material culture may be grounded in a variety of processes that demand investigation; we need to examine Peirce's ideas concerning the different forms of association that may obtain between a sign and its referent.

A sign is something that stands for something else (the referent). For example, a wedding ring, a fingerprint, a portrait, and a cry of pain can all be considered as signs, in that they stand for something else. But the relationship between these signs and their referents is rather different in each case. Peirce not only differentiated among three fundamental modes of association, similarity, contiguity, and convention, but also described these three modes in terms of particular sign types. So, let us look now at Peirce's three basic categories of sign relationship—icon, index and symbol. These terms are absolutely central to any discussion of meaning in material culture, but they do require considerable analysis. As the discussion unfolds, I will be determined not to lose the link between meaning and agency, as meanings are invariably established and negotiated within cultural environments peopled by social actors.[6]

Peirce's tripartite categorization of icon, index, and symbol seems, at first, relatively unproblematic. An icon is a sign that stands for its referent through similarity. This may often be visual similarity, as with landscapes and portraits that are visually iconic of that which they depict. Yet they need not be visual; onomatopoeic words have an aural similarity to that which they represent, for example the "buzzing" of bees. One might also think of sensual icons (the rubber nipple of a baby's bottle) and olfactory icons.[7] Peirce further divided icons into three subtypes, or "hypoicons," consisting of images, diagrams, and metaphors. "Images" he describes as signs that partake of simple qualities, and "diagrams" as signs "which represent the relations, mainly dyadic, or so regarded, of the parts of one thing by analogous relations in their own parts" (Peirce 1932, 2: para. 277). The third type of hypoicon, the metaphor, is a sign representing the character of that which is represented by establishing a parallelism in something else. Later in this chapter, we will investigate the extent to which Peirce's understanding of metaphor corroborates or contradicts other usages (e.g., in rhetoric).

When the relationship between sign and referent is one of contiguity or causality, then the sign is acting as an index. Peirce elicits a wide range of examples of indices, such as a barometer, a weathercock, a footprint, a sailor's rolling gait, a knock on the door, a symptom of disease, a pointing finger, demonstrative pronouns, and adverbs such as "here" and "there." In all these cases, one can see how the relationship between sign and referent is not one of similarity as such, but is attributable to some sort of physical connection—the weathercock represents the direction of the wind due to a direct physical relationship, and the barometer signifies atmospheric pressure through a similar sort of connection. That sign and referent are spatially and temporally connected is also apparent in the case of the pointing finger and the use of demonstrative pronouns. Unsurprisingly, defining the index is rather more complicated than this, as will be explored in due course.

The third category of sign is the symbol, in which sign and referent are mediated by some formal or merely agreed-upon link, irrespective of any physical characteristics of either sign or referent (Deacon 1997, 70–71). The most obvious examples of symbols are in language—a particular letter is a symbol for a sound, and a word is a symbol for an idea. There is nothing intrinsic to the word "dog" that can explain why it symbolizes a canine; it is merely an agreed-upon link within a particular linguistic convention (and other languages use "chien" or "Hund"). Material objects can also act as symbols—a wedding ring is a formal convention symbolizing a marital agreement.

As Deacon stresses, no object is intrinsically iconic, indexical, or symbolic, but is interpreted as such. There is nothing inherently symbolic about a wedding ring; the relevant cultural knowledge is required for it to be appropriately understood as a symbol. Even icons demand a certain amount of knowledge to be correctly interpreted, as in the case of trick drawings, when the icon which is depicted is not perceived until the viewer is informed of its presence. Context is also important, as Sonesson (1998) emphasizes through the example of the car, which may only become an icon of itself in certain circumstances, that is, when exhibited in a car showroom.

Furthermore, the same object may be understood variably as icon, index or symbol, in different situations, according to the perspective and intentionality of relevant social agents.

How robust, then, are these three categories of sign? And are they all equally important in our attempts to clarify the nature of meaning in material culture? The last sign type discussed, the symbol, is not only relatively uncommon in material culture, but is also reasonably straightforward in terms of its definition. Both icon and index, however, are not only much more fundamental to the construction of material culture meaning, but also rather more difficult to define. Thus the majority of the following analysis will focus upon icons and indices. In attempting to characterize these two sign types, I shall draw heavily on the work of art historian Goran Sonesson.[8]

Indices

The most basic stumbling block with regard to the index is the ambiguity over its definition—is its relationship between sign and referent one of physical (spatiotemporal) connection, contiguity, or causality? Peirce defines the index primarily in terms of contiguity, but in some of his writings he appears to define the relationship more in terms of causality, for example, when he says that an index "denotes by virtue of being really affected by that object" or that an index "could not continue to be a sign if its object were removed" (cf. Sonesson 1989, 38–39). This ambiguity has created much debate over the true status of the index as a sign. In the various examples given by Peirce, the manner in which sign and referent are related through contiguity and/or causality seems very variable. For example, one might say that the direction of the wind "causes" the weathercock to move into a particular position, but one could hardly maintain that the object at which a finger is pointing "causes" the finger to point. Let us explore these and other examples more fully.

Weathercocks, barometers, and thermometers are all signs that act as "indicators" of their referents; in each case there must be a physical, spatio-temporal connection with the referent for the sign to function (Figure 5.2). One might, moreover, characterize the link as causal. Contiguity in and of itself hardly seems sufficient. The symptom of a disease, or indeed a cry of pain, may well fall into the same category. Peirce seems to have classified this subset of indexical signs "reagents." He uses the example of when water

Figure 5.2. Weathercock as a "causal" index or "reagent." Photograph by the author.

and camphor are put together into a bucket in order to indicate whether the bucket is clean; here, too, there is a causal, physical, spatiotemporal connection between sign and referent.

Can demonstrative pronouns, adverbs such as "here" and "there," and a pointing finger also be included in the above category of indices? There are indeed certain similarities—the finger and that to which it points enjoy a spatiotemporal connection, in that the link is instantiated in a given place and time. However, the link is not so much a direct physical connection as an indirect contiguity. Moreover, the referent does not "cause" the sign in the direct physical way that the wind causes the direction of the weathercock to shift (Figure 5.2). There is, in fact, little by way of causal relationship in the operation of shifters (demonstrative pronouns) and pointing fingers as signs. How can we characterize this class of indexical sign? Sonesson (1989) argues that with such signs their indexicality is created spontaneously, at the precise moment when the finger points or the pronoun is uttered. It is the enunciation of the sign expression that creates the referent of the sign, and thus instead of describing states of affairs the signs create them. Sonesson (1989, 53) therefore calls such signs "performative" indices.

The weathercock, barometer, and thermometer, in contrast, simply describe a state of affairs rather than creating one. Sonesson would state that, unlike a pointing finger, such indices require a certain amount of prior knowledge if their indicative role is to be correctly read. The same might equally be said of a symptom of a disease or a cry of pain: they describe a state of affairs, but they also require a degree of knowledge if that state of affairs is to be appropriately understood. But might it not also be argued that the pointing finger, too, demands a certain degree of knowledge, however minimal, if it is to be successfully deciphered as a communicative act? Thus even the "purest" performative indices require some prior knowledge to be understood.

Sonesson, however, maintains something of a dichotomy between what he has dubbed performative indices on the one hand, and "abductive indices" on the other. This latter category encompasses indexical signs requiring prior knowledge to be understood. An example he uses is that of the rolling gait of a sailor. The observer has to make a series of abductions based on his/her knowledge of the social agency of sailing in order to grasp that a rolling gait is an index of a sailor. Another example is the use of a loaf of bread on a signpost to denote the presence of a bakery; one needs to have enough acquired cultural knowledge to understand the connection between loaves and bakeries (Figure 5.3). Sonesson's distinction between performative and abductive indices seems to parallel that devised by Peirce between reagents (see above) and designations, the latter covering those indices which stand for things with which the mind is already acquainted.

This does seem to be a useful axis through which we can understand better the operation of indices. However, it would be unwise to create a dualism between "pure" performative indices and "pure" abductive indices. It certainly seems that some indices, such as linguistic shifters and pointing fingers, are heavily performative, requiring only the minimum of abduction. Other types of sign that are still largely performative demand rather more abduction, for instance, a symptom of a disease, a cry of pain, and weathercocks, barometers, and thermometers. The example of the loaf

Figure 5.3. Loaf signifying a bakery—an abductive index. Photograph by the author.

signpost indicating a bakery would involve a rather more equal balance of abduction and performance—it is abductive in relying upon prior knowledge of the connection between loaves and bakeries, yet is also performative in terms of its emplacement, presumably contiguous with the bakery itself (and thus has some of the properties of a pointing finger). One can also think of indices that are heavily abductive and only minimally performative: for instance, a rolling gait as an index of being a sailor may persist on land, even when the rolling sea is distant in time and space, in contexts where there is no physical connection or contiguity whatsoever. Although there is no contiguity to speak of, there is what Sonesson describes as "factorality" (1998, 308–11). This rather unwieldy term describes the relationship between a part and the whole; the whole in this case is the social role of "sailor," the part is the sailor's gait. Sonesson argues that it is abductive indices that build upon such factoralities, whereas performative indices tend to involve relationships of contiguity between sign and referent. And as we have suggested that performative and abductive aspects may combine in indices, so it follows that contiguity and factorality together play a part, to differing degrees.

Sonesson confines his discussion of the performative and the abductive to solely indexical signs. However, in turning our attention now to icons, it emerges that these, too, may well involve both performative and abductive aspects.

Icons

As already stated, icons represent their referents mainly by virtue of their similarity; the similarity may be visual, oral, aural, olfactory, or tactile. The icon is considered by some to be a particularly problematic class of sign, partly because "similarity" is an extremely broad church that may include almost anything (Mitchell 1986, 56). Mitchell also cites criticisms made by Nelson Goodman regarding the status of icons as signs, to the effect that resemblance is neither a necessary nor a sufficient condition for representation (cf. Goodman 1970). Indeed, as Goodman notes, resemblance is symmetric whereas representation is not. He gives as an example automobiles coming off a production line—every car *resembles* every other car, but none of them *represents* another (Mitchell 1986, 57). Yet this is precisely the point made above—that a car will only become an icon of itself in certain circumstances, for example when placed in a car showroom (Figure 5.4). So, for Goodman to say that resemblance is not in itself sufficient for representation is of course absolutely correct; but this does not jeopardize the status of the icon as a sign.

The concept of the icon has received even harsher criticism from other quarters, notably from Umberto Eco, who has suggested getting rid of iconic signs altogether (Eco 1979). His main concern appears to be that "icon" encompasses far too broad a range of phenomena to be at all meaningful as a category: "Iconic signs are partially ruled by convention but are at the same time motivated; some of them refer to an established stylistic rule, while others appear to propose a new rule" (1979, 216). Eco's use of the term "motivated" needs some explanation—Mitchell suggests that " 'motivated' signs have a natural, necessary connection with what they signify; 'unmotivated' signs are arbitrary and conventional" (Mitchell 1986, 58). Eco's comments therefore appear to provide a rather striking parallel

Figure 5.4. Showroom car as icon. Photograph by the author.

to those of Sonesson on the distinction between abductive and performative indices. Abductive indices are those that require prior cultural knowledge in order to be understood. Some iconic signs may also be, as Eco claims, partially ruled by cultural convention—the car in the showroom is a case in point—one would have to understand the role of showrooms in order to interpret the car as an icon.

With performative indices, the meaning is created spontaneously, at the precise performative moment when the finger points (see above). Relatively little cultural knowledge is required to understand the meaning in such indices—therefore a correspondence may exist between these indices and the icons Eco describes as "motivated," in that in both cases the connection between sign and referent is natural and necessary. Thus it is possible to circumvent Eco's criticisms of the icon. Rather than it being a ragbag collection of unconnected phenomena, the icon can be seen to incorporate a range of possibilities on a continuum between motivated and unmotivated, between natural and conventional, and between performative and abductive. By way of example, the nipple of a baby bottle may count as a natural, motivated, performative icon, whereas a car in a showroom is a rather more conventional, unmotivated, and abductive icon.

Icon and Index Combined

A number of issues arise from the discussion so far. In focusing on indexicality and iconicity separately, their interconnections have been somewhat neglected. The relationship between these two sign categories does need to be examined, not least because some objects appear to be acting as icons and indices simultaneously. Photography is one of the most obvious examples, and was indeed discussed by Peirce himself. Photographs are iconic since they bear a perceived visual similarity to that which they represent. Yet at the same time they are indexical, in that "the resemblance is due to the photographs having been produced under such circumstances that they were physically forced to correspond point by point to nature" (Peirce 1955, 106). Being simultaneously icon and index, the photograph differs from a "true" icon insofar as the directness of its physical creation seems "to short-circuit or disallow those processes of schematization or symbolic intervention that operates within the graphic representations of most paintings" (Krauss 1985, 203). Dubois (1990) has argued that the photograph should be considered primarily as an indexical form of representation, even though it may subsequently be understood as icon and/or symbol too.[9] A photograph may thus be an "iconical index." Photography is thereby distinct from other systems of representation such as painting and drawing, which are iconic, and writing and language, which are symbolic (Dubois 1990).

This said, some artworks merge different representational forms, combining, for example, drawing with photography. The iconic and the indexical are fused to form a composite semiosis. Yet photography is not the only indexical mode embodying "traces" or "imprints"; Krauss (1985) draws attention to a work by Marcel Duchamp called *With My Tongue in My Cheek*. As shown in Figure 5.5, it is in one sense a conventional self-portrait, in that the artist has sketched his profile to create a graphic, iconic likeness of himself. However, on top of this drawing he has added a relief area of chin

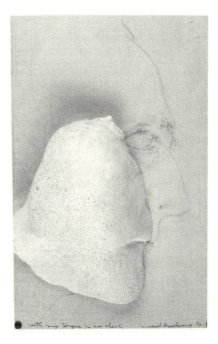

Figure 5.5. Marcel Duchamp, *With My Tongue in My Cheek* (1959). Copyright ©
2003 ADAGP, Paris, and DACS, London.

and cheek, cast from his own face in plaster. Duchamp has fused an iconic
representation of himself with an indexical impression to create a self-
portrait that is "split along the semiotic axis of icon and index" (Krauss
1985: 206). Even though this work does not involve photography in the
strict sense of the term, it can be described as "conceptually photographic";
one could say that much of Duchamp's art is devoted to "index logic"
(Dubois 1987, 232; 1990).[10]

Both the photograph and the plaster cast involve a process of imprinting that seems to be key to the creation of indexical meaning in these art
media. But it is not only in art that we can recognize such processes. Phil-
ippe Dubois (1987) introduces the very interesting example of a tanned
body; this is quite similar to the photograph in that the skin's surface
changes color in reaction to light, not unlike a photographic emulsion. The
sunlight leaves its trace, its "empreinte lumineuse," on those parts of the
skin's surface that are exposed. Tanned skin is thus indexical of exposure to

sunlight. The relationship is not, though, in any way iconic—the tan does not resemble sunlight. In this way the skin differs from photographs which are "iconical indexes." Other forms of impression may, however, be iconical indexes, such as fingerprints. It is indexical because it involves a process of imprinting and, as with both Duchamp's plaster cast and a photograph, relies upon a precedent contiguity between the finger and the print.

But in what sense is it iconic? Sonesson (1989) argues that the fingerprint is not solely indexical but is also iconic in that it bears a visual resemblance to the network of lines on the fingertip. However, this would seem to contravene an important part of Peirce's definition of the icon: that the similarity between sign and referent should *not* be a result of one of them having an influence on the other. This should have implications for semiotic analyses of photography; how, in this case, can a photograph be considered at all iconic? The solution would appear to be that offered by Dubois: to conceive of the photograph, and any other form of trace, as primarily indexical, while allowing for the possibility that it may subsequently be perceived as iconic and/or symbolic too (and in this way one may have iconical indexes—like the photograph, or indeed the fingerprint).

Another point Sonesson raises is that the fingerprint also involves "factorality," in that it is a part standing for the whole; not so much the whole finger, nor the whole body, but the whole person, the individual. Therefore, a degree of abduction is required, in that one needs to have understood the human body at a certain level in order to grasp that each fingerprint is unique to a given individual.[11] Perhaps this discussion can be usefully extended through a consideration of other means by which the body may be represented. How do exuviae, for example hair and nail clippings, come to be meaningful in terms of referencing the body? First, it seems reasonable to argue that there is nothing particularly iconic about them—they do not bear a visual resemblance to the person. Neither are they indexical in the sense of being imprints of the person or parts thereof. Yet they surely display indexicality in terms of both a prior physical connection to the body, and also factorality, in that they are in a part-whole relationship to the body. But does this mean that in no context can a strand of hair reference a person iconically? Gell would suggest that, in context, a strand of hair could certainly come to be seen as iconic of an individual, insofar as it could feasibly bear a perceived visual similarity to the referent. Even more conventional icons, such as drawings and paintings, tend to involve factorality, since only a part of the whole is ever represented.

Relationship	Semiotics	Rhetoric
similarity	icon	metaphor
contiguity	index	metonomy
factorality	symbol	synecdoche

Figure 5.6. Terms from semiotics and rhetoric.

Metonymy, Synecdoche, and Metaphor

The question of the relationship between iconicity, indexicality and factorality brings us very conveniently to the key concepts of metonymy, synecdoche and metaphor. The connection between these phenomena, from the domain of rhetoric, and those of icon, index and symbol from semiotics, is often rather difficult to fathom (see Figure 5.6). How compatible are they? The work of Jonathan Culler (2001) is most useful in tackling this question, drawing upon the work of Stephen Ullman, Roman Jakobson, and Umberto Eco in particular. Ullman (1964) posits that metaphor is based on a relationship of similarity while metonymy is based on a relationship of contiguity. One might, as Christopher Tilley notes, liken a human life to that of a flower, and describe someone as "in full bloom," or as "withering away" (Tilley 1999, 5). These metaphors are thus based on a relationship of similarity. If, however, one were to describe someone as a "hired gun," this image draws on the contiguity of person and gun, and is hence an example of metonymy (Tilley 1999, 5). This set of connections can be taken still further, once it is realized that similarity is also the basis for iconicity, and contiguity the basis for indexicality. It thus becomes possible to draw a link between metaphor and iconicity on the one hand (both based on similarity), and metonymy and indexicality on the other (both based on contiguity).[12] This point is indeed anticipated by Roman Jakobson (1956), who similarly argued that indexicality, insofar as it is based on contiguity, is connected with the rhetorical figure of metonymy.[13]

Jakobson also chose, somewhat controversially, to include the rhetorical device of *synecdoche* within the category of metonymy. He took this course even while acknowledging that synecdoche involves a part-to-whole relationship rather than one of contiguity. However, Sonesson (1998, 308–11) has an interesting proposition to help resolve this incompatibility. Synecdoche overlaps rather conveniently with Sonesson's concept of factorality, in that both revolve around part-to-whole relationships. Meanwhile, metonymy and contiguity can be matched up without any problem. Thus in the same way that contiguity and factorality are subsumed as two dimensions under the overarching banner of indexicality, so can metonymy and synecdoche be seen as two separate (though often overlapping) aspects of indexicality. That metonymy (contiguity) and synecdoche (factorality) fulfill different functions is aptly demonstrated in the example of the crown and the king. A crown is a metonym for a king if the latter is considered a physical person with whom the crown is in spatial contiguity, but is a synecdoche if royalty is seen to be primarily an office of which the crown is a significant part. The functions are different, even if the object itself comes to be ambiguously defined (Sonesson 1998, 415–16).

Jakobson was controversial in another way, too: he put forward the idea that metaphor and metonymy were two poles of language in a relationship of competition. Culler (2001) notes the contrast with the approach of Ullman, for example, which considered that the metonymical could on the whole be subsumed within the metaphorical. It also goes against the perspective adopted by Gerard Genette, who saw metaphor and metonymy (particularly in the work of Proust) as interpenetrative (Culler 2001, 215). The argument over the relationship between metaphor and metonymy becomes much more complex, of which more can be found in Culler. But what does seem clear is that the difficulties in understanding their interactions are comparable to those encountered in fathoming the relationship between iconicity and indexicality.

This is perhaps a rather roundabout means of discussing metonymy, synecdoche and metaphor in material culture. It does, however, serve to emphasize the importance of interconnecting the different traditions within which material culture meaning has come to be examined. As the work of Culler, Jakobson, and Sonesson cited above shows, it is possible to draw links between the frequently divergent traditions of semiotics and rhetoric, but more often than not their separation leads to inconsistencies. Tilley (1999), for example, in one of the most important contributions recently to deal with metaphor in material culture, defines metonymy as a transfer of meaning within a domain, while metaphor involves a transfer between domains. As such, he argues, there is a hierarchical relationship between the two, with metaphor often building upon metonymy. Yet, as is apparent from the above discussion, it is far from certain that metaphor and metonymy are related in this way; the issue requires far more discussion. Ullman subsumed metonymy within metaphor, Genette described them as inter-penetrative, and Jakobson polarized them. From a rather different perspective, Deacon (1997) posits a hierarchical relationship between icon, index, and symbol, with symbolic meaning building upon indexical meaning, and indexical meaning upon iconic. If we accept that metaphor is conceived as a form of icon, and metonymy is allied to indexicality, then, in Deacon's scheme, the hierarchical relationship between metaphor and metonymy finds itself completely reversed from the position envisaged by Tilley. Quite simply, a lot more thought needs to be devoted to characterizing the relationships between metaphor and metonymy, and between iconicity and indexicality, instead of specifying a priori what those relationships are.

So what are we to make of Tilley's versions of metaphor and metonymy in material culture? How much does his analysis suffer from the failure to integrate or at least compare these processes with those devised in semiotics? I would say substantially. For example, he states that "in the most general sense metaphor involves comprehending some entity from the point of view, or perspective, of another" (1999, 4). Yet this statement more or less covers all forms of meaning, and all those categories of signs of which metaphor is but one subgroup. Metaphor therefore seems like a rather odd place to start, but then, as Tilley admits, "metaphor has become a figure for figurality in general";[14] he quickly goes on to explain that "this is the manner in which the term will function in the present account." This relative lack of interest in defining terms may explain why the relationship between metonymy and synecdoche is poorly characterized, and why the connection between metaphor and the semiotic concepts of icon, index and symbol receives no mention. Thus, the very variable processes through which material culture comes to be meaningful are barely systematized.[15]

Metaphor and Cognition

Tilley's approach suffers from its failure to incorporate semiotic theory. However, there does seem to be some promise in his commitment to understanding meaning as an embodied process, drawing upon both phenomenology (e.g., Merleau-Ponty 1962), and cognitive psychology.[16] In relation to the latter, Tilley places the notion of an embodied mind, that is to say a mind operating within the context of bodily experience and cultural understandings, as one of the cornerstones of his whole approach to metaphor.[17] Unfortunately, Tilley does himself no favors in relying almost exclusively for his cognitive slant on the work of just two cognitive psychologists, George Lakoff and Mark Johnson (Lakoff and Johnson 1980; Johnson 1987; Lakoff 1987). Their approach, which posits a constitutive role for metaphor, such that deep conceptual metaphors structure understanding, has come under significant criticism (e.g., Strauss and Quinn 1997, 143–44). The critique by Strauss and Quinn does seem to show that Lakoff, Johnson and others, far from enabling an embodied approach to metaphor, only end up casting it as an inherently internalist and static phenomenon. Indeed, Strauss and Quinn (1997, 265, n. 11) accuse Lakoff (1987) of using the term "embodied" with considerable inconsistency. Tilley's rather underdetermined cognitive perspective on metaphor and meaning thus appears to run the risk of contradicting itself.

It may be interesting in this light to discuss further some of the cognitive aspects of metaphor, particularly in relation to some of the arguments put forward by Strauss and Quinn (1997), and indeed those in Chapter 3 regarding neural networks and semantic maps (Spitzer 1999). These models may still be internalist, but they do hold the potential for flexible responses. In this way it may be possible to introduce a degree of flexibility into the rigid schema of Lakoff and Johnson, in which they propose that metaphor involves a mapping from a source to a target domain. The source domains are familiar, often of the physical world, whereas the target domains are abstract and conceptual. For example, we tend to understand "anger" as the heat of fluid in a container, and the body is conceived of as the container. So the body acts as the source domain, used as a tangible means of understanding the target domain, anger, an intangible abstraction. Thus a metaphor such as "the anger welled up inside" is intimately connected to the body's familiar physical properties and its position within its environment (one might say the human body "affords" such a metaphor). Now, presumably, the use of such metaphors involving the body's physical properties constitutes an integral part of the mind's understanding of the body. We are in a sense obliged to say this, having argued that an object is understood indivisibly as material, activity, and idea.

Introducing Spitzer's perspective at this point, it appears that the meaning of an object is represented in the brain through its relative position on a semantic map. The position of an object on a topographical map of this sort depends not only upon its material properties but also its projected uses and the ways in which it is understood conceptually. Body parts, for example, are not simply mapped together according to physical similarity: toes and fingers, for example, are quite similar visually, but not at all in the way they are used or conceived. Fingers do not map closely to toes, but they do to hands and arms (Spitzer 1999, 107, 224)—presumably their projected actions—and, indeed, the possible meanings associated with fingers (as opposed to toes) are important in this mapping process. Following Spitzer, it therefore seems likely that these feature maps operate at both tactile and semantic levels, notwithstanding the lack of firm evidence to support such an observation at this stage. Nonetheless, thanks to the emphasis on mapping, it is possible to discern some intriguing possibilities regarding the cognitive basis of metaphor (and indeed other phenomena such as iconicity, contiguity, etc.).

Embodied Meaning and Sociosemiotics

It is not only cognitive science and anthropology that can be profitably brought together; Sonesson has shown the potential for integrating insights from phenomenology and cognitive psychology with semiotics.[18] Sonesson's work is heavily focused upon semiotics, but at the same time he succeeds in integrating what one might call "semantic" concerns. From phenomenology he draws extensively upon the work of Husserl and his concept of a *Lifeworld*, while from cognitive psychology he cites the work of James Gibson on perception, Eleanor Rosch on categorization, and Howard Gardner on the structure of the mind. In considering "all semiotic theories to be basically theories about the spontaneous categorisations taking place in the Lifeworld" (1989, 14), Sonesson is essentially exploring the variable mechanisms whereby meaning is generated. Although his focus is primarily on images, much of his analysis, as is apparent from this chapter, is highly relevant to material culture more generally.

Sonesson's attempt to recombine the pragmatic and the significative dimensions of meaning is mirrored in what has been dubbed a sociosemiotic approach within material culture studies (Thomas 1998a). While S. H. Riggins (1994a, b), for example, does not explicitly integrate phenomenology or cognitive psychology into his version of sociosemiotics, he does demonstrate the indivisibility of functional and symbolic meanings, and the dialogic process whereby objects (artifacts) and subjects (people) cocreate one another socially. Gottdiener (1995) sees sociosemiotics as a means of transcending the idealist assumptions of post-Saussurean semiotics, which has tended to understand artifacts in material culture in terms of their qualities as signs. In seeking to reinstate the materiality of material culture within a semiotic framework, Gottdiener turns pointedly to Peirce as a source of inspiration (an unknowing founder of sociosemiotics?), asserting that "behind the infinite regress of meaning there exists an objective referent" (Gottdiener 1995, 25).[19] Coming from a rather different perspective, Tobin Nellhaus too emphasizes the extent to which Peircean semiotics is effective at grounding semiosis as a practical action in the real world (Nellhaus 1998). Nellhaus's goal is to effect a marriage between critical realism and semiotics, an objective that seems very much consistent with the sociosemiotic project.[20] As was stated earlier in this chapter, Peirce's work represents a peculiarly apt starting point for any attempt to bring together the pragmatic and the significative, given that his philosophical writings deal explicitly and presciently with both.

The contributions of Sonesson, Gottdiener, Riggins, and Nellhaus inhabit different disciplines (art history, sociology, philosophy), and yet there is much common ground between them. A further striking parallel can be found in yet another discipline, anthropology, in the work of Alfred Gell, and in particular in his book *Art and Agency* (1998). Yet what is rather extraordinary is that Gell apparently rejects semiotic, language-based approaches to art (particularly Panofsky's iconographic approach) in order to replace them with an embodied, agent-based approach (D'Alleva 2001, 80). Indeed, Gosden stresses "the shift Gell makes from an analysis of meaning to the analysis of effect" (Gosden 2001, 164). From this angle, Gell's project does not offer any promise at all for a reconciliation of the pragmatic and the significative. And yet it is essentially Saussurean semiotics that Gell is so keen to avoid; as it happens, his approach is very much consistent with many of the principal tenets of Peircean semiotics, as espoused by Sonesson, Gottdiener, Riggins, and Nellhaus, among others. In particular, there are some rather remarkable links to the work of Sonesson; just as Sonesson places indexicality, abduction, and agency at the center of his discussion, so Gell bases much of his argument on this crucial triple connection. It is fascinating that Gell weaves these components together without any mention of the work of Sonesson, and with relatively little mention of Peirce. On the one hand, the way in which Gell develops his ideas on indexes and the abduction of agency suggests a clear knowledge and use of the tradition of Peircean semiotics. On the other hand, if this is the case, he does not stay particularly close to it, with his idea of the "index" going well beyond the way in which it was intended by Peirce. In fact, in Gell's book *Art and Agency*, Peirce attracts just two mentions in the book's index (pp. 13, 14), and none of his work is found in the bibliography. Whatever the degree of consciousness with which Gell used Peirce, the upshot is that his work does offer a potential basis for an articulation of the pragmatic and the significative in material culture theory. Moreover, it is Gell (rather than Sonesson, for example) who is having the greater impact upon archaeology and material culture studies, principally because archaeology has traditionally enjoyed close links with anthropology, and because many of his examples are taken from both "art" and material culture. We shall be hearing rather more about Gell's important work in the following chapter.

Recap

In this chapter we have sought to add another dimension, the semiotic, to the question of how humans think through material culture. We have examined the complex associative relationships of similarity, contiguity, factorality, causality, and convention that end up binding together objects, actions, and ideas in networks of structure and flow. One possible, if somewhat harsh, criticism of some of the approaches outlined in this chapter is that there is scope for integrating much more of some of the more recent and exciting developments from cognitive science (some of which were touched upon in previous chapters). For example, having learned from our focus on icon, index, and symbol that objects, actions, and ideas come into diverse associations, based on similarity, contiguity, factorality, causality, and convention, we might begin to ask if these *networks* of association find themselves reflected in some sort of cognitive structure. And might not this be of considerable use to our efforts to understand the relationship between brain, body, and world? Some discussion of such questions took place in the section on neural networks in the previous chapter, but they are questions that appear not to have been very often addressed.

Most of our theoretical building blocks are now in place. It is high time we set out to test their applicability to specific case studies, from not only archaeological but also contemporary contexts. This will be the focus of the next two chapters.

Chapter 6
Thinking Through: Meaning in Modern Material Culture

Once again his head began to whirl with the sad round of removers and undertakers, property agents and their customers, plumbers, electricians, painters, decorators, tilers, and carpet-layers: he began to think of the tranquil life of things, of crockery chests full of wood shavings, of cartons of books, of the harsh light of bare bulbs swinging on their wires, of the slow installation of furniture and objects, of the slow adaptation of the body to space, that whole sum of minute non-existent, untellable events— choosing a lamp-stand, a reproduction, a knickknack, placing a tall rect- angular mirror between two doors, putting a Japanese garden in front of a window, lining cupboard shelves with a flower-printed fabric—all those infinitesimal gestures in which the life of a flat is always most faithfully encapsulated, and which will be upset from time to time by the sudden— unforeseen or ineluctable, tragic or benign, ephemeral or definitive— fractures of an ahistorical daily grind: one day the young Marquiseaux girl will run off with the Réol boy, one day Madame Orlowska will leave again for no apparent reason, for no real reason either; one day Madame Altamont will fire a revolver at Monsieur Altamont and the blood will spurt onto the glazed hexagonal tiles of their octagonal dining room: one day the police will come to arrest Joseph Nieto and will find hidden in one of the brass spheres on his large Empire bedstead in his bedroom the fa- mous diamond stolen long ago from Prince Luigi Voudzoï.

—Georges Perec

In Perec's novel *Life, a User's Manual* there are many passages like the one above in which the human and nonhuman inhabitants of a Paris apartment block are described in infinite detail. This example is ap- propriate here both for its French authorship and for its minute focus on everyday objects in a Western industrial setting. Other French authors, ad- mittedly in a somewhat different guise, have also recently been writing about the role of mundane artifacts in the contemporary Western world.

These authors are, however, sociologists and anthropologists such as Latour, Lemonnier, Warnier, Kaufmann, Chevalier, Semprini, and Bonnot, to name but a few. Through their use of anthropological techniques they have managed to rescue from obscurity a facet of our lives that is often taken for granted, and place the study of modern material culture firmly on the agenda.

Why have the mundane artifacts of contemporary living been overlooked? After all, the spaces of the contemporary world are dense with objects. Some of these objects seep into us, others cocoon us, while others radiate out from us like networks. Many find an intimate connection such that they are incorporated into human living systems, and from which systems they subsequently render themselves inseparable, metaphysically as well as physically. Given this infiltration, it is something of a surprise that we have not progressed very far in understanding the social dimensions of Western material culture. One explanation might be the assumption that the material culture of contemporary capitalism is more diverse and more technically complex than at any other stage of human history, thus rendering it fundamentally "other." Yet anthropologists such as Latour would argue that in some regards it differs very little.

However, it is not as if anthropologists have long been studying the material culture of "traditional" non-Western societies and only belatedly coming to turn their techniques on Western societies. An explicit focus on material culture has actually been rather lacking in ethnography too. Even though this manque has been particularly acute in the Anglo-American tradition, there have, until the relatively recent boom, been fewer ethnographic studies of material culture in the French tradition than one might have expected. Nevertheless, the overall lack of ethnographic studies of material culture, particularly in Britain and the U.S., has been a source of frustration to many archaeologists, dearly wishing for such studies to help them analogically in their interpretation of past material culture. It is this state of affairs that prompted some archaeologists to seek out ethnographic material themselves, conducting field studies of contemporary "traditional" groups in an effort to understand some of the dynamics of material culture patterning. Such an exercise can be traced back to the 1960s and 1970s, with the work of archaeologists such as Binford, Gould, and Yellen in the first instance, followed by Hodder, Miller, and others thereafter, albeit with a rather different set of questions. It is thus that "ethnoarchaeology" was born (see David and Kramer 2001).

Ethnoarchaeology has since developed in a number of directions and has illuminated a wide range of themes, such as regional settlement patterns, activity areas within sites, the use of architectural space, and the production, consumption, and discard of various kinds of artifact, with ceramics and lithics the most commonly studied (David and Kramer 2001). In terms of geographical area, many parts of the world are now covered, with a particularly intense focus on Africa and parts of Asia. The theoretical orientation toward material culture adopted in these diverse studies varies according to a number of factors, but an interesting development can be traced from an initial concern in the 1960s and 1970s with the "pragmatic" dimensions of material culture, to an increasing emphasis in the 1980s and 1990s on its "significative" aspects. This change is, of course, related to the emergence first of processual archaeology and then of post-processual archaeologies. The focus of the former is behavior and its material correlates, or what may be termed the "phenomenal order," while that of the latter is cognitive-symbolic systems, the "ideational order" (David and Kramer 2001, 38–39).[1] The latter emphasis is, moreover, consistent with work done in the 1980s and 1990s not by ethnoarchaeologists but by anthropologists, particularly those in the French tradition of the "anthropology of techniques" (Lemonnier 1986). Within this tradition the anthropology is written on its own terms, with no concern in aiding archaeologists with their interpretative frameworks.

Thus in many ways ethnoarchaeology (and certain strands of anthropology) provide us with some of the best material when it comes to understanding the meaningfulness of material culture in "traditional" social settings in the present. Such work has had a profound influence in the genesis of the current book, as the author's first forays into the study of material culture were ethnoarchaeological in nature, involving the study of pottery production in the North-West Frontier Province of Pakistan (Knappett 1994). Clearly, I could, and perhaps should, choose to elaborate upon an ethnoarchaeological case study in this chapter as a means of exploring the pragmatic and significative meanings of artifacts in a contemporary setting. However, in order to overturn the assumption that only ethnographies of traditional societies supposedly little affected by industrialization and globalization can provide such opportunities, I shall resist taking this obvious path. Essentializing traditional societies as somehow more pristine than our own is a dangerous exercise, as David and Kramer have emphasized (2001, 24). Insights can come from contemporary Western material culture too, and it is for this reason that I shall detail below a case study that has as its focus industrial Western products. This case study, taken from the work of

Bonnot (2002), also enables us to see how the meanings of artifacts are not fixed, but may shift substantially over time and through space. It transpires that even industrially mass-produced, mundane products can be valued aesthetically. The relationship between the everyday and the aesthetic is given further consideration through the course of this chapter, and finally provides the cue for a reentry into a discussion of material culture in non-Western as well as Western societies. This discussion is facilitated in no small part by the work of Alfred Gell, already mentioned in the previous chapter. Overall, then, the aim of this chapter is to tackle *meaningfulness* in contemporary material culture.

Let us reiterate how the present theoretical approach has been built up over the course of the previous five chapters. It is a key tenet of this book that in order to understand how humans *think through* material culture, be it in the present or the past, we are much in need of an integrated theoretical framework, one that uses insights derived from diverse fields: cognitive science, ecological psychology, anthropology, sociology, and semiotics, to name a few. Let us remind ourselves of the essential tenets of this theoretical perspective. One of its key goals is to insist that the meaning of an object arises in the articulation of its pragmatic and significative dimensions; in other words, in the coming together of the material and the mental, the functional and the symbolic.[2] The means of accessing this articulation were in part developed in Chapters 2 and 3, where we sought to develop the idea of the human being as a bio-psycho-social living system in which mind, action, and matter together form an integrated "vertical" axis. This idea constituted the basis for a proper understanding of the intimate relationship between human and artifact. In Chapter 4, we acknowledged that this connection is rarely, if ever, between a human and an individual artifact, but that numerous human and nonhuman entities are invariably entangled in "networks." The idea that the connections inherent in these networks are quite variable in character formed the subject of Chapter 5; some of the relationships connecting entities include resemblance, contiguity, factorality, causality, and convention.

The methodology I wish to use in presenting the Bonnot case study grows out of this integrated theoretical framework. But before proceeding with the case study, I need to convey my methodology as straightforwardly as possible. There are quite a number of different, albeit interconnected points to keep in mind, and if we were to plunge straight into a detailed case study based on an actual body of material the complexities might simply be too much to handle. Thus, I shall employ a simple technique, which in-

Figure 6.1. Coffee cup. Photograph by the author.

volves taking an everyday artifact, indeed a Western industrial product, with which most of us are familiar. And as we shall, in the next chapter, be looking at Minoan cups, it seems appropriate to choose a cup as our contemporary analogy. We shall therefore consider the everyday artifact that is the coffee cup (Figure 6.1). I am not drawing on any particular case study of coffee cups, but simply on my own experiences. Only once this simplified, hypothetical example has been used shall we confront more complicated real-world scenarios, drawn from sociology, anthropology, science and technology studies (STS), art history, and an emergent field dubbed "material culture studies." The proposed methodological scheme begins by focusing on the coffee cup's physical affordances; then we turn to its physical, semantic, cultural, and logical constraints; then we place it in its associative networks by assessing its iconicity and indexicality.

Affordances

Starting with the coffee cup's physical affordances, the idea is to ascertain these "directly," pretending the absence of cultural knowledge. It is hard to know where to start, but let us say that because of its flat base and low center of gravity the coffee cup has stability—it can be placed on a flat surface such as a table where it will remain (it is unlikely to roll off, or to be blown off by a gust of wind). The coffee cup, no doubt in part because it is designed to be impermeable to hot liquids, is also hard and rather brittle—if for some reason it were to fall off the table it would probably break into fragments on impact. This does of course vary with the material used and the thickness of the cup's walls, but as the cup's purpose is to be raised to the mouth for consumption it is usually not too heavy and thus not too thick-walled. This leads us to another of its affordances—it is easily manipulable in the hand and is of a size and circumference that maximizes its graspability. Indeed, one might even say that it is easily "cupped" in the hands. Not that this would be a particularly good idea when the cup is full of hot coffee, as its walls conduct heat in such a way that it is often too hot to hold directly. For this reason the coffee cup is furnished with a handle that, not being in direct contact with the hot contents of the cup, remains somewhat cooler to the touch. The handle has a finger-sized hole that increases its graspability; one should also note the handle's placement, vertical and close to the rim, to afford tipping when drinking. Its characteristics also mean that it is equally well grasped in the left hand as in the right.

These are some of the canonical affordances of the coffee cup. The expectation is that in a context where a human protagonist was faced with the possibility of consuming a hot beverage and had to choose between various available artifacts from which to consume, the coffee cup as described would presumably announce "directly" to the user its appropriateness to the task at hand. This should occur regardless of the particular corpus of cultural knowledge acquired by the user in question. Given another context altogether, the coffee cup may offer up other kinds of affordances. It may, quite simply, be used for the consumption of not only hot but also cold liquids. Its solidity means that it lends itself to the propping open of a door. This characteristic, and its manipulability, even render it suitable for throwing at someone to whom one wishes to do harm.

Constraints

But there inevitably exist what we might call "indirect" factors impinging on our perceptions of the coffee cup. Norman (1998) refers to these as physical, semantic, cultural, and logical constraints. For example, some obvious physical constraints come into play. The cup has to be used a certain way up, and can only contain the amount of liquid its size allows (although physical constraints are more direct than indirect). Logical constraints might militate against the use of a coffee cup as a projectile weapon (its tendency to smash rendering it useless subsequently, or useless for drinking at least). There might exist semantic constraints, which Norman says, "rely upon the meaning of the situation to control the set of possible actions" (Norman 1998, 85; see Chapter 3 above): although a coffee cup could conceivably be used simultaneously by a group of people, it is commonly of a size that renders it suitable for individual consumption. As this situation would appear to contain an element of cultural convention, there may well be some overlap between this and what are called "cultural" constraints. An example of the latter might concern the sorts of hot and cold liquids that are deemed appropriate for consumption from such a vessel. There are cultural constraints tacitly discouraging the use of coffee cups for the consumption of cold drinks, particularly alcoholic ones; however, the degree to which protagonists are mindful of such constraints could vary considerably from one context to another.

Among the different kinds of constraint mentioned, it is those of a cultural nature, in particular, that arise from the various associations that coffee cups hold, acquired due to their entanglement in networks of meaning. Objects find themselves embroiled in such networks through a range of processes, as described in Chapter 5: iconicity, indexicality, and symbolism. Let us now treat the coffee cup from each of these perspectives in turn.

Iconicity

Starting with *iconicity*, in what ways can the coffee cup be seen as physically similar to other artifacts? Physical similarity is not purely about the visual—one might also consider other senses: hearing, smell, taste, and touch. Although the coffee cup might very well be closely associated with particular sounds, smells, tastes, and textures, such properties are rather less likely to belong to the cup itself. Thus the principal way we can assess the iconicity of the cup is through its visual features. Let us then consider three aspects: the shape/size of the cup, the material of which it is made, and its decoration. A number of objects are of comparable shape to the coffee cup and may be connected to it in an associative network. For example, a type of vessel of roughly the same size and shape, and also with a vertical handle, is a teacup. This may very often also be in the same material—ceramic. An-

Figure 6.2. Coffee cup, wine glass, and water glass. Photograph by the author.

other vessel of broadly similar shape and size with vertical handle is the beer mug, although it is, of course, often made of glass rather than ceramic. Other vessel types may be more loosely related: for example, it may be quite apparent from the shape and size of a wine glass that it, like the coffee cup, is intended for individual consumption of liquids (Figure 6.2). However, not only is it made of glass, but it also does not have a handle, and is commonly of a rather different shape (with a stem).

In terms of decoration, the surfaces of the coffee cup may be adorned with designs more commonly seen on other types of artifacts (e.g., textiles), and thus iconic connections to other artifactual categories may form in this way, too. The point is that one can see how various kinds of artifacts may be more or less brought to mind due to their visual similarity with the coffee cup; and, not only do the objects spring to mind, but, presumably, so do the activities and ideas that are indivisible from them.

Indexicality

A second mode of association to examine is *indexicality*—to what extent is the coffee cup an index for various other objects, activities, and thoughts?

Figure 6.3. Coffee cup and contiguous objects. Photograph by the author.

In this regard one must consider relationships of contiguity, causality, and factorality, as described in Chapter 5. One obvious relationship of contiguity concerns the coffee contained in the cup. Other objects that may often be contiguous to the coffee cup include spoons, sugar, napkins, and coffee table (Figure 6.3). There is also an element of factorality here—taken together certain objects may form something of a set or whole, the whole in this case being the "ritual" of drinking coffee. Thus the coffee cup is part of the whole and is thus in a relationship of factorality to that whole.

A further aspect of indexicality relates to the production of the coffee cup rather than its consumption. The object is an index of an investment on the part of the producer, and indeed one might characterize the relationship as a causal one (rather than one of contiguity or factorality). The producer's activities "caused" the vessel to take its final form, and these activities are, to a greater or lesser degree, indexed in the finished product. This last point reminds us that, given our commitment to the idea of symmetry between humans and nonhumans, we must take into account not only the "objects" that the coffee cup indexes but also the human agents that may be implicated. Just as a particular producer may be indexically associated with the coffee cup, so, through consumption, may certain individuals or social groups become connected with the object. It is imaginable that a particular gender, age, ethnic, occupational, or status group may develop an association with the artifact in question.

Let us pursue one of the above points a little farther. It was suggested that the coffee cup as an artifactual category may find itself associated with other artifacts, for instance, sugar bowl and coffee table (Figure 6.3). These objects are in a close spatial relationship with the coffee cup, but they also fall into other kinds of spatial contexts. It may be that the coffee table on which the coffee cup tends to sit is placed within a certain sort of space. Is it located in the center of the room or off-center, is it surrounded by chairs or is it free-standing? And then there is of course the nature of the room itself and its role within the context of the building as a whole. The term "coffee table" generally implies a particular kind of object to be found in a sitting room or lounge, but of course coffee cups may also be placed on dining tables in dining rooms, dining tables in kitchens, or kitchen tables in kitchens. However complex and changing the various spatial contexts of the coffee cup may be, they are a key component of its (indexical) meaning.

Spatial context also suggests temporal context. The coffee cup may constitute an index of certain times of the day, of the week, and perhaps even of the year. The object itself is implicated in the flow of time in other ways too. Perhaps it is worn through repeated use—a repaired handle, a chipped rim, many coffee stains. It may also be of a style and a material that testify to the fact that it was produced some time ago. In these ways the coffee cup indexes its own life history, which has become ingrained on its physical surfaces.

Finally, we must briefly consider the symbolism of the coffee cup. The formal linguistic convention through which the object is symbolized is the term "coffee cup." Thus, at this level, word associations may arise with other phrases involving "coffee" or "cup." Another way symbolism operates in relation to this object is when an icon of a coffee cup is used as a formal convention on signposts, often representing to motorists that they are approaching a café. In this system of iconic symbols various icons are used, and therefore, they too may find themselves associated with the coffee cup.

An Everyday Object?

The example of the coffee cup needed to be simple in order to convey a methodology—that of analyzing affordances, constraints, iconicity, and indexicality. Many potential complexities were suppressed, not least among them the *mutability* of objects. We neglected to entertain the possibility that the meaning of the coffee cup may shift over time, or that it might at a single time not have the same meaning to different social groups.[3] These are not assumptions unique to our simple hypothetical example—there is a more widespread tendency to believe that the status of ordinary objects lies in their physicality and is thus somehow intrinsic. A coffee cup is ontologically an everyday object, a fate it simply cannot avoid. Not all kinds of objects are thus damned: art objects, it is claimed, derive their meaning not from their use-value but from their sign-value. The free-floating quality of sign-value means that the art object can be much more readily reassigned a new meaning. Quite simply, the everyday object is designed to be pragmatic (and hence nonsignificative), while the art object is designed to be significative (and hence nonpragmatic).

And yet design is not always respected. This we should know from those cases in which everyday objects are elevated to art-object status thereby acquiring sign-value (Duchamp's urinal being the archetypal and by now somewhat clichéd example), and in which works of art are reclaimed for pragmatic purposes, thereby acquiring use-value (e.g., metal sculptures melted down for scrap—see Bonnot 2002, 231–33). Objects *can* escape the intentions of their creators—they have a mutability that often sees them move between the categories we impose upon them. These categories derive from our own deep-seated assumptions about objects, or from our refusal to pay them much serious attention. The dualism constructed between the everyday object and the art object is just one of a series of dualities that are not unrelated. We have already spoken of the dichotomy between the pragmatic and the significative and between use-value and sign-value; mention could also be made of the stark division between the functional and the symbolic discussed in Chapter 1 (e.g., Flannery and Marcus 1993), or the classic split between gift and commodity. Nonetheless, there are some notable scholarly attempts to overcome such dyads. As long ago as 1958, Simondon explored the relationship between the technical and the aesthetic nondualistically; yet it is only quite recently that his contribution to the philosophy of techniques has received the attention it deserves (e.g., Hottois 1993; Combes 1999; Chabot 2002). In terms of more current attempts at challenging the duality between everyday objects and art objects, the work of Gell (1999) and Bonnot (2002) stands out.

Although with the coffee cup it may seem unlikely that it will ever be anything other than an everyday object, the whole point is that there is nothing intrinsically stopping it from one day becoming an art object. And this is exactly what Bonnot's analysis reminds us is perfectly possible; he takes a class of ceramic objects and shows how, in the space of a few decades, they change from mass-produced everyday items to individually valued quasi-art objects. It emerges quite clearly that, rather than there being different kinds of objects, there exist different registers of objecthood that certain artifacts may enter and exit at various times. Such a perspective encourages us into three healthy views: to see the status of objects as transitory rather than fixed; to imagine that the status of objects relies not only on the objects themselves but on the manner of their articulation within human-nonhuman networks; and to conceive of objects as leading lives that may be eventful and multiphased.

Indeed, a closer look at the work of Bonnot would be beneficial at this stage, allowing us to see how artifacts can slip between different categories as they find their positions newly configured within subject-object networks. His is one of the few examples of an analysis of material culture that pays very close attention not only to the agency of the subjects who produce, exchange and consume objects but also to the materiality of the objects themselves. Too many studies end up focusing solely on the relational position of the object at the moment of purchase (as could be said of many studies of consumption, critiqued by Dant 1999).

Bonnot's study is of stoneware vessels manufactured in the Saône-et-Loire region of France between the mid-nineteenth and mid-twentieth centuries, with a particular focus on the Bourbince valley. The vessels consisted largely of bottles for beer, liqueurs, mineral water, and ink, pots for conserving processed foods such as jam, mustard, and pâté, as well as numerous products for storing chemicals and pharmaceuticals (Figure 6.4).

Stoneware was especially suitable in that it was very hard and durable (fired to 1300°C), was treated with an impermeable glaze, and could be hermetically sealed. To meet the needs of burgeoning mass consumption the stoneware factories had to produce flawless, highly standardized wares in great quantities. After the Second World War, however, new materials for packaging were introduced, such as industrial glass, cartons, and aluminum cans, effectively spelling the end for the large-scale manufacture of stoneware. Between the 1950s and 1970s this class of pottery effectively disappeared, no longer produced or consumed, with those that had already been produced, if not already discarded, ending up in attics and cellars where they gathered dust for a few decades. But the 1980s saw a rise in various types of second-hand markets—such as flea-markets and garage sales—at which bric-a-brac and sometimes antique items were bought and sold. Stoneware bottles and pots reemerged from attics and cellars and found

Figure 6.4. Stoneware vessel types made in Bourbince valley (Bonnot 2002).
Courtesy of Écomusée du Creusot-Montceau.

their way back onto the market, albeit this time within a rather different sphere of exchange from that in which they were initially embroiled. Rather than being sold in bulk and valued for their functionality, they were, and indeed are, now offered as individual pieces and valued for their aesthetic appeal (Figure 6.5). Indeed, in some cases, a slight difference in the shape or the color of the slip can individualize a piece, despite it being mass-produced and more or less identical to thousands of other examples. Bonnot suggests, however, that in such objects the real beauty comes more from knowledge of the antiquity of the artifact and its local heritage.[4] Moreover, the author is a curator at a local eco-museum that collects such pieces of stoneware and exhibits them as emblems of the region's (mostly industrial) heritage. He is thus able to observe the museum's contributory role in elaborating new value schemes for these objects.

What if we were to subject Bonnot's material to the same kind of analysis as was applied to our hypothetical coffee cup? Although Bonnot does not talk in terms of affordances and constraints, or of iconicity and indexicality, his analysis is so rich that we can pick up most aspects sufficiently well. Let us briefly and nonexhaustively run through these criteria. The physical affordances of stoneware are principally its hardness and its imper-

Figure 6.5. Stoneware vessels as aesthetic objects (Bonnot 2002). Courtesy of Écomusée du Creusot-Montceau.

meability. The former property comes in large part from its high temperature firing. The firing also contributes to the ware's impermeability: at this high temperature the slip partially vitrifies to form a glaze. The glaze is not only impermeable but also very smooth and hence easily cleaned. Thus, stoneware physically affords the storage of liquids and also reuse. A number of different shapes are made, each shape having its own affordances. Tall slender bottles have characteristics suggestive of certain kinds of use (Figure 6.6). Their slender shape makes them graspable even in the absence of a handle. Their narrow necks and mouths mean they can be easily sealed and hence lend themselves to storage; the narrowness presupposes liquids rather than solid materials. With their graspability and relatively high center of gravity they lend themselves to pouring. However, the very narrow neck (combined with the heaviness of stoneware) makes it difficult to judge how much liquid is inside.

Open-mouthed jugs (pichets) do not have this drawback, and they too afford pouring, given their spout with vertical handle placed opposite. However their rather more open mouth makes them unsuitable for storage. Other shapes such as terrines have few specific design features, rendering them functionally adaptable.

Figure 6.6. Tall slender bottles—physical affordances? (Bonnot 2002, pl. 44). Courtesy of Écomusée du Creusot-Montceau.

Turning now to the constraints of stoneware, physically speaking, the artifacts' hardness can be a weakness—it makes them vulnerable to chipping and breakage. Their heaviness can also be somewhat constraining, especially if a large jug full of water is to be poured. Some bottles were originally designed to contain mineral water and others alcohol; although there may be no physical reason why a bottle designed for water might not instead be used for alcohol, or vice versa, cultural constraints may limit this kind of crossover (Bonnot has some evidence to the contrary, however!). Although in the first instance they were made to contain products such as pâté, terrines do not seem to be under any particular cultural constraint that restricts their use; Bonnot reports their reuse in food preparation (e.g., washing salad and fruit).[5] However, "saloirs," large jars used for salting and storing pork and originally kept in the cellar, are not reused in domestic contexts; cultural notions of hygiene mean they are often "banished" to the garden (Bonnot 2002, 184). In choosing where to place stoneware objects no longer in use, Bonnot notes that many households still keep kitchen items (such as jugs) in the kitchen, even though there is nothing physically preventing them from being used for decorative purposes in the sitting room. Cultural considerations make this inappropriate—the kitchen items are judged to be more "at home" in the space where they once served. This consideration of the placement of stoneware in domestic space allows us to move the discussion on to *indexicality* (we shall skip *iconicity*, as there is not much information readily available concerning the physical resemblances stoneware may or may not have with other objects). In particular we can discuss the role of *contiguity*, that is, how the meaning of stoneware vessels derives in part from the entities, human and nonhuman, with which they find themselves contiguous. Bonnot devotes a whole chapter to this topic, what he calls the "mises en scène des choses." He is acutely aware of the ways social space in the household is constructed through objects, and shows us how stoneware objects are strategically located as elements within a system of domestic space (for details, see Bonnot 2002, 181–221). This is also an area explored in detail by Chevalier (1992) and Riggins (1994b).

Another aspect of indexicality is *causality*. The production activities responsible for the creation of stoneware objects can be seen as causally related to them. Given that production of stoneware no longer takes place in the Bourbince valley, it has become part of local history. As such, there is also a degree of factorality involved—stoneware objects represents a much larger whole, a set of community values and a cultural heritage that can be contrasted with the modern world that has replaced it.[6] Largely superseded now by plastics and other modern materials, stoneware comes to be emblematic of a different era. This phenomenon by which ideas find themselves crystallized in objects and their surrounding networks of human-nonhuman relations is reminiscent of a case cited in Chapter 3—the "Berliner key" described by Latour (2000). It is through everyday examples of this kind that the codependency of idea, activity, and material really hits home—in the case of stoneware the very artifacts themselves serve as catalysts for a discourse on local heritage. And once again our leitmotif—that humans think through material culture—emerges strongly.

Art Objects

Bonnot's analysis shows that over time the status of stoneware objects changes as they begin to fulfill significative rather than pragmatic roles (involving a change from use-value to sign-value). In their original contexts of production and use the chances of such objects being considered in any way aesthetically pleasing were presumably rather slim. This is not to say that they were not meaningful, of course, but they must have seemed very far from being art objects. Originally they were mass-produced items sold in bulk. Now individual pieces are sought after by collectors or included in the local eco-museum. Stoneware vessels have been subtly reconfigured, in some quarters at least, as items of aesthetic interest (Figure 6.5). The eco-museum is in part responsible, consciously or unconsciously, for providing a symbolic commentary on these objects, imbuing them with value as emblems of local heritage. Unlike another type of industrially produced ceramic item, Marcel Duchamp's urinal, these objects have not been torn from their everyday context and thrust suddenly under the gallery lights to be displayed as artworks. The process of reevaluation is not only far less dramatic but more gradual and negotiated. Placing these stoneware objects in an eco-museum does not make artworks of them; it does nonetheless constitute part of an ongoing discourse as to the changing status of these kinds of objects. Crucially, Bonnot overcomes the tendency to label objects either mundane or magical by refusing to construct a rigid boundary between the different statuses of objects, and embracing the idea of fluidity between the everyday and the aesthetic.[7] For example, he argues that rather than talking of an object's intrinsic function, one should describe instead its "initial functional destination."[8] The position adopted by Bonnot has some extremely interesting parallels in the work of Gell, particularly in his efforts to link the aesthetic and the technical.

Gell (1992, 1996, 1998, 1999) too challenges the divide that is habitually drawn between everyday objects and art objects. His reasoning is that such a divide opens up because we are slaves to aestheticism. The object judged aesthetically superior evokes a world of meaning beyond the reach of the more mundane artifact. Thus stoneware bottles, ceramic urinals, and other banal items are condemned to a meaningless fate by virtue of their aesthetic inferiority. Even if such artifacts were considered by their users to possess a certain aesthetic appeal, this would not suffice to qualify them as artworks because they were not intentionally manufactured as such. Gell (1999, 159) argues that the aesthetic approach is fundamentally at loggerheads with the anthropological; he advocates a rejection of aesthetics as a methodology. His radical alternative is to consider art as a component of technology. All technical procedures have the capacity to "enchant" to some degree, in that the viewer may be at a loss to understand the technical virtuosity behind the creation of an artifact.[9] What art does is simply carry farther the enchantment that is immanent in all kinds of technology. In that poetry, sculpture, painting, and music are "technologies" that somehow specialize in enchanting, taken together they may be said to form what Gell dubs a "technology of enchantment."

If according to Gell's definition an artwork is an object that enchants through its technical virtuosity, neither the urinal nor the stoneware pot would seem to qualify. Their meaningfulness resides predominantly in their functionality. And yet Gell's system is such that no manufactured object is inherently excluded—there is enchantment immanent in all kinds of technology, even Western industrial technology. Indeed, Gell's approach here serves to exemplify a point expressed earlier in this chapter—that case studies from the contemporary West may be just as informative regarding the nature of material culture as those drawn from ethnographies of traditional societies. In paying relatively little attention to this Western/non-Western distinction, and moving between Western and non-Western art in a single breath, Gell implies, in the spirit of the Latour, that the West is not fundamentally "other."

Furthermore, when Gell talks of artworks and artifacts, he does not essentialize the differences between them. And when we look more closely at Bonnot's account of stoneware production, we see that the firing process is regarded with a certain mystery.[10] Subsequent collectors also find aesthetic appeal in the products. It would be stretching the point to say that the objects possessed enchantment, but one can at least see that even the most unlikely objects have the potential for enchantment. And, almost as importantly, the supposed primacy of function need not be any barrier at all to enchantment. Even though we may tend to assume a mutual exclusivity in the Western art-world, Gell claims that art may overlap with function; an example he develops at some length to impress this upon us concerns an exhibition of African objects in a New York gallery, amongst them a Zande hunting net (Gell 1996, 1999). Let us now take a brief look at this case (Figure 6.7).

Gell is reacting primarily against the opinion expressed in the exhibition catalogue, by the art philosopher Arthur Danto, that the hunting net's evident designed functionality precludes it from proper consideration as an artwork. The possibility that the hunting net was designed by its maker with functional rather than aesthetic ends in mind should according to Gell be neither here nor there in the twentieth century. Western art became well accustomed to the notion of functional objects as art, ever since Duchamp's ready-mades. Such objects are considered not on aesthetic but rather on "interpretive" grounds; they qualify as artworks when evaluated within a system of ideas espoused by the Western art-world (Gell 1999, 187). Why

Figure 6.7. Zande hunting net—functional and/or aesthetic? (as used in Gell 1996), Neg. 3444(2). Photograph by J. L. Thompson. Courtesy of the Library, American Museum of Natural History.

then does Danto not accept the hunting net in the spirit of the ready-made? There are two possible reasons. First, for him there is no artist in sight, and artistic intention is obviously key. However, he does seem to overlook the possibility that the exhibition's curator, anthropologist Susan Vogel, may fit this role. Second, the object in question is "exotic," imported from outside the Western tradition, and so does not hold the "historic and iconographic resonances" (Gell 1999, 211) that allow for its interpretation. Gell points out that the flip side of this "exotic" quality is an ignorance of African ethnography; the idea that the hunting net is a purely functional object fails to take into account the symbolic importance of such nets in hunting, which often either forms part of specific rituals or is undertaken in a ritualized manner (Gell 1999, 197).

Danto's dichotomization of artworks and artifacts is but one example of a much broader tendency to which Gell is reacting. He is keen to develop a single overarching framework that can be equally applied to all kinds of objects, be they artworks or artifacts. The "aesthetic" approach of Western art history has in his opinion failed in this regard, incapable of extending itself consistently to all candidate art objects, including the ones that may be considered aesthetically unappealing. His subsequent move is to reject the aesthetic viewpoint altogether and to develop a "methodological philistinism," which consists of "taking an attitude of resolute indifference towards the aesthetic value of works of art" (Gell 1999, 161). He proposes to replace aestheticism with another overarching framework, an anthropology of art truly capable of dealing with all kinds of objects, whether Western and non-Western. The key to such an anthropology of art is to ask of artworks what we have always asked of artifacts—what do they *do*? Gell thereby shifts the focus away from an analysis of *meaning* toward the analysis of *effect* (Gosden 2001, 164; see also Thomas 2001, 4). He is effectively denying the semiotic study of the significative meanings of artworks, in favor of an action-centered study of their corporeal, pragmatic qualities.

Gell's critique, however eloquent, is problematic in some regards. His skepticism toward aesthetic approaches and his adoption of what he has called "methodological philistinism" are a rather extreme position, one that has provoked some robust responses. An immediate riposte came from Spring (1997), who questioned Gell's apparently rather limited definition of "aesthetic." Gosden (2001) believes that rather than maintain the term "art" and reject "aesthetics," as Gell does, we would be better advised to do exactly the opposite. D'Alleva (2001) takes issue with Gell's rejection of metaphor and metonymy, and indeed all kinds of symbolic meaning in art. It seems that in propounding his action-centered approach Gell may have been rather too quick to announce the demise of aestheticism within the anthropological study of art.

There is clearly an attraction in finding a perspective that is somehow unified, with the capacity to deal with all kinds of objects. And, although Gell succeeded in creating an overarching framework capable of treating artworks and artifacts on the same terms, he achieved this by emphasizing the pragmatic qualities of artifacts and artworks at the expense of their significative qualities. There are clear reasons why Gell followed this anti-aesthetic path; in his reckoning, the aesthetic, the semiotic, and the linguistic were inseparable bedfellows. In trying to distance his work as far as possible from the linguistic/semiotic tradition, Gell, therefore, could not help but also reject the aesthetic. Fortunately, however, as we have seen in the previous chapter, not all semiotic approaches have to be linguistic and derived from the Saussurean tradition; Peircean semiotics, in stark contrast to the Saussurean system, is avowedly phenomenological. Moreover, it is very much consistent with Gell's project.

With this in mind, we need to take steps to reconcile aestheticism with an action-centered approach, building on many of the points developed in Chapter 5. One means may be to differentiate consistently between aesthetic *effect* and aesthetic *intention*. These are terms used by Genette (1999) in defining "the aesthetic relation," and his observations are very helpful in this context. Many kinds of object can have an aesthetic effect on a viewer, but this quality alone does not make them artworks. What differentiates art objects from other objects, according to Genette, is that they embody an artistic "intention," or that they are thought by the viewer, rightly or wrongly, to have such an intention:

> Whenever the subject of this relation, rightly or wrongly and to whatever degree, takes this object for a human product and ascribes to the person who produced it an "aesthetic intention," that is, the aspiration to achieve an aesthetic effect, or "candidacy" for aesthetic reception, the object is received as a work of art, and the relation takes the more specific form of an artistic relation or function. (Genette 1999, 222)

This does not mean, however, that, with regard to the Zande net, Danto was right. First, Danto's dichotomization of the aesthetic and the functional is unnecessary—an object can certainly be both, and intentionally so. Second, even if Danto was right and the producer of the net had no aesthetic intention, this does not take account of the intentionality of the exhibition's curator, the anthropologist Susan Vogel. In a similar vein, the industrial urinal is not produced with much aesthetic intention; but it is the intentionality of Duchamp that the viewer tries to understand when confronted with his famous artwork in a gallery, and not the intentionality of its industrial manufacturer. If we consider the relationship between Vogel and the Zande net as comparable to that between Duchamp and the urinal, in that both objects are essentially "ready-mades" (Gell 1999, 192), then the viewer is surely not mistaken in seeing an aesthetic intention within the Zande net.

Gell's approach can certainly be reconciled with, and clarified by, the distinction made by Genette between aesthetic effect and aesthetic intention. Ironically, Gell argues that, since artworks can in fact be defined in terms of their evocation of "complex intentionalities," anthropologists should abandon the aesthetic notion of artworks (Spring 1997). Yet Genette shows through his term "aesthetic intention" how intentionality can be absolutely intrinsic to an aesthetic approach. The viewer confronted with an artwork seeks to understand the nature of the agency behind its creation. This is in fact close to Gell's ideas on art as technology, and of the relationship between artwork, creator, and viewer: "the attitude of the spectator towards a work of art is fundamentally conditioned by his notion of the technical processes which gave rise to it, and the fact that it was created by the agency of another person, the artist" (1999, 172).

Thus, both Genette and Gell stress that the viewer is looking through the work to the agency (or intentionality) within and behind it. Another area of overlap in their approaches concerns the relationship between artworks and everyday objects. In constantly reminding us that "art is not the only occasion for the aesthetic relation" (1999, 223), Genette refuses to construct an impenetrable boundary between the domain of the art object and that of the everyday object. From the above it should be clear that this also satisfies one of Gell's major concerns (not to mention Bonnot).

Magical Objects

The dichotomization of art objects and everyday objects in Western culture means that we are hard-pressed to see the artistic in the everyday, despite the best efforts of Gell, Bonnot, Genette, and others to insist that there is a continuity between the two. As part of his thoroughgoing attempt to demonstrate that industrial and traditional material cultures are not all that different after all, Gell uses anthropological examples as a means of encouraging us to see the potential for convergence. We are presented with an example that we can grasp as "artistic"—the carving of a Trobriand canoe board—a process requiring such technical virtuosity as to render the object enchanting. But Gell's real concern here is to shift the discussion toward the realm of magic, and in particular to argue for a convergence between the categories of "art" and "magic." He highlights how the technical/artistic process of carving is suffused with magical rites that aim to make the process as effortless and efficient as possible. Magic in a sense sets the ideal standard for technology. Even though the magical goes beyond the boundaries of the real, it takes the real as a base point: as Gell comments, "it is technology which sustains magic, even as magic inspires fresh technical efforts" (1988, 9). By inserting the ideal/magical in the real, the ideal becomes part of the very fabric of the real; a Trobriand garden's "real" function is to produce yams, but this does not mean that it is at the same time incapable of possessing magical properties. The hope is that through this intimate entanglement the real may grow closer to the ideal. The ideal is thus constantly evoked even if never realized; and this interpenetration of the ideal and the real is, contrary to Western expectations, probably the rule rather than the exception.[11] Within the category of "the ideal" we may include

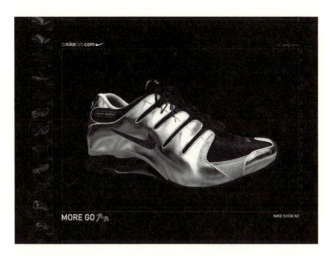

Figure 6.8. Nike running shoe—a magical artifact? Courtesy of Brand Communications, Nike Inc.

both art and magic: they are categories that coincide. Just as art may be characterized by its ability to transcend the technical schemas of the spectator, so may magic be similarly defined.

When we try to think about Western examples it is difficult to entertain the idea of "magical" production, except perhaps in the case of artworks; the artistic act of creation may be seen to have magical qualities. Where everyday objects are concerned, however, the ability to see anything remotely "magical" within them requires the eye of faith. For example, the stoneware described by Bonnot hardly appears enchanting, yet even here, in the midst of seemingly purely technofunctional industrial production, there are hints of magic in production, judging by some informants' descriptions of the "mystery" of the firing process. Today, high-tech consumer products can involve technical "wizardry" far beyond the layperson's comprehension: technical virtuosity, as we read above, is a source of enchantment. Thus there may be something magical in the engineering of the running shoe—so light as to make running almost perfect—a merging of the ideal and the real. And, as if the engineering of the shoe itself were not enough, the consumer is provided with a symbolic commentary that idealizes the shoe, suggesting it is as much magical as real (Figure 6.8). The branding and advertising of the product, managed with particular success by Nike during the 1980s and 1990s, serves to create around the artifact and its technology a mythical world (Katz 1994; Goldman and Papson 1998). Nike offers "an occasional glimpse of a re-enchanted, sometimes magical relationship with the world" (Goldman and Papson 1998, 148).

Social commentators tell us that advertising is an industry of the symbolic, centered on manipulating the meanings of *l'objet-signe*. The sign-value of the object is portrayed as responding to its own set of symbolic dynamics, to the extent that the relationship between image and reality in such artifacts and technologies is ignored or assumed (e.g., Baudrillard, critiqued by Dant 1999). It is as if mere association with the sign content of the running shoe is enough to transform body and mind. Yet one might very well argue instead that the imaginary world projected in the symbolic commentary of advertising is unattainable without the artifact/technology itself. Acquisition in itself is not enough; one must at least wear/embody the shoe if it is to transform body and mind. Surely the most effective form of symbolic commentary is that which conjures up an imaginary world with *some* bearing on the real, rather than amplifying the discrepancy between the real and the imaginary. Nike, for example, promotes athletics as an avenue for both physical and spiritual development, both immanence and transcendence; the brand's sign value is built on "the gap between the everyday and the spectacular" (Goldman and Papson 1998, 167).

Gell (1988) has commented upon the similarities between advertising in Western consumer society and magic in traditional societies. He would argue that the symbolic commentary elaborated around a Nike running shoe is akin to the magical incantations associated with the Trobriand garden; both summon up a utopian world. In the anthropological example the magical is firmly attached to particular technical systems; in the creation of a Trobriand garden, or indeed of a Trobriand canoe board, these two dimensions are almost impossible to disentangle.[12] In a similar way, the myth-making that is advertising (operating through the manipulation of iconic, indexical, and symbolic associations), strives to create a particular image of how object, body, and mind should unite perfectly.[13] In promulgating the ideal of the Nike running shoe as an indivisible, "magical" union of technology, body, and mind, the design process and the image-making process are surely very much intertwined, driving each other on. Even though Gell suggests that advertisers, propagandists, and image-makers are the magicians of modern technological culture, a good case can be made for casting the designers and technologists as magicians too.[14]

And then the question for us becomes, "how are we to understand the *meaning* of objects that exhibit technical virtuosity and/or symbolic elaboration?" From the perspectives of both Bonnot and Gell, it would follow that their meaning does not fundamentally operate any differently from that of "everyday" objects such as stoneware pots. The methodology we have used, in which affordances, constraints, iconicity, and indexicality are brought together, should apply equally well to artifacts occupying all kinds of registers, from the banal to the magical. What essentially emerges is that objects in these registers experience different relations in respect to other objects, activities, and knowledge/ideas.[15] The differences between everyday, art, and magical objects may thus lie in these network-like configurations; for an object to pass from one register to another requires a reconfiguration of the network topology (a deterritorialization?).

Concluding Remarks

Even though we are often told that consumption today revolves entirely around the sign-value of objects within symbolic frames of reference, such an observation fails to recognize the complex articulation of object symbolism and object functionality, a key relationship in need of scrutiny in all material culture. Much of this chapter has been about overcoming entrenched dualisms of this kind; indeed, it is a theme pursued ever since the first chapter in which we railed against the separation of functional from symbolic meanings. We have also discussed this duality in terms of the pragmatic vs. the significative, use-value versus sign-value, the real versus the imaginary, and technology versus magic. What emerges instead of duality is in fact fluidity, to the extent that in material culture these extremes are often codependent. The pragmatic and the significative interweave, the imaginary is embedded in the real, and magic "haunts technical activity like a shadow" (Gell 1999, 181). These relationships of codependency rather than of separation should take us back to the argument outlined in Chapter 3, that material culture invariably entails a codependency of mind, action, and matter.[16]

I hope to have underlined some of the challenges we face in understanding the interface in modern culture between mind, agency, and object. The very rapid and seemingly unpredictable changes occurring in certain areas of modern technology, such as genetic engineering and communications, create both enormous excitement and trepidation. These technologies should force us to think long and hard about the boundaries between the real and the imaginary, and to elaborate as full a picture as possible of how humans "think through" material culture. And yet despite some of the new challenges of contemporary technology, there are many ways in which the material culture of today is not so very different from that of the past. There should be no need to use two entirely different theoretical frameworks for tackling material culture, one for the modern/postmodern world, and one for the premodern world. Indeed, it is the goal of this chapter to tackle aspects of contemporary material culture from a perspective that can also be fruitfully applied to the past; this will be demonstrated in the next chapter through the elaboration of an archaeological case study.

Chapter 7

Archaeological Case Study: Drinking Vessels in Minoan Crete

We now follow through on the ideas developed in previous chapters and apply them to bodies of archaeological material. The aim, of course, is to reveal some of the ways in which meanings in past material culture may be accessible to us. There are obvious challenges and problems that the prehistoric archaeologist in particular faces when seeking to situate certain categories of artifact or activity in networks that are distributed across matter, body, and mind. But despite the lacunae that exist when dealing with only the material traces of past societies, it is nonetheless possible to undertake impressive reconstructions of cultural networks over both space and time. The temporal perspective, particularly over the medium to long term, is of course a unique strength of the discipline.

As already mentioned, the theoretical groundwork for this task has been put together piece by piece over the course of the preceding chapters. A few lessons in particular ought to be kept to the fore. For example, we must remember the codependency of mind, action, and matter that inheres in material culture; these connections are fundamental to the human ability to cognize and perceive the affordances and constraints of artifacts in their contexts. Indeed, so inseparable are mind, action, and matter that, at times, to say that humans "think through" material culture runs far deeper than trite wordplay. With these "vertical" connections in mind we must set about assessing the horizontal networks in which objects find themselves, not forgetting that the connections holding such heterogeneous networks together are of variable character, based on the semiotic relationships of similarity, contiguity, causality, factorality, and convention. It is essential to keep these multiple connections to the fore as they contribute to the rapprochement between materiality and signification by which considerable stock has been set in previous chapters. As noted in Chapter 5, it is in its articulation of the links between the object as sign and the object as material

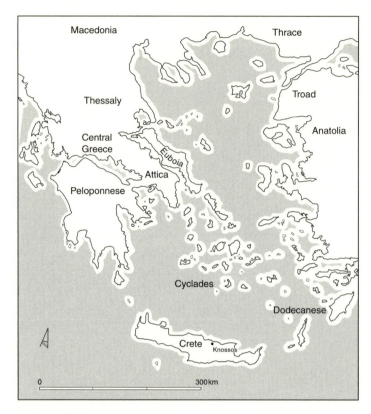

Figure 7.1. Map of the Aegean.

that a theory of material culture should be judged (Warnier 1999, 28). One final point is that it is not only artifacts that are implicated in material culture but also humans; an acceptance of the symmetry between humans and nonhumans means that either can be treated as agents or artifacts.

The case study I present derives from my research on the material culture of Crete (Figure 7.1) during the Middle Bronze Age (Figure 7.2). It focuses on a class of material culture that is so common as to be almost definitive of Minoan-ness: ceramic drinking vessels. These artifacts are variable over space and time in technology and style, exhibiting patterns of variation that are associated with a whole series of other changes in production and consumption within Minoan society more generally. It is in exploring the pragmatic and significative properties of ceramic drinking ves-

First Palace Period	Protopalatial	MM IB	1900 BC
		MM IIA	
		MM IIB	
Second Palace Period	Neopalatial	MM IIIA	1700 BC
		MM IIIB	
		LM IA	
		LM IB	1450 BC

Figure 7.2. Chronological chart showing Middle Bronze Age.

sels within these broader human and nonhuman networks that we may move toward an understanding of their meaningfulness.

Object Studies in Aegean Prehistory

In order to grasp the novelty of what is proposed—a search for meaning in Minoan material culture—we must give some thought to the status quo of technology and material culture studies in Aegean prehistory. This has been something of a growth area, with a number of innovative approaches to a range of materials, such as metal (Nakou 1995), stone tools (Carter 1994, 1998), and especially pottery (Whitelaw et al. 1997; Day et al. 1997; Day and Wilson 2002; Knappett 1997). These studies break the mold of traditional perspectives on techniques and objects through the discussion of socioeconomic dimensions such as specialization, centralization, and the organization of production. But questions of *meaning* only rarely enter into such studies. This is in part because of the character of the material with which these studies tend to be concerned: they have not, on the whole, tackled the production technology of "art" objects with iconographic scenes. Whether it be representational frescoes, sealstones, relief stone vases, or indeed certain kinds of figurative pottery such as Marine Style (Marinatos 1993; Driessen and Macdonald 1997, 61–64), most of these material culture forms, conventionally considered under the heading "Minoan art," are deemed to be *intrinsically* meaningful and symbolic. Being art objects, the assumption is that they were clearly produced with aesthetic intention by their creators.

Although not intrinsically meaningful or symbolic, some "non-artis-

Figure 7.3. Neopalatial conical cups. Photograph by the author. Courtesy of the British School at Athens.

tic" objects are thought to acquire meaning in ways such as their use in special contexts. One such context is burial: objects consumed during the ritual activities surrounding burial may well become symbolically charged. Thus two examples of work on production technology in which the issue of symbolism does arise are both concerned with burial assemblages: Tristan Carter's work on the production and consumption of obsidian (1998) and the work of Day and colleagues on the Early Minoan pottery from the Ayia Photia cemetery (Day et al. 1998). Whereas the former may be somewhat unique in considering both the production *and* consumption activities of certain tomb artifacts (obsidian blades) to be symbolically charged, the latter appear to see symbolism only in the consumption phase.[1] Another kind of consumption context through which otherwise "meaningless" artifacts are thought to become symbolically charged, is ceremonial feasting. The classic case from Bronze Age Crete is the Neopalatial conical cup (Figure 7.3), a mundane and ubiquitous type of ceramic drinking vessel often found in ritual contexts such as tombs and peak sanctuaries. For earlier periods, Day and Wilson highlight the "symbolic value" of vessels used in conspicuous consumption at Early and Middle Minoan Knossos (Day and Wilson 1998; Wilson and Day 2000; Day and Wilson 2002). But it is only through their central role in feasting ceremonies, that is, in ritual consumption contexts, that the objects in question acquire meaningfulness; they are not argued to have any *intrinsic* meaningfulness or symbolic value.

Thus, one can see that symbolism and meaning really only raise their heads in relation to objects that fulfill either one of two criteria (ideally, both): either "art" objects that are iconographic and hence deemed to be intrinsically meaningful from the moment of their production, or objects that are tied up in consumption contexts that have a ritual, ceremonial, or religious character. In both cases there is assumed to be a kind of conscious communication going on, whether at the moment of production or of consumption. This position seems very close to that set up by Flannery and Marcus (1993) in their attempt, discussed in the first chapter of this book, to limit the scope of cognitive archaeology to the domains of cosmology, religion, ideology, and iconography. Activities in these domains are considered symbolic and communicative, and for Flannery and Marcus the term *cognitive* only applies to these areas. One can only surmise that they are interested solely in *conscious* levels of cognition (with language, presumably, as the ultimate example). Flannery and Marcus do admit that other more mundane activities may require "intelligence," but such activities do not require conscious thought, and so do not fall within the remit of cognitive archaeology. If one were to employ the distinction between *connaissance* and *savoir-faire*, one might say that Flannery and Marcus only acknowledge the former as being cognitive. Of course, we may not agree with Flannery and Marcus's narrow conception of cognitive archaeology or with their simplistic equation of cognitive = conscious = symbolic. And indeed those scholars pursuing "chaîne opératoire" approaches within a cognitive framework may disagree quite violently. But what is more important to us here is the implication that *everyday* artifacts are nonsymbolic and hence nonmeaningful. They are presumably just functional.

Somehow this set of assumptions also seems to be pretty firmly entrenched in the way objects are treated in Aegean prehistory. There are hardly any attempts to tackle the meaningfulness of ordinary objects in ordinary contexts. Symbolism and meaning only get attention when the subject matter involves ritual and religion (feasting ceremonies, burials), or iconography (frescoes, sealstones etc.), preferably all these at once. If a Minoan archaeologist is to talk of symbolism, the ideal scenario involves a figurative scene in a ritual context. And even if one finds an iconographic scene in a nonritual setting, the desire to read it as ritual is nonetheless overwhelming (e.g., the Theran frescoes—Sherratt 2000; see also Knappett 2002b).

There is a sense, then, that meaning is somehow exotic, mysterious, and unattainable. As was discussed in the opening chapter, prehistorians have long been nervous about meaning, feeling that it is beyond their reach. Of course this runs in tandem with the idea that meaning resides largely in the mind as an internal mental representation, and that the recovery of ancient mind is thus a step too far for the prehistorian. As a corollary, meaning is seen to occupy a different sphere of abstraction over and above objects and behavior. It is somewhat ironic that prehistorians tend to be both *materialists* and *mentalists*. Even though we think through materials, we tend to maintain a dichotomy between the realms of the artifactual and the ideal. And this can in large part be attributed to the Cartesian legacy, whereby mind is considered to be primary and internal, with environment broadly construed as secondary and external. One of this book's central arguments is that when we begin to explore more fully this notion of thinking through material culture, we may see that mind and cognition are not necessarily confined to the brain but seep out into the body and the world. Equally, body and world are constantly and ineluctably drawn into the process of cognition. If we accept this, the materialist/mentalist duality melts away. We arrive at a middle ground that acknowledges the materiality of things as well as the properties of the human body and mind in the creation of meaning. People and things bring each other into being in a dialogic process. It is this kind of rapprochement between mind and matter, between thoughts and artifacts, that is needed if we wish to tackle the meaningfulness of all kinds of objects, be they mundane or magical.

Therefore, what follows now is an exploration of how, in prehistoric contexts, different kinds of objects come to be meaningful. While we will examine both everyday objects and artworks, it is important to bear in mind that no object belongs intrinsically to either category—these registers of objecthood possess a degree of fluidity as to which objects belong within them. Some objects may be produced as everyday, mundane items (their initial functional destination), but may through time come to be experienced as magical or aesthetic. Conversely, objects initially destined to be "artworks" may lose their sign-value and come to have a primarily functional role. So-called "everyday" objects are not separated by a fixed boundary from other categories of objects, such as art objects or magical objects; there is fluidity between these different registers, with any given object able to acquire status as a certain kind of object as quickly as it can lose it (Löfgren 1996; Gell 1999; Bonnot 2002). Thus, between production and consumption there may be "slippage." Moreover, as Gell emphasizes for the Zande hunting net (see previous chapter), an object does not have to be produced with the intention of being either functional or aesthetic. The two may very frequently be interpenetrative. And this interpenetration applies to all things, from mass-produced wares to the unique art object—it is simply the balance that alters. This means that the mundane and the magical do not occupy fundamentally different ontological categories, but rather represent points on a continuum that can be assessed equivalently. Indeed, in the analytical framework that follows, the notion of equivalency is fundamental. This is largely facilitated by Gell's ideas on the technology of enchantment and technical virtuosity, and Genette's on aesthetic effect and aesthetic intention, as discussed in the previous chapter.

The Minoan drinking vessels on which our focus now falls certainly appear to occupy widely differing registers, from the mundane to the magical, from the everyday to the aesthetic. The plain and often rather crude goblets and cups seem in some ways a world apart from the elaborately decorated Kamares cups. And yet not only do these different classes share a number of features in terms of their production technology, they are also often very closely linked in their consumption contexts. Thus Minoan drinking vessels are very well suited to an analysis of how objects come to occupy different registers. Moreover, in that such vessels are clearly suited to individual consumption, there is a very apparent human dimension implicated in the patterns of "nonhuman" artifactual variability. It is not so much the cup that is the focus, but the hybrid form of individual-with-cup (see comments by Latour discussed in earlier chapters on the hybrid human-nonhuman agency of man-with-gun) that takes shape within the context of certain kinds of consumption activity in Minoan Crete.

Minoan Drinking Vessels

Minoan drinking vessels, that is, cups and goblets (with and without handles respectively), are found at sites all over Crete throughout the Middle Bronze Age. But when and how do they develop? If we look back to the Early Bronze Age, the third millennium B.C., there are some interesting observations to be made. Individual drinking vessels, predominantly goblets, first appear during the Early Minoan IIA period; before this time, in Early Minoan I, there are large chalices and serving bowls that seem to be indicative of communal rather than individual consumption (Day and Wilson 2002, 149–52). From Early Minoan IIA onward, indeed until the onset of the

First Palaces, individual drinking vessels continue to occur in large deposits suggestive of feasting (Day and Wilson 2002). Despite the large quantities involved, however, these vessels exhibit a remarkable homogeneity, with very little variation in typology or quality. The goblet takes a rather standard form in each period and is always of a moderate level of production skill and quality, neither extremely finely made nor extremely crude.

Although Day and Wilson argue that there is a fundamental continuity in feasting practices into the Protopalatial period, I would say that the picture in fact changes quite dramatically. Not only do the types of cups proliferate, but we see the joint appearance of very low quality and very high quality drinking vessels (Macdonald and Knappett forthcoming). These changes coincide rather precisely with the first emergence on Crete of significant social hierarchies institutionalized in palaces and states. It is in part for this reason that drinking vessels have been chosen for this case study—they are emblematic of a much broader and more far-reaching set of sociopolitical developments. A case in point in this regard is one particular type of drinking vessel known as the carinated cup (Figure 7.4). As is true of the first palaces as a whole, they appear quite suddenly in the first phase of the Protopalatial period (Middle Minoan IB). Thereafter they are rapidly established as one of the principal drinking vessels of Middle Minoan II, before disappearing during Middle Minoan III. The vessel type is found all over the island for about 200 years. The shape does undergo alterations over this period, but the essential idea remains the same throughout.

To what extent, then, can we recreate some of the meaningfulness of ceramic drinking vessels as produced, exchanged, and consumed nearly 4,000 years ago in Minoan Crete? Quite substantially, I would say, if we keep in mind the co-implication of their pragmatic and significative dimensions, and the codependency of humans and nonhumans in networks. We can set about this through a systematic assessment of their affordances and constraints on the one hand and their iconic/indexical/symbolic associations on the other, much as we attempted, rather simplistically perhaps, with the coffee cup example in the previous chapter.

Affordances and Constraints

The Minoan cup, of whatever type, is a vessel not unlike the modern coffee cup in certain features. Having a flat base and a low center of gravity it has stability on level surfaces. Being made of well-fired clay, it is reasonably

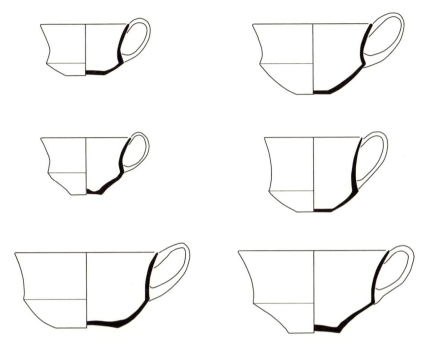

Figure 7.4. Examples of Minoan carinated cups (after MacGillivray 1998). Courtesy of the British School at Athens.

solid. However, as it is earthenware, not stoneware or porcelain (neither of which existed in Minoan times), it is somewhat less solid than the modern coffee cup. This is further exacerbated by the fact that it tends on the whole to have thinner walls, which also make it rather more prone to breakage when dropped. Its capacity, ranging roughly between 0.1 and 0.5 liters, is broadly similar; it was presumably designed for individual consumption. That the Minoan cup invariably possesses a vertical handle might be taken to indicate a primary use in the consumption of hot liquids. In this it may appear to differ from the goblet, a class of drinking vessel without handle. Yet the presence or absence of handle for cups and goblets respectively probably does not correspond quite so neatly to a distinction between hot and cold liquids. Although Minoan cups, and indeed goblets, are often treated with a reasonably thick slip at both interior and exterior, they do not have the impermeability that one might expect of a vessel used for hot liquids. The position of the handle is comparable to that of the coffee cup's handle, seemingly pointing to a physical affordance for tipping. Although the handle can be a little on the delicate side, the Minoan cup possesses good manipulability and graspability (features also true of goblets).

Thus in a situation in which the consumption of a liquid was the principal activity at hand, the Minoan cup would announce itself as a suitable object for such ends. But given other contexts, alternative uses would announce themselves. Some possibilities were suggested in our discussion of the modern coffee cup, and it is perhaps unnecessary to invent similar situations for the Minoan cup. But one might at least note that some classes of Minoan cup do actually have a spout at the rim (lateral to the handle), seemingly enhancing an affordance for pouring, perhaps into another vessel, rather than just tipping.

What about the physical, logical, semantic, and cultural constraints that may have in practice restricted the use to which the Minoan cup was put? It is difficult to know quite what physical or logical constraints may have been at work, except for the rather obvious ones mentioned in relation to the modern coffee cup. As for semantic constraints, one also imagines that the suitability of the form for individual consumption would have precluded its use by a group. This apparently straightforward point is very important for the current discussion—the strong potentiality of the form for individual and individualizing consumption. Indeed, despite the considerable range of cups found at most Protopalatial sites, Minoan cups are almost always of a size and capacity highly suited to individual consumption. For example, although at the palatial center of Malia around thirty different cup types appear to have been in use simultaneously (Poursat and Knappett in press), many of them are largely equivalent in their functional affordances. This strongly suggests that consumers must have been faced with various cultural constraints as to which contexts were appropriate for the use of different kinds of cups. Perhaps different cups were deemed appropriate for consuming different types of liquid (water, wine, hot infusions?), or for use at particular times and in specific social settings. It may also be the case that these different types were quite interchangeable and that the choice of cup was more a matter of personal preference and taste. A further factor to consider is the organization of production—maybe there were different workshops that sought to differentiate their products from one another by specializing in particular styles and shapes. As we explore this case study in greater depth some of these possibilities will emerge as more or less likely. The bewildering variety in cup types and their numerous associations we now examine within the semiotic framework of iconicity, indexicality, and symbolism.

Figure 7.5. Crudely made carinated cups from Knossos. Photograph by Kathy May. Courtesy of the British School at Athens.

Iconicity

Beginning with iconicity, we must ask what material culture categories Minoan cups resembled? As stated earlier, iconicity is not necessarily just about visual similarity, it is also about other sensual similarities—touch, taste, sound, and smell. Some of these may well have been important as far as the contents of the cup are concerned; however, for the cup itself, the visual is likely to preoccupy us more than any other sense. And, as with the modern coffee cup, we need to take account of three dimensions: material, shape/size, and surface treatment. Minoan cups do not vary greatly in material, tending to be made in fine buff clay fabrics. Yet these fine buff clays are not always treated with the same degree of care when it comes to fashioning them into a pot. Some of the cups we encounter are rather clumsily constructed; their thick, irregular walls and inelegant shape point to a striking lack of skill and effort invested in their production (Figure 7.5). Others, meanwhile, occupy the other extreme, so finely made as to beggar belief— the very thinnest of walls, indicative of a sensitive mastery of the clay body (Figure 7.6). These latter examples are also invariably the vessels with the most elaborate shape and decoration, what might easily be dubbed "art-

Figure 7.6. Thin-walled polychrome carinated cup (after MacGillivray 1998). Courtesy of the British School at Athens.

works." In terms of their physical form they bear little relation to the cruder types, and any "iconic" connection occurs only at the broadest level. Nonetheless, these two extremes of the "mundane" on the one hand, and the "magical" on the other are linked technologically by a series of intermediate forms, such that it is impossible to draw an absolute boundary between them.

Minoan cups exhibit considerable variability, not only in their technology but also in their shapes and surface treatments. In terms of shapes, a wide range is commonly encountered, with straight-sided cups, carinated cups, and hemispherical cups, not to mention handleless forms such as tumblers and goblets (Figure 7.7). Moreover, within each of these broad categories a number of subtypes exist; at Malia, for example, there are ten different versions of the carinated cup in use during Middle Minoan IIB.

Different shapes physically resemble objects in other material culture categories to greater or lesser degrees. The carinated cup in particular is usually considered by Minoanists to be a primarily metallic shape that is imitated in clay, not only because of its carinated shape, but also because of its thin walls and delicate ribbon handle. Even though metal vessels are

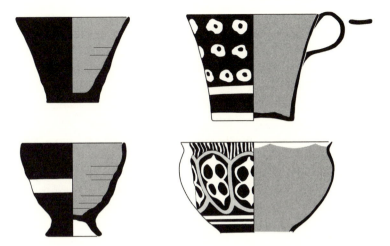

Figure 7.7. Various types of Minoan drinking vessels from Knossos: tumbler, goblet, straight-sided and hemispherical cups. Courtesy of the British School at Athens.

very rarely found in the Middle Minoan period, it is thought that this is illusionary, a result of recycling and poor preservation rather than an actual rarity at the time. The idea is that while the carinated cup makes very good sense as a metal shape, it is far less suited to being made in clay. Thus, it is argued, the main reason this shape is made in ceramic at all is because it is aping those made in metal (principally silver and bronze), which would have been extremely valuable, far more so than any pot. In short, not only is there an iconic relationship between ceramic and metal carinated forms, but this relationship is exploited so that some of the value of the metal originals rubs off on the ceramic imitations (we shall explore this further below, in the discussion of indexicality).

Thought must also be given to variation in surface treatment and details of shape. Some cups are highly polished and elaborately decorated, while others are roughly finished and entirely plain. Much more will be made of these patterns of variation in the section on indexicality. But in terms of iconicity, the surface treatments of different cup types appear to relate in varying degrees to other material culture categories. At most Minoan sites, carinated cups are very rarely decorated except for an all-over dark slip that is quite often lustrous. The intention behind this may have been to create a sheen or luster iconically reminiscent of metal vessels (although one must note that Phaistian potters appear to buck this trend by decorating carinated cups with complex polychrome motifs). By comparison, it is interesting to observe that other cup types that owe somewhat less to metal originals, such as straight-sided and hemispherical cups, are much more commonly decorated with quite complex motifs; at Malia in Middle Minoan IIB such forms are frequently decorated with bands and spaliform motifs that owe little to metal, and perhaps more to textiles.

Another craft medium with which such cup types display associations is stone. Throughout the Minoan period, stone vases are one of the most distinctive categories of material culture. Most are made from serpentine, a soft and easily worked stone that is widely available in many areas of Crete (particularly central Crete). Stone carinated cups are extremely rare, although not totally unknown (Warren 1969, type 17C—eight catalogued examples, of which two have crinkly rims). Other ceramic cup types do, however, show closer affinities with the medium of stone, in terms of both shape and decoration. The hemispherical cup, for example, is rather better known than the carinated cup as a type of stone vase (Warren 1969—25 catalogued). Moreover, a number of ceramic examples have decoration that looks very much as if it is inspired by stone—white dots on a dark ground mimicking the effect of some kinds of serpentine; veining imitating breccia; or wavy lines mimicking banded tufa, a form of calcite.

Yet some types of drinking vessels do not find themselves iconically associated with any particular material culture category. These may be plain and undecorated, simple in shape, and not especially carefully made. Although there are plenty of such examples in the Protopalatial period, it is the Neopalatial conical cup that answers perfectly this description (see Figure 7.3). There are no gestures being made to other crafts, no intentional aesthetic investment. It would seem that iconicity is not much of a factor for such mundane artifacts. At the other extreme, the very finest Kamares cups, laden with aesthetic intention, seem to flag madly their physical similarity to metal, stone, or textiles. But there is no question of a fixed boundary between the aesthetic and the everyday; some seemingly ordinary cups, and many carinated cups by no means superbly made, are making gestures toward other crafts. Clearly, different cup types have variable iconic relationships with other material culture categories. The iconic qualities of the carinated cup, and indeed of other cup types to which it is related, are rather complex, with some aspects of their meaningfulness deriving from their connectivity within human-nonhuman networks. But this process is not the sole preserve of the magical, aesthetic artwork.

Indexicality

In this section we turn to the indexical properties of Minoan cups, exploring the areas of contiguity, factorality, and causality (as discussed in Chapter 5). With what artifacts and agents do they tend to find themselves spatially contiguous? Owing to the nature of archaeological contexts, this is not usually a question that can be answered with any degree of precision. However, thanks to the unique preservation conditions of certain Minoan assemblages (e.g., from Malia and Knossos), it is possible to tackle this question more satisfactorily than might otherwise be the case.

Contiguity

First, we should explore what kinds of cups tend to be found together. Interestingly, there is not a very clear spatial separation in consumption contexts between mundane cups and their more "aesthetic" counterparts. Indeed, quite the opposite: they are very often found together, as if to accentuate their differences. Perhaps one of the most striking examples comes from the first phase of the Protopalatial period at Knossos. Here a large MM IB deposit composed of 200 vessels, of which approximately 150 were for drinking, was found concentrated in a small area in the west wing of the palace (Macdonald and Knappett forthcoming). It seems that during this early phase the findspot of the cups may actually have been just outside the palace, possibly on its monumental south façade.

Among the drinking vessels a number of types are represented, including goblets (Figure 7.8), straight-sided cups, and carinated cups. And within each of these categories there is a remarkable hierarchy of quality. That is to say, the quality ranges, among the goblets for example, from some extremely crudely made types, through two levels that are of moderate quality, right up to the very finest eggshell ware. Although this highest rung is absent in the straight-sided and carinated cups, these types too show a very wide range of quality. Moreover, this qualitative hierarchy is pyramidal in character: the crudest vessels are also the most abundant, and the very finest are very rare (only one eggshell ware goblet exists).

Given that each of these drinking vessels would have been associated with an individual person during a consumption activity, it is hard to avoid drawing the conclusion that an individual drinking from the crudest type of goblet must have been far removed in status from the individual drinking from the eggshell ware goblet. The latter type of goblet, being conspicuously

Figure 7.8. Drinking goblets from Knossos MM IB deposit. Photograph by Kathy May. Courtesy of the British School at Athens.

unique, is individualizing; the former type, being a kind of "lowest common denominator," is deindividualizing. Some facet of Minoan social hierarchies finds itself crystallized in this assemblage. The individual-with-cup is a hybrid human-nonhuman form; even if either element is removed, that which remains still holds some flavor of the other. The bringing together changes both parties. If we imagine that Minoan social status may at times have been a fluid and fuzzy phenomenon, the use in ceremonial contexts of objects of widely differing character coming into close association with individual protagonists would surely have anchored those statuses more securely.

This Knossian deposit is a rather extreme example of a phenomenon that is in fact widely represented in Minoan Crete—the cooccurrence of drinking vessels of widely differing quality. They may not always be found in such close proximity and with such blatant differentiation, but the dynamic can certainly be traced at other sites and in other periods. At the palatial center of Malia, for example, one building complex dubbed "Quartier Mu" (Figure 7.9) has revealed drinking cups from a variety of contexts, found in situ in some rooms and fallen from upper stories in others (Poursat 1992, 1996).

Sometimes a number of whole examples of a certain type are found grouped together; in the case of carinated cups, no more than 15 have been

Figure 7.9. Plan of Quartier Mu, showing location of cup deposit in room I 3a. Plan by Martin Schmid. Courtesy of Jean-Claude Poursat and l'École Française d'Athènes.

found in any single context. In contexts where a number appear together, they are found in association principally with other cup types, and especially with a kind of tall conical cup which is usually the more plentiful. Context I 3a (Figure 7.9), for example, contained 15 carinated cups, but 45 goblets and tall conical cups (Poursat and Knappett in press). This context is some kind of small cupboard or chest adjacent to one of the main "public" rooms within the building, probably serving some ritual function. Given the number of drinking vessels involved, it seems quite likely that they were destined for use in some sort of ceremony involving conspicuous consumption. One might note, however, that other types of drinking vessels, such as straight-sided or hemispherical cups, which tend to be elaborately decorated, are not found in association. This suggests that individualizing cups were perhaps inappropriate in whatever ceremony was taking place—relative social status was not being accentuated, in contrast to the ceremony associated with the Knossian deposit discussed above.

It is rarely the case that only cups are found together. Usually in a single context there are other types of vessels too, vessels for pouring, storing, and cooking. This is certainly true of the Quartier Mu I 3a context already described—alongside the cups are saucers, scoops ("puisettes"), and various types of jugs. Although they are not frequent enough to constitute a true set, there does seem to be a consistent association of sorts. One might also point to the vessels other than cups found in the Knossos Early Palace deposit mentioned above—a few open bowls, a single cooking pot, a single amphora, and a number of pouring vessels, in particular bridge-spouted jars. These bridge-spouted jars, of which there are only thirteen, display the same kind of hierarchy of quality as do the cups and goblets, with a number of crudely made examples and a single very finely made specimen. Thus one can put together drinking sets to some extent, in which we see certain kinds of cups associated with certain kinds of jugs.

Moreover, one should of course not ignore vessels of other materials found in contiguity with such objects, such as stone and metal vases. There may be not only vessels but also other kinds of ceramic items such as clay loomweights, and indeed clay sealings and tablets. All these kinds of objects have been found in Quartier Mu, but not usually in any significant association with pottery vessels; the clay tablets, for example, are invariably found fallen from an upper story. Other materials to consider are stone tools of both ground and chipped varieties, bone tools, and debris from stone and metal working. The contiguity of objects to architectural features such as benches, hearths, or staircases is another aspect worthy of note.

The question of contiguity arises at various spatial levels which can be described as nested—the location of drinking vessels within a room, the room's position in the building, the building's apparent role within the settlement, and the settlement's stature at the regional level. These nested spatial scales all contribute to the indexical meaning of the artifacts in question. Let us now zoom out for a moment to consider the question at the regional level.

On the subject of the site's regional role, it is possible to make comparisons with assemblages at other sites in the broader region and beyond. Myrtos Pyrgos, for example, is a small village site on the south coast, sepa-

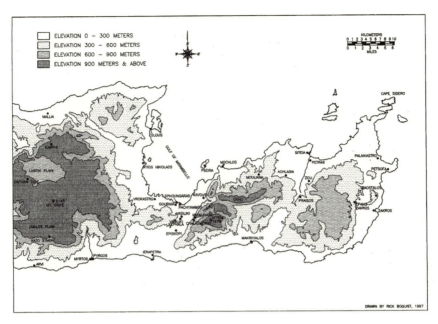

Figure 7.10. Map of east Crete, showing Malia, Myrtos Pyrgos, and other sites. Drawn by R. Boquist. Courtesy of Paul Rehak and J. G. Younger.

rated from Malia by the high mountains of the Lasithi massif (Figure 7.10). At this site, extensive well-preserved deposits have been found dating to the same period as Quartier Mu. Much of the fine pottery, including the carinated cups, is extremely similar to that from Malia, notwithstanding the fact that it is locally made. This has been seen as evidence of a particularly close relationship between the two sites, to the extent that Myrtos Pyrgos may fall within Malia's domain. It appears that Malia was probably a regional political and ritual center to which Myrtos Pyrgos owed allegiance (Cadogan 1990; Knappett 1999a).

Although the fine pottery alone may suggest that similar kinds of ceremonial consumption were taking place at the two sites, consumption contexts at Myrtos Pyrgos are nothing like as well-preserved as at Malia, rendering it impossible to identify drinking sets or precise locations of use. However, the diversity of drinking and pouring vessels at Myrtos Pyrgos is comparable to that of Malia, with carinated cups occurring alongside a range of hemispherical cups, straight-sided cups, bridge-spouted jugs, and beaked jugs. Moreover, there is the same mimicking of more valuable metal

Figure 7.11. Crinkly-rimmed kantharos from Myrtos Pyrgos, containing miniature kantharoi. Courtesy of Gerald Cadogan and the British School at Athens.

forms, as evidenced in the exceptional crinkly-rimmed kantharos displayed in Heraklion Museum (Figure 7.11; also Cadogan 1977–78; Knappett 2002a). It would appear that the different kinds of drinking vessels at the site fulfilled a similar role and had a comparable set of cultural meanings as at Malia, despite the difference in status between the two sites.

In continuing our discussion of contiguity, the temporal context acts as a complement to this spatial perspective. It is an interlinked dimension in which the object may be considered to possess indexical properties. In other words, do Minoan cups come to serve as indexes of a particular time as well as place? At Malia, and indeed in Minoan contexts as a whole, fineware cups are not often found in contexts later than the period in which they were produced. That is to say, it is rare to find cups of MM IIA style in a MM IIB context. This might in part be due to the high risks of breakage of such vessels—they simply did not last very long. Moreover, there are few if any attempts at curation, indicating that even fine ceramic cups were expendable and easily replaced. As far as is possible to tell, carinated cups are no exception: all those found in the MM IIB Quartier Mu destruction levels seem to have been produced in that same period. The point is that cups from earlier periods are not used to hearken back to earlier times, as Bonnot (2002) suggests is sometimes the case with twentieth-century stoneware (see previous chapter).

Figure 7.12. Amphora imported to Malia from the Mirabello region. Courtesy of Jean-Claude Poursat and l'École Française d'Athènes.

This said, other vessel types at Malia do survive in use for long periods. Among the storage pithoi from Quartier Mu are some that are clearly of Prepalatial type and technology—meaning they must have been manufactured some three hundred years earlier (Poursat and Knappett in press). It may simply be that storage vessels are more physically resilient than tableware, but there may have been some conscious curation involved too. A further aspect to consider is that many storage vessels at Protopalatial Malia were actually imported from other parts of the island, notably the south coast, and the Mirabello region some 45 km to the east (Figure 7.12). This may have added another layer of meaning to curated storage vessels: from not only another time but another place. Conversely, this is rarely the case with carinated cups—those consumed at Malia were almost exclusively local products. Perhaps table wares simply had to be (indexical) of their own time and their own place.

It has to be said, however, that at neither Malia nor Myrtos Pyrgos does the archaeological evidence lend itself to a detailed examination of the carinated cup's history. Deposits belonging to the appropriate phases (MM IB and MM IIA) have yet to be clearly defined. At the palatial center of Knossos, though, there are many carinated cups from deposits belonging to these earlier phases. These show not only that carinated cups were popular in MM IIB, but that they were just as prevalent in MM IIA, and indeed in MM IB, their first real phase of use (c. 1900 B.C.). Owing to the pronounced ceramic regionalism between north-central and east-central Crete, carinated cups at Knossos are rather different from those at Malia and Myrtos Pyrgos in both shape and decoration (see Figures 7.4–7.6; also MacGillivray 1998). Nonetheless, some evidence points to a similar use for carinated cups. They tend to form part of large sets of cups found in stores within or close to the palace, seemingly being kept for certain occasions at which time they would all be brought out for conspicuous consumption in the form of ceremonial feasting (Day and Wilson 1998). One good example we have already discussed—the large stock of drinking vessels (included among them a number of roughly made carinated cups) from the west wing of the palace dated to MM IB (Figures 7.5, 7.8). It seems probable that such a set was only used periodically, perhaps at particular times of the month or year. This is of course another (temporal) level at which these objects may have come to represent or be indexical of a certain time.

Factorality

Let us now tackle a second aspect of indexicality—the ways Minoan drinking vessels represent a part of a larger whole (factorality). The nature of the whole of which the drinking vessel was a part seems to have changed significantly during the Early Bronze Age. It has been argued that there is a shift in emphasis during Early Minoan IIA away from communal toward individual consumption (Day and Wilson 2002). The whole that the drinking vessel represents stops being the community and instead becomes the individual. Yet, through the rest of the Prepalatial period, no single individual or set of individuals is marked out as different, as all drinking vessels are very much equivalent in type and quality. In the Protopalatial, however, we observe what appears to be the growth of individualization in consumption—some drinking vessels become very clearly set apart from the rest, as a pronounced hierarchy of quality sets in. If the drinking vessel is a part of a whole, then the whole has become the status of the individual within the community.

Another way such objects manifest factorality is in their capacity to serve as an index for a certain sort of consumption activity, even in the absence of that activity. The question of skeuomorphism raised in the discussion of the iconic properties of the carinated cup is relevant here. It was noted that the ceramic carinated cup appears to be aping vessels made in precious metals such as silver or bronze. One presumes that a valuable metal vessel of this type would not have been accessible to all segments of the population at all times, and it may well have been an index par excellence of prestigious elite consumption practices (an index of a certain social group). Thus a ceramic cup, which one assumes would have been intrinsically less valuable, can take on some of the value of the metal vessel it seeks to emulate. The skeuomorphing clay carinated cup may then also have been an index of aspiration (and thereby indexing ideas as well as objects and people).

Causality

A further element of indexicality concerns causality—we have seen in Chapter 5 how with some indices there is a *causal* relationship between sign and referent. One way of approaching this is to consider the manufacturing processes that caused Minoan cups to take on their form as finished objects. Their very substance, the clay fabric, can reveal their place of origin; analyses have shown that drinking vessels consumed at Minoan sites were almost always locally produced at the site itself (as noted earlier). The techniques employed and the energy invested also find themselves indexed in the objects themselves. For example, the process of smoothing and slipping a carinated cup results in a metallicizing lustrous finish. The thin walls and crisp shape are in no small part thanks to the fact that they are wheel-made, and indeed the carinated cup as a type only appears with the introduction of wheel technology. It is not only the wheel and wheel technology that are implicated, but also the particular artisanal groups involved; in the earliest Protopalatial phase not all potters were using the wheel, and so it may have been that the carinated cup was an index in and of itself of certain classes of skilled artisans.

Given the contribution of production processes to the meaningfulness of an object, a more detailed investigation of the wheel technique is in order. The connection is a natural one in that Minoan cups were on the whole made on the wheel. By focusing on the dynamics of a technique we accentuate the importance of *action* to object meaning.

A Technological Turn—The Wheel Technique

It is widely agreed that wheel-made pottery is first attested on Crete during the first phase of the Protopalatial period, that is to say Middle Minoan IB (c. 1900 B.C.).[2] This means that, along with the carinated cup, its appearance coincides with the emergence of the first Minoan palaces and states; the adoption of wheel technology thus takes on significance within a broader context of major sociopolitical change. Despite this, the technology itself has been relatively little studied, such that its temporal and regional development is only sketchily understood. A major study of the wheel and other pottery forming techniques has, however, formed the focus of a project conducted by the author (see Knappett 1999b; Knappett in press; Poursat and Knappett in press).

Given the evident technical expertise already possessed by Minoan potters in the Prepalatial period, the introduction of the wheel technique during the Protopalatial could have led to an immediate transformation of the entire Minoan ceramic tradition, both in terms of quantity and quality. Although a priori the technique could have been used in many different ways and for many different shapes, we find in practice that it was actually heavily constrained to certain configurations. For example, the wheel (Figure 7.13) was used in the first instance for small vessels such as cups and goblets and only subsequently for larger vessels such as jugs and jars.[3] Moreover, it takes roughly four hundred years for some of the larger storage jar shapes to be made using the wheel, and even then not all potters but only some take this step. What factors were at work constraining a more rapid and widespread uptake of the wheel innovation?

It is not only the case that the first vessels made on the wheel were small ones such as cups and goblets; it is also true that in its initial stages the technique was applied as much to high-quality vases destined for elite consumption as it was to more everyday items (Knappett 1999b). Even the

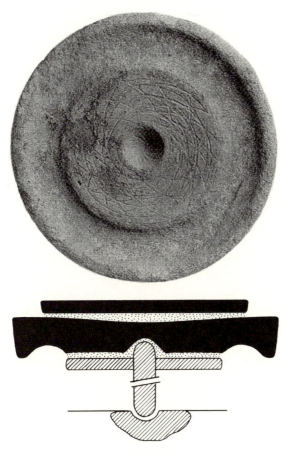

Figure 7.13. Potter's wheel from Quartier Mu and a hypothetical reconstruction of the wheel in use. Courtesy of Jean-Claude Poursat and l'École Française d'Athènes.

very finest eggshell wares, astonishing in their technical virtuosity, were made on the wheel. That the first wheel-made Minoan vessels are not necessarily mass-produced wares seems to indicate that economic efficiency was probably not the driving force behind the adoption of the new technique. This flies in the face of most established wisdom concerning the wheel innovation. In terms of the causal, indexical connections between the technique used and the object produced, this must surely be of considerable importance.

So, why was the wheel first used for small vessels, and why those of high quality in particular? Dealing first with the question of vessel size, the physical affordances of the technique and the equipment must have played a part. This is rather hard to establish given that the technique is a dynamic coming together of human and nonhuman, a complex interaction of mind, action and matter. But it is quite possible that initially wheel devices were not sufficiently stable to cope with the manufacture of large vessels. Given what we know of Minoan wheels (Evely 1988), it is reasonable to suppose that there may have been problems creating a stable pivot.[4] Naturally, not all the responsibility lies with the device; it is also up to the potters to find ways to make the most of the tools at their disposal, or indeed to develop the tools to suit their needs. One way around such a problem is for the potter to have an assistant turn the wheel, a solution devised by some Sinhalese potters in Sri Lanka (personal observation by the author).

Such physical constraints aside, there must have been significant cultural considerations affecting a potter's decision to adopt the wheel technique. That technological choices are as much sociocultural as technical is by now reasonably well established in socioanthropology. Drawing on extensive ethnoarchaeological research in Africa, Olivier Gosselain (2000) makes the important point that, of all the techniques used by a potter, forming techniques tend to be the most resistant to change. This is in part because "these gestures are 'motor habits' mastered through repeated practice during early learning and subsequently internalized" (Gosselain 2000, 192). Given that pottery forming methods are therefore generally acquired at a young age and from close relatives, they "should reflect those most rooted and enduring aspects of social identity, such as kinship, language, gender, and class subdivisions" (Gosselain 2000, 193; see also Figures 7.14, 7.15). With this in mind, the extremely long tradition of coil-building in Minoan Crete cannot be taken lightly; the transition to the wheel technique, even if incorporating elements of the existing coil-building tradition, would in all likelihood have been a culturally loaded decision. There may have been an impact upon consumers too, accustomed to using coil-built pots. Yet, apart from being among the least malleable of all the potter's methods, forming techniques are also the least conspicuous as far as the consumer is concerned. Some users may nonetheless have perceived differences in the look and feel of wheel-made pots as opposed to coil-built ones; this being so, one can imagine a possible reluctance on behalf of consumers toward pots not made in the "traditional" coil-built style.

One might also give some thought to those iconic and indexical aspects of the wheel technique that may not have had any direct impact on

Figure 7.14. One of the six main shaping techniques used in sub-Saharan Africa. Courtesy of Olivier Gosselain.

the finished objects themselves. In terms of iconicity, what, if anything, did the technique physically resemble? Similar rotative devices might have been used in other craft technologies, perhaps in the manufacture of stone vases (Warren 1969, 161–62), or of certain kinds of sealstones (Betts 1989).[5] It seems, however, that such techniques were first applied to stone only in the MM III period. Although it may not be possible to enter into an in-depth discussion of the iconicity of the technique itself, instructive here are Sillar's observations on the preparation of clay by potters in the Andes (Sillar 1996). He shows that the same pounding and grinding techniques are used for clay and grain, and that the physical similarity between these activities, performed in each case by women, has cultural meaning that can be carried across different cultural domains. Another example in which the physical appearance of a technique bears significance comes from iron technology in sub-Saharan Africa; an iron-smelting furnace when in use physically (and metaphysically) resembles a woman in childbirth—the furnace is even adorned with breasts and scarification patterns to make it more iconic of a woman (Childs 1991). As far as pottery forming techniques are concerned, Mahias (1993) describes how in India certain methods can act as powerful

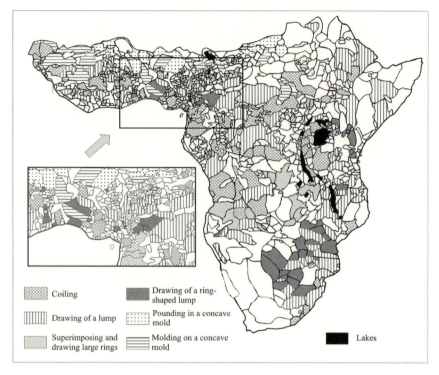

Figure 7.15. Sub-Saharan distribution of the six shaping techniques. Courtesy of Olivier Gosselain.

metaphors of ritual purity or pollution because of their physical resemblance to techniques used in other domains:

> In Orissa the Magadha potters regard as inferior those who "detach an unfinished pot from the wheel by means of a string, thus leaving a hole at the bottom." This . . . is equated with the snapping of the umbilical cord of a new-born baby. (Behura 1978, 290; quoted in Mahias 1993, 176)

Confronting next the question of indexicality, we can discuss aspects of contiguity, factorality, and causality. Starting with the first of these, with what other activities was the wheel technique spatially contiguous? During the period in question we have very little "on the ground" evidence for craft locales or "workshops." Even in the single best-preserved example, the potter's workshop that forms part of the Quartier Mu building complex at

Malia (Poursat 1996), it is not possible to go into too much detail as to which activities were spatially contiguous with the use of the wheel. One complete potter's wheel (see Figure 7.13) and a fragment of another were indeed discovered, but because they were found fallen from an upper story and not in situ it is difficult to say very much about the nature and place of their installation (Poursat 1996, 111, pl. 50a-b). That no kiln has been found in the vicinity might indicate that some if not all stages of the production process occurred elsewhere, at a location removed from the workshop. Nonetheless, one should note that the potter's workshop is similar architecturally and in very close proximity to four other workshops that cluster around the principal buildings of Quartier Mu (see Figure 7.9; also Poursat 1996). In these workshops evidence for the working of metal (tools and vessels) stone (seals and vases) and bone (tools) has been found, some of which was definitely happening "sur place." Notwithstanding the problem of specifying the exact location of pottery manufacture, it seems that the technique may have been contiguous with a whole range of other craft techniques in various media. The complex interaction of different craft media is a phenomenon that is evident in the pottery too (e.g., skeuomorphism).

Of course not all the pottery in use in the settlement of Malia was made by this single workshop of Quartier Mu; there were undoubtedly other production locales in the town. Judging from the pottery alone, one can say that the wheel was clearly not confined to any single production outlet, but was in widespread use by Maliote workshops. At the broader regional level too, the wheel is by no means a technique confined to Malia, but is found widely and, moreover, used in very similar ways across much of the island.

As with the Minoan cup, we can place the wheel technique in a temporal context. Although we suggested that, for example, the carinated cup could in a sense be seen as an index of the First Palace Period, this is much less clearly so with the wheel: the technique carries through into the Second Palace Period and indeed beyond, to the end of the Bronze Age. Nevertheless, in the initial stages of its use, during the Middle Minoan IB period, the technique may well have had indexical qualities. Only very few potters used the technique at this early stage, and only for a limited number of forms, predominantly cups and goblets in fine wares destined for some kind of elite consumption. Perhaps the technique spoke quite clearly of the fact that only a select group of potters had access to the necessary knowledge and expertise; moreover, these were the only ones willing and able to make the necessary capital investments and take risks (Knappett 1999b). One might argue there is an element of *factorality* here, of the part representing the whole. If the wheel is the part, then the whole it represents is specialized knowledge, and quite probably elevated status as a result (see Helms 1993). Yet it did not take long for the technique to spread, and its potential for signifying distinction thereby evaporated.

What may we say about the third element of indexicality, causality? We can simply reverse the logic used for the Minoan cup. There we said that the object was causally linked to the production processes that brought it forth. Here we can say that what "causes" production is consumption (the two are in a continuous feedback loop). Thus particular consumer demands ultimately contributed to the adoption of the wheel. One might note that one of the advantages of wheel techniques is that they facilitate the creation of thinner vessel walls; this would have been a desirable feature of ceramic vessels meant to mimic closely much more valuable metal prototypes (e.g., Figure 7.11). And it is perhaps no coincidence that one such skeuomorphing type, the carinated cup, appears almost hand in hand with the wheel technique. In that such vessels (their metal equivalents, at least) were being produced for use by elites in conspicuous consumption, one could say that the wheel is, in a sense, an index of elite demand and attached production. Where factorality and causality are concerned, both artifacts and agents are implicated; thus the meaningfulness of the wheel technique comes to be distributed across hybrid networks comprised of humans and nonhumans.

Symbolism

It should be apparent that indexicality is the most important of the semiotic processes through which connections multiply across networks and artifacts (and techniques) acquire their meaning. Moreover, the phenomenon of skeuomorphism shows how iconic and indexical properties may sometimes interact quite closely in the construction of meaning. Now that we come to deal with the third principal semiotic process, symbolism, we are reminded how insignificant it may be when it comes to meaningfulness in material culture. This category elicits very little discussion, not least because we have no idea whatever of the formal conventions of language by which cups were known in Minoan Crete. Some common objects are represented with ideograms in the scripts of the time (Cretan Hieroglyphic and Linear A), but the cup is not one of the symbols used in either system. Nor do there appear to be any representations of cups in the iconography of seal-stones, wall paintings, and so forth. For wheel technology we encounter many of the same limitations. While we must presume the existence of significant symbolic connections for both objects and actions, in this context they are something of a closed book.

The Mundane and the Magical, the Everyday and the Aesthetic?

The kinds of Minoan cups that take pride of place in museum collections are those in "eggshell" ware, so-called because of their extremely thin walls. These rare vessels, hemispherical, straight-sided, or carinated in shape, are the finest products of the Kamares tradition; they are very light and delicate, with intricate polychrome decoration (see Figure 7.6), and often impressed and embossed with relief patterns imitating metalwork. Undeniably, they have aesthetic appeal and were produced with aesthetic intention; they must surely have been highly valued in Minoan times too.

And yet it is difficult to create a clear delineation between these special "art" objects and the more mundane types of cup found in much greater quantities in all Minoan settlements. There is a clear technological continuity between them, in terms of clays, forming techniques, and surface treatments. Indeed, it is quite possible that the same potters were responsible for making these different classes of such widely differing quality. It is as if the potters simply decided in some instances to carry their work further, to push the boundaries at which they habitually stopped; it may have been that only the most skilled were capable of going all the way. But we can see here the value of a crucial point made by Gell, and raised in the previous chapter: what art does is simply carry further the enchantment which is immanent in all kinds of technology.

The artful technologist extends beyond the limits of the real into the realms of the magical. The very finest Kamares cups are indeed enchanting, as one marvels at the unreal skill needed to make such objects (and many modern potters would certainly struggle). For the potter to make such thin walls on the wheel is almost inconceivable, to the extent that some scholars have argued that they must have been mold-made (although this is unlikely). But crucially, the production processes behind the finest eggshell ware vessels are connected to those used for the more humble carinated cup—it is probable that the very same potters were responsible for both. So what is it that differentiates them? One might argue that although both the carinated cup and the finest eggshell ware have some aesthetic effect, only the latter may have been created with aesthetic intention (Genette 1999, see previous chapter). Beguiled by the work and the intentionality of the agency behind it, the viewer is drawn into receiving the object as an artwork. The carinated cup would seem to display less technical virtuosity; it does not immediately present itself as a candidate for aesthetic reception. This does not mean that these objects can be set apart as categorically different; even if the carinated cup was not actually produced with aesthetic intention, the viewer may perceive it and consider it as an art work nonetheless. The key is that the viewer may in some circumstances confuse aesthetic effect for aesthetic intention. And, in that the everyday object can certainly possess an aesthetic dimension, there is no saying that it can never be taken for art, Duchamp's urinal being the classic case in point (see previous chapter). The continuity between the plainest and the finest cups, what one might describe as a kind of interpenetration, provides the potential for the real to grow closer to the ideal.

This fluidity between the everyday object and the art object (and indeed the magical object) was emphasized in the previous chapter through the work of Bonnot, Gell, and Genette. Its importance lies in the fact that no object is condemned to remain in a given object category, but may move between registers. Although it may seem that some Minoan objects, particularly during the Protopalatial period, are intrinsically aesthetic, and others are intrinsically mundane, this is not quite the case. The mutability that these objects in fact possess arises because they do not have their meaning imprinted solely during the production phase; meaning arises from their position within "networks" of production and consumption practices performed by various social actors. These networks are prone to constant and subtle reconfigurations affecting the regard in which the object is held. As Genette says, quoted by Bonnot, it is the relation that makes the object aesthetic and not vice versa.[6]

This being the case, the obvious challenge before us is to sum up what "the relation" might be in the case study outlined above. We have seen that at the beginning of the Protopalatial period a pronounced distinction arises between the artistic and the mundane within a single broad category of object—Minoan drinking vessels. These objects are used in particular ways to crystallize emergent hierarchies and the relationships between personal and group identity; they effectively materialize the processes of individualization and de-individualization in consumption, as was apparent in the case study from Knossos. However, this was a particular kind of context most probably connected with highly public ceremonial activity. In other less public contexts, however, such objects do not retain these meanings: they are rarely used side by side to convey social status in quite such striking opposition. In the Malia case study, for example, we considered the kinds of cups found in semi-public and private contexts within the building complex of Quartier Mu. There did not appear to be any contexts in which very fine and very plain cups were used side by side to accentuate difference among the users. Carinated cups and plain goblets are found within ritual/ceremonial contexts (e.g., I 3a; see Figure 7.9), but there are no fine ceramic drinking vessels in sight. This changes the relational position of the object, and hence its meaning: the plainest goblet or cup, reconfigured in such a way, may easily take on an aesthetic dimension. It is not solely the intrinsic qualities of the object itself that create an aesthetic situation or moment; it is the overall configuration of the network that renders the object aesthetic.

The eggshell ware Kamares cup does not have a fixed meaning in relation to the plain goblet; their position and meaning in relation to each other changes according to context, for example from public to private. In a public context, a given user, let us imagine one of high rank, may only ever use one particular kind of elaborate drinking vessel. This object may be appropriate to the single public role that the user fulfills. In other, more private scenarios, that same user may very well embody a number of different roles and thus use a range of different drinking vessels, ones that in public might only be associated with individuals of lesser status. Whatever the case, one can see how the development of personal and communal identity is not something that is worked out first among humans and then transferred to the nonhuman domain—the two domains coimplicate each other and intermingle. The individual using the cup is changed by it, becoming a hybrid entity of individual-with-cup. By the same token, the cup is changed by the individual, embroiled within a network of connections that may spread far beyond that single consumption moment.

Conclusions

It is not only magical or aesthetic objects that possess meaning. Mundane or everyday objects can have meaning, too. Most important, their meaningfulness is not categorically different from that of magical or aesthetic objects. As long as we follow Gell's warning of not being slaves to aestheticism, the meanings of all kinds of objects should be comprehensible within the same overall framework. Such statements only represent the first steps toward a fuller understanding of meaning in ancient material culture. And yet when we look at how the everyday and the aesthetic are generally separated in archaeological studies of material culture, Aegean prehistory included, these are large steps to be taking.

The above discussion has not furnished the reader with *the* meaning of Minoan drinking vessels. But to look for such a singular meaning would be to fall prey to the fallacy that meaning resides solely within the object, rather than within the human-nonhuman networks in which it is entangled. Nevertheless, we should resist the kind of radical relationality critiqued in Chapter 2; it is also crucial to appreciate the role that the materiality of the object plays in its positioning relative to other entities in heterogeneous sociotechnical networks (not unlike the case of Proust's madeleine). Minoan drinking vessels, with their various resemblances, contiguities, and causalities, find themselves within particular networks that contribute to the ways in which they are perceived/conceived as a category in the Minoan world. We need to be asking the right kinds of questions if we are not to be disappointed by the answers.

When accounting for artifactual meaning, considerable attention needs to be devoted to the meshing of the pragmatic with the significative. Such an effort represents part of a broader struggle to overcome the dualism between the materialist on the one hand and the mentalist on the other. In this context, the attempt in this book to reconcile ecological psychology with sociosemiotics through the concept of affordances may be one way forward. And it is not just these two fields that are compatible, but also cognitive science, phenomenology, practice theory, and so on. If we are to move forward in our understandings of material culture in the past, present and future, we must work on this compatibility. The prospects for interdisciplinary projects of this kind are considered in the concluding chapter.

Chapter 8
Conclusions

L'opposition dressée entre la culture et la technique, entre l'homme et la machine, est fausse et sans fondement; elle ne recouvre qu'ignorance ou ressentiment. Elle masque derrière un facile humanisme une réalité riche en efforts humains et en forces naturelles, et qui constitue le monde des objets techniques, médiateurs entre la nature et l'homme.

—Gilbert Simondon

Nearly fifty years ago Gilbert Simondon reacted in these forceful terms against the general tendency in Western culture to dichotomize society and technology, mind and matter, human and machine. Simondon was something of a rare breed, a philosopher with an almost archaeological concern for objects and techniques. Yet, falling in the cracks between academic disciplines, he has gone largely unnoticed. His critique is of course somewhat unfair to anti-Cartesian philosophers such as Husserl, Heidegger, and Merleau-Ponty, hardly unaware of the problems of dichotomizing mind and matter. Yet, as powerful as their contributions are, none devoted very much attention to material culture. And philosophy, not to mention psychology, anthropology, and sociology, has continued until only relatively recently to turn a blind eye to objects and techniques. The psychologist working with the mind and the anthropologist concerned with social representations may both be fully aware that mind and matter are not as cleanly separated as Cartesianism made out; nonetheless, they do not find means of effectively bridging the gap. Thus the artifactual and the technical remain in a separate sphere of little significance to their own endeavors.

But what of archaeology? Of all disciplines this is surely one that could never be similarly accused: does not the archaeologist work with nothing but objects? And yet this "nothing but" is the crux of the matter. The archaeologist's ultimate interest, allegedly, is past attitudes and ideas, but as these are deemed to occupy a domain distinct from that of the material, the common assumption is that they can only be indirectly extrapolated. Aspiring to mentalism but condemned to materialism, it is hardly surprising that many archaeologists have given up on the former altogether. Those who participate in the recent trend in archaeological theory to borrow substantially from phenomenology should, one might have thought, be rather more optimistic. And yet the philosophers on whom archaeological phenomenologists draw, notably Heidegger and Merleau-Ponty, tend not to provide the kinds of methodologies that archaeologists require if they are to succeed in articulating the material and the mental.

This is by no means to underestimate the significance of phenomenology as a serious challenge to the Cartesian legacy. The point, rather, is that archaeological theory may have overemphasized its importance at the expense of other philosophical approaches equally able to contribute to a fuller understanding of material culture. One might mention here the ecological psychology of James Gibson as dealt with in Chapter 2, or indeed the pragmatic semiotics of Charles Peirce discussed in Chapter 5. Neither scholar could be described as contemporary, but both have been underexploited in archaeological theory. However, many of the developments traced in this book are recent and ongoing, none more so than in cognitive science. It is only really in the 1990s, with the contributions of scholars like Norman, Hutchins and Clark, that a situated and distributed approach to cognition has come to the fore as a challenge to the dualistic perspective espoused by representationalism. Dualism is also being challenged in other fields, as material culture comes increasingly into view as a subject of study; the more anthropologists and sociologists direct their focus upon the boundary between mind and matter, between human and nonhuman, the fuzzier that boundary becomes.

Most important, the anti-Cartesian reactions are not occurring in isolation in these various disciplines. That phenomenology has had quite an impact on anthropology and sociology is not entirely surprising, but that it is also filtering into cognitive science (Petitot et al. 2000) is as unexpected as it is encouraging. Another coupling one might have wished for rather than expected is that between phenomenology and semiotics (Sonesson 1989; Csordas 1994, 1999). There are other marriages that are proving healthy and fruitful even when apparently unlikely not all that long ago, such as those between biology, psychology, and anthropology (Ingold 2000). These and other interdisciplinary cross-fertilizations, such as that represented by the emerging field of "material culture studies," constitute the most remarkable of recent developments. It is hoped that this book has contributed to this development by suggesting new paths and intersections, in the belief that they are a powerful stimulus to further fruitful explorations of the relationship between mind and matter. I would argue that to understand how humans think through material culture we cannot avoid drawing upon as wide a range of disciplines as possible, creating in the process an articulated framework and not a rag-tag collection of odds and ends.

And thus with our leitmotif of "thinking through material culture" the archaeologist need not be reduced to the unhappy state of being a frustrated mentalist condemned to materialism. If we accept that mind and matter achieve codependency through the medium of bodily action, then it follows that ideas and attitudes, rather than occupying a separate domain from the material, actually find themselves inscribed "in" the object. Moreover, as the bodily activities of intentional human agents draw in and coimplicate objects, subsequently the latter cannot be neatly separated, and we are confronted by what are effectively hybrid forms (we may even go so far as to class objects as bodily and cognitive prosthetics). Objects are bound up in humans in their guises as biological, psychological, and social beings, as bio-psycho-social totalities.

The intermingling of the human and nonhuman adopts different forms and can be distributed over space in patterns of association that are both structured and fluid. This hybrid combination of structure and flow is characteristic of the network as a topological form. It is important to try to characterize the patterns of association in terms of networks because there are implications for the nature of meaning.

Our approach to meaning seeks above all to incorporate the pragmatic and the significative. The study of sign relationships is key to the understanding of meaning, although not as envisaged by Saussure; his highly influential semiology may work for language, but is not well suited to the study of meaning in material culture. It simply does not allow for the pragmatic dimension, the world of the real inhabited by solid objects bumping up against human bodies. Peirce's semiotics, however, is a different story; indeed, his approach to the study of signs was very clearly not only pragmatic but also phenomenological (or "phaneroscopic"). The groundedness of Peircean semiotics has been well explored recently by the likes of Sonesson, Gottdiener, Parmentier, Nellhaus, and Csordas (see Chapter 5), scholars working in a range of disciplines. The importance of achieving a rapprochement between the pragmatic and the significative, between *l'objet-corps* and *l'objet-signe*, has also been stressed by French anthropologist Warnier (1999a, b, 2001), who suggests that the work of Parlebas, for example, on the meaningfulness of motor habits, is fundamental in this respect.

What we have sought to do is develop a preliminary methodology that takes explicit account of all these points and can be applied to bodies of material culture in the past as well as the present. It is a matter, essentially, of dealing with both affordances and associations in nondualistic fashion, of seeing the intimate interdependency between these two aspects. For example, the shift in meaning that stoneware undergoes (Bonnot 2002) is a transformation in the object's physical and at the same time significative position within a network of material and social relations. The Minoan carinated cups discussed in Chapter 7 possess physical properties—resemblances and contiguities—that are constitutive of their meaning. Their pragmatic and significative dimensions are interdependent. Humans may be physically absent from the Minoan and indeed other archaeological contexts, but they are there metaphysically and structurally. To refer back to the comment made by Latour cited in Chapter 2, "consider things, and you will have humans . . . consider humans and you are by that very act interested in things" (Latour 2000, 20). The nature of sociotechnical networks is such that the human and the nonhuman bring each other into being. In that an artifact holds and encapsulates both action and thought, archaeologists have always needed to be mentalists, even if trapped by their materialist shackles and unable to see how both could ever be possible. In this regard, to define "cognitive archaeology" as a special branch of archaeology seems a redundant exercise. We should not need to proclaim cognitive archaeology as an archaeology of the future—archaeology should always have been cognitive. And yet there have been major obstacles preventing such a perspective. Until now, that is. It is only relatively recently that the possibility has arisen for drawing together major developments from a whole range of fields, as discussed above. An interdisciplinary venture of this kind can make a full-fledged cognitive archaeology a reality. There is an enormous amount to learn from other disciplines, and indeed a great deal that archaeology can itself contribute to a fuller understanding of material culture. This book is little more than an initial stumbling step in what can become an exciting new direction in archaeology and material culture studies more generally.

Notes

Chapter 1. Introduction: Thinking Through Material Culture

Epigraph: Auster (1989, 122).

1. This is also a criticism sometimes made of processual archaeologists today, with Renfrew, for example, accused of seeing meaning as predominantly individual and subjective (Lucas 1995). Interestingly, an overemphasis on the individual is an accusation that has also been leveled at post-processualists (Renfrew 1994, 6).

2. Note that others have chosen to create two categories within "savoir-faire"—Pelegrin (1990) distinguishes between *ideational* savoir-faire and *motor* savoir-faire. Pelegrin, however, does not split "connaissance" into discursive and nondiscursive.

3. Hodder does indeed note: "we still have very little idea of how know-how or practical knowledge works and how it relates to the more general and abstract levels of meaning" (1992, 206).

4. "Nous savons maintenant que les techniques du corps et l'engagement dynamique dans la culture matérielle s'articulent aux representations. Nous savons que cette articulation n'est ni univoque, ni nécessaire, ni à sens unique. En fait, nous savons qu'il y a une articulation, mais nous ne savons pas comment elle fonctionne" (Warnier 1999a, 34).

Chapter 2. Animacy, Agency, and Personhood

Epigraph: Tolkien (1991), 319–320. Sauron and the ring bring each other to life. Their respective fates are inextricably bound together. Sauron needs the ring, and the ring needs Sauron to become powerful; their agencies are joint and distributed. The ring's connection to the place of its creation is indissoluble: it can only be destroyed if cast back into the fires of Mordor.

1. The work of Tim Ingold, who describes humans as ecological organisms and at the same time social persons (Ingold 2000, 2–3), is of fundamental importance to many of the themes discussed in this chapter. Yet, whereas Ingold deals first with the ecological and social aspects of humans and then subsequently with the psychological, in this chapter I approach matters in a different order, tackling first the ecological and psychological and only thereafter the social. This, in part, reflects the idea expressed by Mauss that the psychological capacities of the individ-

ual are intermediary between the biological and the social (Mauss 1936; Warnier 1999a, b).

2. The distinction between agent and person is discussed in a comparable way in Taylor (1985).

3. Capra 1996. Much of the discussion that follows on the nature of "living systems" is drawn from his work.

4. The roots of systems thinking can be traced back to the early twentieth century, when biologists, frustrated with the dualistic arguments over form and substance, strove to reconcile form and substance and understand their articulation (Capra 1996, 27). Of course they go further back than this, to Kant and indeed Aristotle.

5. Capra (1996, 82) stresses that the *network* is the characteristic pattern of organization of all living systems. The concept of network is one we shall come back to, as it forms the main focus of Chapter 4.

6. I am grateful to Tim Ingold, not only for drawing the mycelia example to my attention, but also for asking "what if biology had developed its concept of the organism not based on mammals but on mycelial fungi?"

7. Hayles (1999) notes that during the 1980s and 1990s, Varela distanced himself from the idea of closure, and gradually became involved in "Artificial Life" research. Aspects of this research domain are discussed in chapter three.

8. An emphasis on the open flow of matter and energy through a system was much more a feature of Prigogine's work on dissipative structures (Capra 1996). Indeed, Capra feels that by combining the approaches of Maturana and Varela and of Prigogine one can understand living systems as being simultaneously open and closed: open in terms of structure and substance but closed in terms of organization and form (Capra 1996, 169).

9. Capra (1996) stresses that in autopoietic networks and dissipative structures something else besides organization and structure is implied, and that something is *process*.

10. Cf. also Goodwin (1994), and Ingold (2000, 19) who argues we should "treat form as *emergent* within the life-process."

11. A termite mound is an example of "niche construction," an idea developed in Laland et al. (2000).

12. That the entire colony and mound together function as a superorganism, that is to say with all the attributes of an organism writ large, finds graphic demonstration in Turner's description of how termites respond when their mound is damaged by a predator or a rainstorm (2000, 188–89).

13. We might also give some thought to the converse of this: not only are human beings increasingly technologized (especially computer technology—implanting of chips), but technologies are increasingly humanized (especially in "artificial life" technologies, with computers being given "bodies"—see Geary 2002). See also Brooks who claims "the distinction between us and robots is going to disappear" (2002, 236).

14. See also Potter (2002), "Mind over Metal."

15. Strain and Neuberger (2002, 1005): "Patient plasma is circulated extracor-

poreally through a bioreactor that houses liver cells (hepatocytes) sandwiched between artificial plates or capillaries."

16. Some of these new hybrid types do not start off as either organism or artifact, but are simultaneously both from the very outset. Real nervous tissue is being connected directly to electronics. Steve Potter at Caltech (2002) merges biology with silicon: he has thousands of neurons growing in wells etched in silicon.

17. But note the recent example of the man who, instead of having a prosthetic arm fitted, had the arm of another man surgically grafted on. Suffering from psychological problems as a result, the man has now chosen to have the arm removed.

18. While also bearing in mind the question of whether the boundary between humans and nonhumans is organizationally as well as structurally "open" (see Capra 1996).

19. This may, very broadly speaking, tally with the distinction Strathern draws between agents and persons: "the person is construed from the vantage points of the relations that constitute him or her; she or he objectifies and is thus revealed in those relations. The agent is construed as the one who acts because of those relationships and is revealed in his or her actions" (Strathern 1988, 273).

20. Another possible example might be a potter at the wheel forming a vase out of a centered mass of clay—the hands of the potter almost melt into the clay, much as the blind man's hand "merges" with his stick.

21. Although one might note that humans seem perfectly capable of treating objects as psychological agents and social persons without imputing to them any sort of biological animacy. Hence the incredible and astonished reaction when idols or statues believed to have spiritual life start showing signs of biological life, such as tears or blood (Gell 1998, 122).

22. In this regard a potential comparison to the Automatic Turk is the subject of the 1999 film *Being John Malkovich*, directed by Spike Jonze. A puppeteer inexplicably finds himself able to enter into the mind of the movie star John Malkovich from which he can control the star's actions. John Malkovich thus becomes a marionette whose strings are being pulled from the inside, and the deception is total (see Knappett 2002a). One might also note the psychological effects upon the puppeteer, perhaps akin to the experiences of the operators of the Automatic Turk.

23. The psychological, social, and philosophical implications of the merger of man and machine are also addressed by Geary (2002) in *The Body Electric*.

24. Quoted by Lee and Brown (1994, 772). One might note too the distinction between the human *species* on the one hand and the human *condition* on the other, discussed by Viveiros de Castro (1998, 472).

25. See in Chapter 3 the use of another example by Latour, that of the Berliner key.

Chapter 3. Cognition, Perception, and Action

1. The term "connectionism" is more or less interchangeable with "parallel distributed processing" and "neural networks."

2. Well summarized by Kosslyn and Koenig (1992, 18), and Elman (1998, 488). First, in computers the processor is clearly distinct from stored memory (not the case in brains). Second, computers act as instructed according to rules, whereas brains discover new strategies and are not strictly rule-based. Third, processing in computers consists of discrete operations executed sequentially—this does not seem to be how brains work.

3. Another example of an approach that sits between semantic and connectionist approaches is schema theory, especially in the form put forward by Strauss and Quinn (1997; see also Westen 2001). Although schema theory is essentially internalist, when combined with connectionism it does have the capacity for flexible responses in the face of changing environmental situations.

4. It is perhaps therefore understandable that van Gelder and Port (1995, 38) cite Gibsonian ecological psychology as a major source of inspiration for dynamical approaches. See also discussion in Chapter 3.

5. One might, at least, speculate that behind the mapped structure of semantic memory there may exist self-organizing neural networks flexible enough to resonate with (and piggy-back on) external structures "out there" in the world. Moreover, external structures are often manipulated and ordered by humans so that they support internal information processing even more effectively. In other words, a human tendency to exploit the potential for *natural mappings* (Norman 1998) in the environment can become an active process of creating external *cultural mappings*. So, if there is mutual feedback between structure in the cultural environment and the structure of self-organizing feature maps in the brain, then the implications for material culture theory are most interesting. At the very least, it provides us with a possible neuroscientific perspective on the idea that brain, body and environment together forming a kind of network, along what we have described as a "vertical axis." See also, in this respect, Chazal (2000) for his idea of "resonance."

6. As is indeed also the case for van Gelder and Port (1995).

7. As was mentioned earlier, in such a view, the divisions often made between cognition, perception, and action seem to lose much of their significance.

8. As is apparent in the quote, such reasoning is not always confined to artifacts but may extend to organisms too. This includes not just animals such as slugs but presumably humans too. Humans may be seen to "design" themselves as objects, altering their own properties (through clothing, cosmetics, surgery) so as to channel the sorts of "projections" that people are able to make about them.

9. Although Costall notes that people with "visual agnosia" have great difficulties in perceiving the affordances of everyday objects. In a more recent article, he also suggests that this difficulty with affordances might also be extended to autism as a whole (Williams and Costall 2000), even though the problems autistic people have in dealing with objects have been underestimated, due to the common emphasis on the social difficulties they experience.

10. For example Michaels and Carello (1981); Reed (1988a, b, 1991); Costall (1981, 1997); Heft (1989); Noble (1991, 1993); Norman (1998); Glenberg (1997, 4); Clark (1997, 50–51).

11. Note too its importance in the work on perception by the anthropologist Tim Ingold (2000).

12. As one might imagine, some objects exhibit much greater elasticity in their affordances than others; indeed consumers too are variably elastic in their responses to objects.

13. Ingold (2000, 168, n.6), quoting Gibson (1979, 139).

14. Kirsh defines an affordance as a "dispositional property of a situation defined by a set of objects organised in a set arrangement, relativised to the action repertoire of a given agent. Agents perceive an affordance when they recognize that one of their possible actions is feasible in a situation" (Kirsh 1995).

15. That is to say, in the terms of our earlier discussion, humans are not just corporeal beings with *animacy*, but also mindful, intentional beings with *agency*.

16. As an aside, one might consider research by Gallese and Goldman (1998) on the neural activity within the brain of a macaque. When the macaque sees an experimenter pick up a slice of apple and bring it close, certain neurons fire. However, quite different neurons are activated when the macaque just sees the same object lying in a tray. The implication would seem to be that the macaque does not directly perceive the slice of apple as affording eating except in certain contexts. The macaque's understanding of what an object *is* depends on context. Going back to a point made earlier in the chapter, one might equally well say that the shape of a Tetris zoid only has affordances within the context of the game Tetris.

17. This is of course reminiscent of the supposed tendency of processual archaeology to focus on functional not symbolic meanings (Hodder 1986, 124).

18. We referred to Heft's work above in the context of the relationality of affordances.

19. For other work in this tradition and with clear links back to the Soviet psychology of Vygotsky (and indeed Luria and Leontiev), see Cole (1996) and Holland et al. (1998).

20. This example may be compared with another used by Latour—that of the gun, which is cited in Chapter 2 as a means of demonstrating Latour's "symmetrical" approach to the interactions between humans and nonhumans. Before the gun comes into human hands, it has little agency as an artifact; but once held, it in turn transforms the agency of the human. There is a degree of symmetry in their coming together; not all the power lies in human hands. Similarly, the key is embedded within a set of social practices in such a way that any agency that exists is distributed between human and nonhuman entities. The human holds the key but the key also has a hold on the human.

21. The distribution of meaning across networks is a theme that will be investigated in Chapters 4 and 5.

22. In this way design and productive manufacturing may be seen as revelatory processes, in which the inherent qualities of materials are brought forth out of concealment into unconcealment (cf. Heidegger 1977). See also Dreyfus (1993).

23. Burkitt (1998, 70) notes how Gibson was not particularly attuned to the idea that *socially created* artifacts afford action in a different way from natural objects (such as water), because they already have practice embodied in them. It is also true that Gibson paid relatively little attention to the idea that *agents* as well as objects may possess certain affordances. Given that objects may have the agency properties of humans, we must also agree that humans may sometimes be treated

as objects. This means that in some circumstances humans may be perceived in terms of the affordances they offer for different sorts of action. Reed (1988a) is one scholar who has attempted to push the concept of affordances to cover the animate environment.

24. It is interesting that from a developmental perspective, this phenomenon of "joint attention," as Tomasello refers to it (1999, 62), first appears among children between the ages of nine and twelve months. Before this age, infants can engage with objects, or with people, but not both at the same time.

25. In archaeological parlance, this separation is akin to that commonly made between the *functional* and the *symbolic* meanings of objects.

Chapter 4. The Dynamics of Networks

1. Cf. Chapter 2: "cognition is seamlessly distributed across persons, activity and setting" (quoting Lave 1988, 171).

2. Musso (2001, 195): "la symbolique du réseau se forge dans le double référent des images du corps et de la machine."

3. MTV is one of the global corporations discussed by Naomi Klein in her book *No Logo: Taking Aim at the Brand Bullies*. Moreover, she uses the term "network" in an interesting way, for example: "The logo network may have been designed to maximise consumption and minimise production costs . . . but regular people can now turn themselves into 'spiders' and travel across its web as easily as the corporations that spun it" (2000, 357). One might argue that global corporations are themselves networks of networks, creating a production network on the one hand and a consumption network on the other, with a series of exclusive connections between the two.

4. The capacity of some communication networks to act as if making decisions, and to self-organize to some extent, has led to the assessment that "large-scale networks appear as coherent, almost intelligent, organisms" (Kelly 1996).

5. See Deleuze and Guattari (1988), as discussed below.

6. This is true for other social insects too for that matter, notably termites (Turner 2000).

7. Which means that the colony can simply be referred to as an organism rather than a "superorganism."

8. For the source of this phrase, see discussion below of the work of Deleuze and Guattari (1988).

9. Hofstadter also makes use of the term "heterarchy" to describe nonhierarchical systems such as ant colonies and neural networks.

10. It is interesting to note that ANT shares common ground with "action theory," the distributed/embodied approach to cognition pursued by the likes of Norman, Hutchins, and Clark, and mentioned above in Chapter 3. According to Gomart and Hennion (1999) they share three principal goals. First, they attempt to go beyond an oscillation between action as determining and action as determined. Second, they "seek to describe the actions of humans and non-humans symmetri-

cally" (1999, 223). Third, each strips the subject of its cognitive and cultural capacities and returns them to its surroundings.

11. Here they employ, among other examples, the analogy of the ant colony, which resonates with our discussion earlier in this chapter on this very theme. They remark that "a rhizome may be broken, shattered at a given spot, but it will start up again on one of its old lines, or on new lines. You can never get rid of ants because they form an animal rhizome that can rebound time and again after most of it has been destroyed" (Deleuze and Guattari 1988, 9).

12. See previous note concerning their thoughts on ant colonies. Moreover, we might consider, in the light of our earlier discussion of neural networks, what Deleuze and Guattari have to say about cognition. They suggest that "thought is not arborescent" (1988, 9), and that the brain is "a multiplicity, forming an uncertain, probabilistic system." Extrapolating from this one might even say that neural networks, being an example of a rhizomatic structure, undergo a partial deterritorialization whenever their topographical maps adjust to new sensory data.

13. Fritjof Capra goes as far as to say that "during the second half of the century the network concept has been the key to the recent advances in the scientific understanding not only of ecosystems but of the very nature of life" (1996, 35).

Chapter 5. Networks of Meaning: A Sociosemiotics of Material Culture

Epigraph: Ponge (1977), 221.

1. This perspective is apparent in certain post-structuralist works, e.g., in Derrida, the later work of Baudrillard, and Barthes—cf. comments by Gottdiener (1995, 23).

2. For introductions to Sebeok's contribution, see Petrilli and Ponzio (2001) and Cobley and Jansz (1999, 119–29).

3. "This duality of signs as being both objects in the experiential world with consequences for our behaviour and also cognitive artifacts of consciousness is a fundamental aspect of socio-semiotics" (Gottdiener 1995, 10–11). Gottdiener's use of the word "duality" here is puzzling, as it suggests a degree of separation between the pragmatic and the significative dimensions, the very separation that he is trying to overcome. This ultimate failure to reconcile these two dimensions is in fact a criticism leveled at Gottdiener by Thomas (1998a); see below.

4. The representamen is also referred to by Peirce as the sign. Confusingly, Peirce also referred to the whole system of interpretant/representamen/object as the "sign."

5. In language there are some occasional exceptions, for example, with onomatopoeic words like "buzzing"—the physical characteristics (the sound) of the signifier do relate in a non-arbitrary way to the signified.

6. The perspective of the previous chapter can perhaps be loosely characterized as a semantic one. However, in this chapter we shall adopt a semiotic viewpoint. The semiotic and the semantic are, however, heavily interdependent, as emphasized, for example, by Henrietta Moore in her work on the theoretical relevance

of Paul Ricoeur to material culture theory (Moore 1990, 88–90). In the course of this chapter I shall try to stress the mutualism between semiotics and semantics in the construction of meaning.

7. Note that Bierman (1963) suggests that not all iconic signs are visual and not all visual signs are iconic. Some visual signs may actually be aniconic, for example some (but not all) traffic signs, punctuation signs, and even garments (which may be aniconic visual signs of different ethnic groups). Such signs are usually purely conventional, and thus presumably are operating as *symbols*.

8. For the purposes of this chapter I find the work of Sonesson (art history) more useful than that of Parmentier (semiotic anthropology), even though the latter has explicitly tackled issues of meaning in material culture using Peircean semiotics. Despite the fact that Parmentier's analysis is undoubtedly rich in detail and an invaluable contribution, his use of Peirce is, in my opinion, over-complicated. See comments earlier in this chapter.

9. Dubois (1990, 58): "L'image photographique apparaît d'abord, simplement et uniquement, comme une empreinte lumineuse, plus précisément comme la trace, fixée sur un support bidimensionnel sensibilisé par des cristaux d'halogénure d'argent, d'une variation de lumière émise ou réfléchie par des sources situées à distance dans un espace à trois dimensions."

10. Duchamp's work can be seen historically as the touchstone for the relations between photography and contemporary art (Dubois 1987, 233).

11. A footprint is also an imprint of an individual but, unlike a fingerprint, it is not usually understood to be a reliable index of a particular individual. This might be different, of course, in a culture where each individual wears a unique pair of shoes. Even photography, which may seem to Westerners a "pure" form of representation, demands a degree of cultural knowledge before the image can be successfully understood for what it is.

12. Peirce designated metaphor as one type of "hypoicon," thereby placing it within the category of iconicity.

13. Jakobson (1956) drew connections between metaphor and substitution and the paradigmatic axis of language. He contrasted these with metonymy and combination, and the syntagmatic axis of language.

14. This exact point is also made by Culler: "today metaphor is no longer one figure among others but the figure of figures, a figure for figurality" (2001, 210).

15. A recent and rare exception is represented by the work of D'Alleva (2001). Not only does she examine the interaction of metaphor and metonymy in material culture, she relates these concepts to Peircean semiotics.

16. And Ingold (2000) has emphasized how these two perspectives can arrive at compatible understandings of embodied meaning.

17. Tilley states that "our ordinary conceptual system by means of which we live, think and act is fundamentally metaphorical in nature" (1999, 16).

18. "Taking our inspiration from phenomenology as well as from cognitive psychology, we will argue for a revisionist version of semiotics" (Sonesson 1989, 14). As stated earlier in this chapter, Peirce's original work on semiotics had a phenomenological or "phaneroscopic" basis.

19. Thomas (1998a) identifies a paradox within Gottdiener's approach: it is

relatively straightforward for him to advocate that the material world plays a part in our sociosemiotic analyses, because he implicitly assumes that the material world is much less problematic than the universe of meaning.

20. Nellhaus creates an interesting parallel: Bhaskar, in his development of critical realism, formulates a semiotic triangle consisting of Saussure's signifier and signified, with the addition of the "referent" as the third, "objective" element (missing in Saussurean semiotics). Nellhaus considers Peirce's analysis of the sign to be strikingly similar, as it effectively consists of object (cf. "referent"), representamen (cf. "signifier") and interpretant (cf. "signified").

Chapter 6. Thinking Through: Meaning in Modern Material Culture

Epigraph: Perec (1987), 128.

1. David and Kramer further observe that this distinction may also be considered in terms of two distinct styles of analysis, dubbed "naturalist" and "antinaturalist" respectively.

2. Or, as Warnier puts it, "entre l'objet-corps et l'objet-signe" (1999, 82–83).

3. See Bijker's (1995) work on sociotechnical innovation, and how at certain moments a single artifact, such as the bicycle, may take on quite different meanings for distinct social groups.

4. Bonnot (2002, 141): "l'objet devient beau parce qu'il a été produit dans une usine locale, et parce que cette usine a depuis longtemps fermé ses portes. Esthétique du lieu, esthétique de l'ancien se rejoignent alors pour faire de l'objet usuel un objet esthétique."

5. It seems that stoneware is actually reused quite liberally and without much intervention of cultural constraint: "Cette capacité d'etre utilisé dans plusieurs champs sociaux ou dans plusieurs domaines d'activités quotidiennes se retrouve pour la quasi-totalité des produits de grès" (Bonnot 2002, 170).

6. Bonnot (2002, 165): "les utensiles et leurs utilisations sont autant de repères temporels permettant de se représenter la longue durée et de cristalliser la mémoire collective."

7. Cf. also Simondon (1958, 185): "Tout objet technique, mobile ou fixe, peut avoir son épiphane esthétique, dans la mesure où il prolonge le monde et s'insère en lui."

8. Bonnot (2002, 149): "Il ne peut donc y avoir, selon notre logique, d'objet *intrinsèquement utilitaire*, mais des objets *initialement destinés à être utilisés*."

9. Even though there may be nothing particularly beguiling about a urinal to a Western viewer, such technology might conversely be enormously beguiling to a non-Western viewer unfamiliar with techniques of mass production, etc.

10. Bonnot (2002, 50): "Les fours, dans lesquels se produit l'alchimie, ont acquis une personalité, ils sont comme des géants à qui on a donné nom ou surnom."

11. The intertwining of the material and the imaginary is, according to Warnier, a point developed by Mauss in tying together his work on magic, religion, and bodily techniques. "Mauss, dans son essai sur les techniques de corps, faisait

l'hypothèse que celles-ci sont mises en oeuvre dans le rapport aux arrière-mondes magiques et religieux et, d'une manière générale, dans le rapport aux representations. A ma connaissance, cette idée est tombée en déshérance dans l'anthropologie contemporaine" (Warnier 1999, 164). With regard to this last point, Gell might be an exception.

12. "Entre le souhait et sa réalisation, il n'y a pas, en magie, d'intervalle" (Mauss 1950, 56).

13. Indeed, it is not just through the magic of myth-making that a perfect union is sought; bearing in mind Gell's attempts to link art and magic, a similar process may be observed in contemporary art, and particularly in the work of Antony Gormley, a sculptor who creates molded lead figures from his own body (Hutchinson et al. 2000). His method requires him to maintain his body in a set position while the mold is cast around him. For an effective casting he must stay very still, a practice in which he is skilled thanks to training in yoga. By channeling his mental energy through his body and into the mold that will become a lead figure, Gormley achieves an unbroken flow between mind, body, and matter.

14. Indeed, one might note that, even without branding or advertising, objects/technologies will attract significative elaboration. As the Berliner key example from Chapter 3 showed, an object is invariably idea, action, and matter conjoined. Advertising simply serves to provide a more explicit and conscious level of symbolic commentary.

15. This relational perspective is neatly summed up by Genette in commenting on the nature of aesthetics: it is not the object that makes the relation aesthetic, but the relation that makes the object aesthetic. Genette (1997, 18) cited by (Bonnot 2002, 145): "ce n'est pas l'objet qui rend la relation esthétique, c'est la relation qui rend l'objet esthétique."

16. Despite our commitment to the idea of an embodied/situated mind, we should not forget that ideas can disembody themselves—humans do have the capacity to imagine future events, construct imaginary worlds, etc. (which makes it hard to ignore the arguments of representationalism, as discussed in Chapter 3). We do have to take account of the extent to which not all the meaning of an object resides within it or in its apparent associations.

Chapter 7. Archaeological Case Study: Drinking Vessels in Minoan Crete

1. As Carter (1998, 72) notes, "pressure-flaked obsidian blades fulfilled a primary symbolic role within Mesaran communities, whereas in the Cyclades their production and consumption was concentrated within the domestic arena."

2. Although it has been suggested that the first wheel-made pottery actually occurs earlier, in EM III-MM IA, the evidence for this is both slight and ambiguous. It is only in MM IB that wheel-made pottery is found in any quantity.

3. The technique used for the larger vessels was almost certainly wheel-fashioning—using rotative kinetic energy to finish and shape an essentially coil-built vessel on the wheel (Roux and Courty 1998). Although it has generally been consid-

ered that the smaller vessels were *wheel-thrown* (made entirely on the wheel from a lump of clay), it may well be the case that these too were wheel-fashioned (Knappett in press).

4. Some support for this idea comes in the form of experimental work conducted at Amarna in Egypt (Powell 1995).

5. Betts (1989, 12): "The invention and development of the potter's fast wheel between MM IB and MM II must have produced concomitant innovations in other arts. It is not difficult to imagine the stone-worker taking the rotating axle of the potter's wheel turning it through 90 to the horizontal and rotating it."

6. Enchantment is not fixed by the producer, but is negotiated between producer and consumer (e.g., the matchstick model of Salisbury Cathedral may not be particularly enchanting to adults, but it was to Gell the boy—example in Gell 1992, 1999).

Chapter 8. Conclusions

Epigraph: Simondon (1958), 9.

Bibliography

Akrich, M. 1994. "Comment sortir de la dichotomie technique/société; présentation des diverses sociologies de la technique." In B. Latour and P. Lemonnier, eds., *De la préhistoire aux missiles balistiques: L'intelligence sociale des techniques.* Paris: La Découverte, 105–31.

Albert, R. and A.-L. Barabási. 2002. "Statistical Mechanics of Complex Networks." *Review of Modern Physics* 74: 47. www.arXiv.org/abs/cond-mat/0106096.

Amaral, L. A. N., A. Scala, M. Barthélémy, and H. E. Stanley. 2000. "Classes of Behaviour of Small-World Networks." www.arXiv.org/abs/cond-mat/0001458.

Appadurai, A. 1986. "Introduction: Commodities and the Politics of Value." In A. Appadurai, ed., *The Social Life of Things: Commodities in Cultural Perspective.* Cambridge: Cambridge University Press, 1–62.

Ashby, W. R. 1952. *Design for a Brain.* New York: Wiley.

———. 1956. *An Introduction to Cybernetics.* London: Chapman and Hall.

Ashmore, M., R. Wooffitt, and S. Harding. 1994. "Humans and Others, Agents and Things." *American Behavioral Scientist* 37 (6): 733–40.

Atlan, H. 1979. *Entre le crystal et la fumée: Essai sur l'organisation du vivant.* Paris: Seuil.

Auster, P. 1989. *Moon Palace.* London: Faber and Faber.

Barabási, A.-L. 2002. *Linked: The New Science of Networks.* Cambridge, Mass.: Perseus Publishing.

Barabási, A.-L. and R. Albert. 1999. "Emergence of Scaling in Random Networks." *Science* 286: 509–12.

Bechtel, W. and A. Abrahamsen. 2002. *Connectionism and the Mind: Parallel Processing, Dynamics, and Evolution in Networks.* 2nd ed. Oxford: Blackwell.

Bechtel, W., A. Abrahamsen, and G. Graham. 1998. "The Life of Cognitive Science." In W. Bechtel and G. Graham, eds., *A Companion to Cognitive Science.* Oxford: Blackwell, 1–104.

Behura, N. K. 1978. *Peasant Potters of Orissa: A Sociological Study.* New Delhi: Sterling Publishers.

Betts, J. H. 1989. "Seals of Middle Minoan III: Chronology and Technical Revolution." In I. Pini, ed., *Fragen und Probleme der Bronzezeitliche Ägäischen Glyptik.* Corpus der Minoischen und Mykenischen Siegel 3. Berlin: Gebr. Mann Verlag, 1–17.

Bierman, A. K. 1963. "That There Are No Iconic Signs." *Philosophy and Phenomenological Research* 23 (2): 243–49.

Bijker, W. 1995. *Of Bicycles, Bakelites, and Bulbs: Toward a Theory of Sociotechnical Change.* Cambridge, Mass.: MIT Press.

Binford, L. 1965. "Archaeological Systematics and the Study of Cultural Process." *American Antiquity* 31: 203–10.

Bird-David, N. 1999. "'Animism Revisited': Personhood, Environment, and Relational Epistemology." *Current Anthropology* 40 (Suppl.): 67–92.

Blier, S. P. 1987. *The Anatomy of Architecture: Ontology and Metaphor in Batammaliba Architectural Expression.* Cambridge: Cambridge University Press.

Bloch, M. 1991. "Language, Anthropology, and Cognitive Science." *Man* 26: 183–98.

Bonnot, T. 2002. *La vie des objets: D'utensiles banales à objets de collection.* Paris: Editions Maison des Sciences de L'Homme.

Brooks, R. 1991. "Intelligence Without Representation." *Artificial Intelligence* 47: 139–59.

———. 2002. *Robot: The Future of Flesh and Machines.* London: Penguin.

Bruce, V., P. R. Green, and M.A. Georgeson. 1996. *Visual Perception: Physiology, Psychology, and Ecology.* Hove: Psychology Press.

Buchanan, M. 2002. *Small World: Uncovering Nature's Hidden Networks.* London: Weidenfeld and Nicholson.

Buchli, V. 1995. "Interpreting Material Culture: The Trouble with Text." In I. Hodder, G. Lucas, A. Alexandri, V. Buchli, J. Last, J. Carman, and M. Shanks, eds., *Interpreting Archaeology: Finding Meaning in the Past.* London: Routledge, 181–93.

Burkitt, I. 1998. "Bodies of Knowledge: Beyond Cartesian Views of Persons, Selves and Mind." *Journal for the Theory of Social Behaviour* 28 (1): 63–82.

Busby, C. 1997. "Permeable and Partible Persons: A Comparative Analysis of Gender and the Body in South India and Melanesia." *Journal of the Royal Anthropological Institute* 3 (2): 261–278.

Byers, A. M. 1994. "Symboling and the Middle-Upper Palaeolithic Transition." *Current Anthropology* 35 (4): 369–99.

Cadogan, G. 1977–78. "Pyrgos, Crete 1970–7." *Archaeological Reports*: 70–84.

———. 1990. "Lasithi in the Old Palace Period." *Bulletin of the Institute of Classical Studies* 37: 172–74.

Callon, M. 1987. "Society in the Making: The Study of Technology as a Tool for Sociological Analysis." In W. E. Bijker, T. P. Hughes and T. J. Pinch, eds., *The Social Construction of Technological Systems.* Cambridge, Mass.: MIT Press, 83–103.

Capra, F. 1996. *The Web of Life: A New Scientific Understanding of Living Systems.* New York: Doubleday.

———. 2002. *The Hidden Connections: A Science for Sustainable Living.* London: HarperCollins.

Carelman, J. 1994. *Catalogue d'objets introuvables.* Paris: Livre de Poche.

Carter, T. 1994. "Southern Aegean Fashion Victims: An Overlooked Aspect of Early Bronze Age Burial Practices." In N. Ashton and A. David, eds., *Stories in Stone.* Lithics Studies Society Occasional Paper 4. London: Lithics Studies Society, 127–44.

———. 1998. "Reverberations of the 'International Spirit': Thoughts Upon Cycladica in the Mesara." In K. Branigan, ed., *Cemetery and Society in the Aegean Bronze Age.* Sheffield: Sheffield Academic Press, 59–77.

Chabot, P., ed. 2002. *Simondon*. Paris: Vrin.

Chapman, J. 2000. *Fragmentation in Archaeology: People, Places and Broken Objects in the Prehistory of South-Eastern Europe*. London: Routledge.

Chazal, G. 2000. *Les réseaux du sens: De l'informatique aux neurosciences*. Seyssel: Champ Vallon.

Chevalier, S. 1992. "L'ameublement et le décor intérieur dans un milieu populaire urbain: Approche ethnographique d'une vrai-fausse banalité." PhD thesis, Université de Paris X.

Childe, V. G. 1956. *Piecing Together the Past: The Interpretation of Archaeological Data*. London: Routledge and Kegan Paul.

Childs, S. T. 1991. "Style, Technology, and Iron Smelting Furnaces in Bantu-Speaking Africa." *Journal of Anthropological Archaeology* 10: 332–59.

Chislenko, A. 1995. "Legacy Systems and Functional Cyborgization of Humans." www.lucifer.com/~sasha/articles/Cyborgs.html

Clark, A. 1996. "Philosophical Foundations." In M. A. Boden, ed., *Artificial Intelligence*. London: Academic Press, 1–22.

———. 1997. *Being There: Putting Brain, Body, and World Together Again*. Cambridge, Mass.: MIT Press.

———. 1998. "Embodied, Situated, and Distributed Cognition." In W. Bechtel and G. Graham, eds., *A Companion to Cognitive Science*. Oxford: Blackwell, 506–17.

Cobley, P. and L. Jansz. 1999. *Introducing Semiotics*. Cambridge: Icon Books.

Cole, M. 1996. *Cultural Psychology: A Once and Future Discipline*. Cambridge, Mass.: Harvard University Press.

Combes, M. 1999. *Simondon, individu et collectivité: Pour une philosophie du transindividuel*. Paris: Presses Universitaires de France.

Costall, A. 1981. "On How So Much Information Controls So Much Behaviour: James Gibson's Theory of Direct Perception." In G. Butterworth, ed., *Infancy and Epistemology: An Evaluation of Piaget's Theory*. Brighton: Harvester, 30–51.

———. 1995. "Socialising Affordances." *Theory and Psychology* 5: 467–82.

———. 1997. "The Meaning of Things." *Social Analysis* 41: 76–85.

Csordas, T. J., ed. 1994. *Embodiment and Experience: The Existential Ground of Culture and Self*. Cambridge: Cambridge University Press.

———. 1999. "The Body's Career in Anthropology." In H. L. Moore, ed., *Anthropological Theory Today*. Cambridge: Polity Press, 172–205.

Culler, J. 2001 (1981). *The Pursuit of Signs: Semiotics, Literature, Deconstruction*. London: Routledge.

D'Alleva, A. 2001. "Captivation, Representation, and the Limits of Cognition: Interpreting Metaphor and Metonymy in Tahitian *Tamau*." In C. Pinney and N. Thomas, eds., *Beyond Aesthetics: Art and the Technologies of Enchantment*. London: Berg, 79–96.

Dant, T. 1999. *Material Culture in the Social World: Values, Activities, Lifestyles*. Buckingham: Open University Press.

David, N. and C. Kramer. 2001. *Ethnoarchaeology in Action*. Cambridge: Cambridge University Press.

Dawkins, R. 1982. *The Extended Phenotype*. Oxford: Oxford University Press.

Day, P. M. and D. E. Wilson, 2000. "Consuming Power: Kamares Ware in Protopalatial Knossos," *Antiquity* 72: 350–58.

———. 2002. "Landscapes of Memory, Craft and Power in Prepalatial and Protopalatial Knossos." In Y. Hamilakis, ed., *Labyrinth Revisited: Rethinking Minoan Archaeology.* Oxford: Oxbow Books, 143–66.

Day, P. M., D. E. Wilson, and E. Kiriatzi. 1997. "Reassessing Specialisation in Prepalatial Cretan Ceramic Production." In R. Laffineur and P. P. Betancourt, eds., *TEXNH: Craftsmen, Craftswomen and Craftsmanship in the Aegean Bronze Age.* Liège: Aegaeum 16, 275–90.

———. 1998. "Pots, Labels and People: Burying Ethnicity in the Cemetery at Aghia Photia, Siteias." In K. Branigan, ed., *Cemetery and Society in the Aegean Bronze Age.* Sheffield: Sheffield Academic Press, 133–49.

Deacon, T. 1997. *The Symbolic Species.* London: Penguin.

Deledalle, G. 2000. *Charles S. Peirce's Philosophy of Signs: Essays in Comparative Semiotics.* Bloomington: Indiana University Press.

Deleuze, G. and F. Guattari. 1988. *A Thousand Plateaus: Capitalism and Schizophrenia.* London: Athlone Press.

Derfler, F. J. and L. Freed. 2000. *How Networks Work.* Indianapolis: Que.

Des Chene, D. 2001. *Spirits and Clocks: Machine and Organism in Descartes.* Ithaca, N.Y.: Cornell University Press.

Dietler, M. and I. Herbich. 1998. "Habitus, Techniques, Style: An Integrated Approach to the Social Understanding of Material Culture Boundaries." In M. Stark, ed., *The Archaeology of Social Boundaries.* Washington, D.C.: Smithsonian Institution Press, 232–63.

Dobres, M.-A. 2000. *Technology and Social Agency: Outlining a Practice Framework for Archaeology.* Oxford: Blackwell.

Doyle, R. 1997. *On Beyond Living: Rhetorical Transformations in the Life Sciences.* Stanford, Calif.: Stanford University Press.

Dreyfus, H. L. 1993. "Heidegger on the Connection Between Nihilism, Art, Technology, and Politics." In C. Guignon, ed., *The Cambridge Companion to Heidegger.* Cambridge: Cambridge University Press, 289–316.

Driessen, J. M. and C. F. Macdonald. 1997. *The Troubled Island: Minoan Crete Before and After the Santorini Eruption.* Liège: Aegaeum 17.

Dubois, P. 1987. "Photography and Contemporary Art." In J.-C. Lemagny and A. Rouillé, eds., *A History of Photography: Social and Cultural Perspectives.* Cambridge: Cambridge University Press, 232–53.

———. 1990. *L'acte photographique et autres essais.* Paris: Nathan.

Eco, U. 1979. *A Theory of Semiotics.* Bloomington: Indiana University Press.

Eigen, M. 1971a. "Molecular Self-Organisation and the Early Stages of Evolution." *Quarterly Review of Biophysics* 4 (2/3): 149.

———. 1971b. "Self-Organization of Matter and the Evolution of Biological Macro-Molecules." *Naturwissenschaften* 58: 465–523.

Elman, J. L. 1998. "Connectionism, Artificial Life, and Dynamical Systems." In W. Bechtel and G. Graham, eds., *A Companion to Cognitive Science.* Oxford: Blackwell, 488–505.

Evely, D. 1988. "The Potter's Wheel in Minoan Crete." *Annual of the British School at Athens* 83: 83–126.

Flannery, K. and J. Marcus. 1993. "Cognitive Archaeology." In C. Renfrew, C. Peebles, I. Hodder, B. Bender, K. Flannery, and J. Marcus, "Viewpoint: What Is Cognitive Archaeology." *Cambridge Archaeological Journal* 3 (2): 247–70.

Fowler, C. 2001. "Personhood and Social Relations in the British Neolithic with a Study from the Isle of Man." *Journal of Material Culture* 6 (2): 137–63.

———. 2002. "Body Parts: Personhood and Materiality in the earlier Manx Neolithic." In Y. Hamilakis, M. Pluciennik, and S. Tarlow, eds., *Thinking Through the Body: Archaeologies of Corporeality*. New York: Kluwer Academic/Plenum, 47–69.

Fox Keller, E. 1985. "The Force of the Pacemaker Concept in Theories of Aggregation in Cellular Slime Mold." In *Reflections on Gender and Science*. New Haven, Conn.: Yale University Press, 150–57.

———. 1995. *Refiguring Life: Metaphors of Twentieth-Century Biology*. New York: Columbia University Press.

Gallese, V. and A. Goldman. 1998. "Mirror Neurons and the Simulation theory of Mind-Reading." *Trends in Cognitive Sciences* 2: 493.

Garfinkel, A. 1987. "The Slime Mold Dictyostelium as a Model of Self-Organisation in Social Systems." In F. E. Yates, ed., *Self-Organizing Systems: The Emergence of Order*. New York: Plenum Press.

Geary, J. 2002. *The Body Electric: An Anatomy of the New Bionic Senses*. London: Weidenfeld and Nicholson.

Gell, A. 1988. "Technology and Magic." *Anthropology Today* 4 (2): 6–9.

———. 1992. "The Technology of Enchantment and the Enchantment of Technology." In J. Coote and A. Shelton, eds., *Anthropology, Art and Aesthetics*. Oxford: Clarendon Press, 40–67.

———. 1996. "Vogel's Net: Traps as Artworks and Artworks as Traps." *Journal of Material Culture* 1 (1): 15–38.

———. 1998. *Art and Agency: Towards a New Anthropological Theory*. Oxford: Clarendon Press.

———. 1999. *The Art of Anthropology: Essays and Diagrams*. Ed. E. Hirsch. London: Athlone Press.

Genette, G. 1997. *L'oeuvre de l'art*. Vol. 2, *La relation esthétique*. Paris: Seuil.

———. 1999. *The Aesthetic Relation*. Ithaca, N.Y.: Cornell University Press.

Gibson, J. J. 1979. *The Ecological Approach to Visual Perception*. Boston: Houghton Mifflin.

Glenberg, A. M. 1997. "What Memory Is For." *Behavioral and Brain Sciences* 20: 1–55.

Gofman, A. 1998. "A Vague but Suggestive Concept: The 'Total Social Fact.'" In W. James and N. J. Allen, eds., *Marcel Mauss: A Centenary Tribute*. Oxford: Berghahn, 63–70.

Goldblum, N. 2001. *The Brain-Shaped Mind: What the Brain Can Tell Us About the Mind*. Cambridge: Cambridge University Press.

Goldman, R. and S. Papson. 1998. *Nike Culture: The Sign of the Swoosh*. London: Sage.

Gomart, E. and A. Hennion. 1999. "A Sociology of Attachment: Music Amateurs, Drug Users." In J. Law and J. Hassard, eds., *Actor Network Theory and After.* Oxford: Blackwell, 220–47.

Goodman, N. 1970. "Seven Strictures on Similarity." In L. Foster and J. W. Swanson, eds., *Experience and Theory.* Amherst: University of Massachusetts Press, 19–29.

Goodwin, B. 1988. "Organisms and Minds: the Dialectics of the Animal-Human Interface in Biology." In T. Ingold, ed., *What Is An Animal?* London: Routledge, 100–109.

———. 1994. *How The Leopard Changed Its Spots: The Evolution of Complexity.* London: Weidenfeld and Nicholson.

Gordon, D. 1999. *Ants at Work: How an Insect Society Is Organized.* New York: Free Press.

Gordon, I. E. 1997. *Theories of Visual Perception.* 2nd ed. Chichester: J. Wiley.

Gosden, C. 2001. "Making Sense: Archaeology and Aesthetics." *World Archeology* 33 (2): 163–67.

Gosselain, O. P. 2000. "Materialising Identities: An African Perspective." *Journal of Archaeological Method and Theory* 7 (3): 187–217.

Gottdiener, M. 1995. *Postmodern Semiotics: Material Culture and the Forms of Postmodern Life.* Oxford: Blackwell.

Granovetter, M. 1973. "The Strength of Weak Ties." *American Journal of Sociology* 78: 1360–80.

Graves-Brown, P., ed. 2000. *Matter, Materiality and Modern Culture.* London: Routledge.

Greimas, A. J., 1990. *Narrative Semiotics and Cognitive Discourses.* London: Pinter.

Guare, J. 1990. *Six Degrees of Separation: A Play.* New York: Vintage.

Haraway, D. 1991. *Simians, Cyborgs and Women: The Reinvention of Nature.* London: Free Association Press.

———. 1995. "Cyborgs and Symbionts: Living Together in the New World Order." In C. H. Gray, ed., *The Cyborg Handbook.* London: Routledge, xi–xx.

Hawkes, C. 1954. "Archaeological Theory and Method: Some Suggestions from the Old World." *American Anthropologist* 56: 155–68.

Hayles, N. K. 1999. *How We Became Posthuman: Virtual Bodies in Cybernetics, Literature, and Informatics.* Chicago: University of Chicago Press.

Heidegger, M. 1927. *Being and Time.* Trans. J. Macquarrie and E. Robinson. New York: Harper and Row, reprinted 1962.

———. 1977. *The Question Concerning Technology and Other Essays.* Trans. W. Lovitt. New York: Harper and Row.

Heft, H. 1989. "Affordances and the Body: An Intentional Analysis of Gibson's Ecological Approach to Visual Perception." *Journal for the Theory of Social Behaviour* 19 (1): 1–30.

Helms, M. 1993. *Craft and the Kingly Ideal.* Austin: University of Texas Press.

Hodder, I. 1982. *Symbols in Action: Ethnoarchaeological Studies of Material Culture.* Cambridge: Cambridge University Press.

———. 1984. "Archaeology in 1984." *Antiquity* 58: 25–32.

———. 1986. *Reading the Past.* Cambridge: Cambridge University Press.

————. 1989. "This Is Not an Article About Material Culture as Text." *Journal of Anthropological Archaeology* 8: 250–69.

————. 1992. *Theory and Practice in Archaeology.* London: Routledge.

————. 1993. "Social Cognition." In C. Renfrew, C. Peebles, I. Hodder, B. Bender, K. Flannery, and J. Marcus, "Viewpoint: What Is Cognitive Archaeology." *Cambridge Archaeological Journal* 3 (2): 247–70.

————. 1999. *The Archaeological Process.* Oxford: Blackwell.

————, ed. 2001. *Archaeological Theory Today.* Cambridge: Polity Press.

Hofstadter, D. 1979. *Gödel, Escher, Bach: An Eternal Golden Braid.* New York: Basic Books.

Hogle, L. F. 1995. "Tales from the Cryptic: Technology Meets Organism in the Living Cadaver." In C. H. Gray, ed., *The Cyborg Handbook.* London: Routledge, 203–16.

Holland, D., W. Lachicotte, D. Skinner, and C. Cain. 1998. *Identity and Agency in Cultural Worlds.* Cambridge, Mass.: Harvard University Press.

Hölldobler, B. and E. O. Wilson. 1994. *Journey to the Ants: A Story of Scientific Exploration.* Cambridge, Mass.: Harvard University Press.

Hottois, G. 1993. *Simondon et la philosophie de la "culture technique".* Bruxelles: De Boeck Université.

Hutchins, E. 1995. *Cognition in the Wild.* Cambridge, Mass.: MIT Press.

Hutchinson, J., E. H. Gombrich, L. B. Njatin and W. T. J. Mitchell. 2000. *Antony Gormley.* 2nd ed. London: Phaidon Press.

Ingold, T. 1988. "Introduction." In T. Ingold, ed., *What Is An Animal?* London: Routledge, 1–16.

————. 2000. *The Perception of the Environment: Essays in Livelihood, Dwelling and Skill.* London: Routledge.

Jackson, M. 1989. *Paths Toward a Clearing: Radical Empiricism and Ethnographic Enquiry.* Bloomington: Indiana University Press.

Jakobson, R. 1956. "Two Aspects of Language and Two Types of Aphasic Disturbances." In R. Jakobson, and M. Halle, eds., *Fundamentals of Language.* The Hague: Mouton, 55–82.

Johnson, M. 1987. *The Body in the Mind.* Chicago: University of Chicago Press.

Johnson, S. 2001. *Emergence: The Connected Lives of Ants, Brains, Cities and Software.* London: Penguin.

Julien, M.-P. 1999. "Des 'techniques du corps' à la synthèse corporelle: Mises en objets." In M.-P. Julien and J.-P. Warnier, eds., *Approches de la culture matérielle: Corps à corps avec l'objet.* Paris: Harmattan, 15–27.

Katz, D. 1994. *Just Do It: The Nike Spirit in the Corporate World.* Holbrook, Mass.: Adams Media Corporation.

Kaufmann, J.-C. 1997. *Le coeur à l'ouvrage: Théorie de l'action ménagère.* Paris: Nathan.

Kelly, F. P. 1996. "Modelling Communication Networks, Present and Future." *Philosophical Transactions of the Royal Society of London* A354: 437–63.

Kirsh, D. 1995. "The Intelligent Use of Space." *Artificial Intelligence* 73: 31–68.

Kirsh, D. and P. Maglio. 1994. "On Distinguishing Epistemic from Pragmatic Action." *Cognitive Science* 18: 513–49.

Klein, N. 2001. *No Logo: Taking Aim at the Brand Bullies.* London: Flamingo.

Knappett, C. 1994. "Traditional Pottery Technologies in Two North West Frontier Villages, Pakistan." *South Asian Studies* 10: 99–111.

———. 1997. "Ceramic Production in the Protopalatial Mallia 'State': Evidence from Quartier Mu and Myrtos Pyrgos." In R. Laffineur and P. P. Betancourt, eds., *TEXNH: Craftsmen, Craftswomen and Craftsmanship in the Aegean Bronze Age.* Liège: Aegaeum 16, 305–11.

———. 1999a. "Assessing a Polity in Protopalatial Crete; the Malia-Lasithi State." *American Journal of Archaeology* 103: 619–45.

———. 1999b. "Tradition and Innovation in Pottery Forming Technology: Wheel-Throwing at Middle Minoan Knossos." *Annual of the British School at Athens* 94: 101–29.

———. 2000. "Overseen or Overlooked? Ceramic Production in a Mycenaean Palatial System." In J. Killen and S. Voutsaki, eds., *Economy and Politics in the Mycenaean Palace States.* Cambridge Philological Society Supplementary Volume 27. Cambridge: Cambridge Philological Society, 80–95.

———. 2002a. "Photographs, Skeuomorphs and Marionettes: Some Thoughts on Mind, Agency and Object." *Journal of Material Culture* 7 (1): 97–117.

———. 2002b. "Seeing Is Believing: The False Privilege of Images." Review article on S. Sherratt, ed., *The Wall Paintings of Thera* (2000). *Cambridge Archaeological Journal* 12 (1): 158–61.

———. in press. "Technological Innovation and Social Diversity at Middle Minoan Knossos." In G. Cadogan and E. Hatzaki, eds., *Knossos: Palace, City, State.* London: British School at Athens Studies.

Kosslyn, S. M. and O. Koenig. 1992. *Wet Mind: The New Cognitive Neuroscience.* New York: Free Press.

Kopytoff, I. 1986. "The Cultural Biography of Things: Commoditization as Process." In A. Appadurai, ed., *The Social Life of Things.* Cambridge: Cambridge University Press, 64–91.

Krauss, R. 1985. *The Originality of the Avant-Garde and Other Modernist Myths.* Cambridge, Mass.: MIT Press.

Kus, S. 2000. "Ideas Are Like Burgeoning Grains on a Young Rice Stalk: Some Ideas on Theory in Anthropological Archaeology." In M. B. Schiffer, ed., *Social Theory in Archaeology.* Salt Lake City: University of Utah Press, 156–72.

Lakoff, G. 1987. *Women, Fire, and Dangerous Things: What Categories Reveal About the Mind.* Chicago: University of Chicago Press.

Lakoff, G. and M. Johnson. 1980. *Metaphors We Live By.* Chicago: University of Chicago Press.

Laland, K. N., J. Odling-Smee, and M. W. Feldman. 2000. "Niche Construction, Biological Evolution, and Cultural Change." *Behavioral and Brain Sciences* 23: 131–75.

Latour, B. 1994. "Pragmatogonies: A Mythical Account of How Humans and Non-humans Swap Properties." *American Behavioral Scientist* 37 (6): 791–808.

———. 1996. "Lettre à mon ami Pierre sur l'anthropologie symétrique." *Ethnologie Française* 26 (1): 32–37.

————. 1999a. *Pandora's Hope: Essays on the Reality of Science Studies.* Cambridge, Mass.: Harvard University Press.

————. 1999b. "On Recalling ANT." In J. Law and J. Hassard, eds., *Actor Network Theory and After.* Oxford: Blackwell, 15–25.

————. 2000. "The Berlin Key or How To Do Words with Things." In P. M. Graves-Brown, ed., *Matter, Materiality and Modern Culture.* London: Routledge, 10–21.

Lave, J. 1988. *Cognition in Practice: Mind, Mathematics and Culture in Everyday Life.* Cambridge: Cambridge University Press.

Law, J. 1999. "After ANT: Complexity, Naming and Topology." In J. Law and J. Hassard, eds., *Actor Network Theory and After.* Oxford: Blackwell, 1–14.

————. 2000. "Networks, Relations, Cyborgs: on the Social Study of Technology." Draft version published by the Centre for Science Studies and Dept. of Sociology, Lancaster University, at: http://www.comp.lancs.ac.uk/sociology/soc042jl.html

Law, J. and A. Mol. 1995. "Notes on Materiality and Sociality." *Sociological Review* 43 (2): 274–94.

Le Breton, D. 2001. *Anthropologie du corps et modernité.* 2nd ed. Paris: Presses Universitaires de France.

Lee, N. and S. Brown. 1994. "Otherness and the Actor Network: The Undiscovered Continent." *American Behavioral Scientist* 37 (6): 772–90.

Lemieux, V. 1999. *Les réseaux d'acteurs sociaux.* Paris: Presses Universitaires de France.

Lemonnier, P. 1986. "The Study of Material Culture Today: Toward an Anthropology of Technical Systems." *Journal of Anthropological Archaeology* 5: 147–86.

————. 1996. "Et pourtant ça vole! L'ethnologie des techniques et les objets industriels." *Ethnologie Française* 26 (1): 17–31.

Lewontin, R. C. 1993. *Biology as Ideology: The Doctrine of DNA.* New York: Harper and Row.

LiPuma, E. 1998. "Modernity and Forms of Personhood in Melanesia." In M. Lambek and A. Strathern, eds., *Bodies and Persons: Comparative Views from Africa and Melanesia.* Cambridge: Cambridge University Press, 53–79.

Llinas, R. R. 2001. *I of the Vortex: From Neurons to Self.* Cambridge, Mass.: MIT Press.

Löfgren, O. 1996. "Le retour des objets? L'étude de la culture matérielle dans l'ethnologie suédoise." *Ethnologie Française* 26 (1): 140–50.

Lucas, G. 1995. "Interpretation in Contemporary Archaeology: Some Philosophical Issues." In I. Hodder, G. Lucas, A. Alexandri, V. Buchli, J. Last, J. Carman, and M. Shanks, eds., *Interpreting Archaeology: Finding Meaning in the Past.* London: Routledge, 3–29.

Luquet, G. H. 1913. *Les dessins d'un enfant: Étude psychologique.* Paris: Librairie Félix Alcan.

MacGillivray, J. A. 1998. *Knossos: Pottery Groups of the Old Palace Period.* London: British School at Athens Studies 5.

Maglio, P. P., T. Matlock, D. Raphaely, B. Chernicky, and D. Kirsh. 1999. "Interactive Skill in Scrabble." In *Proceedings of the 21st Annual Conference of the Cognitive Science Society*. Mahwah, N.J. : Lawrence Erlbaum.

Mahias, M.-C. 1993. "Pottery Techniques in India: Technical Variants and Social Choice." In P. Lemonnier, ed., *Technological Choices: Transformation in Material Culture Since the Neolithic*. London: Routledge, 157–80.

Margulis, L. 1997. "Speculation on Speculation." In L. Margulis and D. Sagan, eds., *Slanted Truths: Essays on Gaia, Symbiosis, and Evolution*. New York: Springer Verlag, 113–23.

Margulis, L. and M. McMenamin. 1997. "Marriage of Convenience." In L. Margulis and D. Sagan, eds., *Slanted Truths: Essays on Gaia, Symbiosis, and Evolution*. New York: Springer, 35–46.

Marinatos, N. 1993. *Minoan Religion: Ritual, Image, and Symbol*. Columbia: University of South Carolina Press.

Maturana, H. and F. Varela. 1980. *Autopoiesis and Cognition*. Dordrecht: D. Reidel.

Mauss, M. 1950/1936. "Les techniques du corps." *Journal de Psychologie* 32; reprint in *Sociologie et anthropologie*. Paris: Presses Universitaires de France, 363–86.

McCarthy, P. M. and W. A. Smith. 2002. "Mechanical Circulatory Support—A Long and Winding Road." *Science* 295: 998–99.

McCulloch, W. S. and W. H. Pitts. 1943. "A Logical Calculus of the Ideas Immanent in Nervous Activity." *Bulletin of Mathematical Biophysics* 5: 115–33.

Merleau-Ponty, M. 1962. *The Phenomenology of Perception*. London: Routledge.

Michaels, C. F. and C. Carello. 1981. *Direct Perception*. London: Prentice-Hall.

Milgram, S. 1967. "The Small-World Problem." *Psychology Today* 1: 60–67.

Mitchell, W. T. J. 1986. *Iconology: Image, Text, Ideology*. Chicago: University of Chicago Press.

Mithen, S. 1996. *The Prehistory of the Mind*. London: Thames and Hudson.

Mol, A. and J. Law. 1994. "Regions, Networks and Fluids: Anaemia and Social Topology." *Social Studies of Science* 24: 641–71.

Moore, H. 1990. "Paul Ricoeur: Action, Meaning and Text." In C. Tilley, ed., *Reading Material Culture: Structuralism, Hermeneutics and Post-Structuralism*. Oxford: Blackwell, 85–120.

Musso, P. 1997. *Télécommunications et philosophie des réseaux*. Paris: Presses Universitaires de France.

———. 2001. "Genèse et critique de la notion de réseau." In D. Parrochia, ed., *Penser les réseaux*. Seyssel: Champ Vallon, 194–217.

Nakou, G. 1995. "The Cutting Edge: A New Look at Early Aegean Metallurgy." *Journal of Mediterranean Archaeology* 8 (2): 1–32.

Nellhaus, T. 1998. "Signs, Social Ontology, and Critical Realism." *Journal for the Theory of Social Behaviour* 28 (1): 1–24.

Newell, A. and H. A. Simon. 1956. "The Logic Theory Machine." *IRE Transactions on Information Theory* 3: 61–79.

Noble, W. 1991. "Ecological Realism and the Fallacy of Objectification." In A. Still and A. Costall, eds., *Against Cognitivism: Alternative Foundations for Cognitive Psychology*. London: Harvester Wheatsheaf, 199–223.

———. 1993. "Meaning and the 'Discursive Ecology': Further to the Debate on

Ecological Perceptual Theory." *Journal for the Theory of Social Behaviour* 23 (4): 375–98.

Norman, D. 1998. *The Design of Everyday Things.* Cambridge, Mass.: MIT Press.

Palmer, S. E. 1999. *Vision Science: From Photons to Phenomenology.* Cambridge, Mass.: MIT Press.

Parmentier, R. J. 1994. *Signs in Society: Studies in Semiotic Anthropology.* Bloomington: Indiana University Press.

———. 1997. "The Pragmatic Semiotics of Cultures." *Semiotica* 116: 1–115.

Parrochia, D. 1993. *Philosophie des réseaux.* Paris: Presses Universitaires de France.

———. 2001. "La rationalité réticulaire." In D. Parrochia, ed., *Penser les réseaux.* Seyssel: Champ Vallon, 7–23.

Peirce, C. S. 1932. *Collected Papers of Charles Sanders Peirce.* Vol. 2, *Elements of Logic.* Ed. C. Hartshone and P. Weiss. Cambridge, Mass.: Harvard University Press.

———. 1955. "Logic as Semiotic: The Theory of Signs." In *Philosophic Writings of Peirce.* New York: Dover Publications.

Pelegrin, J. 1990. "Prehistoric Lithic Technology: Some Aspects of Research." *Archaeological Review from Cambridge* 9 (1): 116–25.

Perec, G. 1987. *Life, a User's Manual.* Trans. D. Bellos. London: Collins Harvill.

Petitot, J., F. J. Varela, B. Pacoud, and J.-M. Roy, eds. 2000. *Naturalizing Phenomenology: Issues in Contemporary Phenomenology and Cognitive Science.* Stanford, Calif.: Stanford University Press.

Petrilli, S. and A. Ponzio. 2001. *Thomas Sebeok and the Signs of Life.* Cambridge: Icon Books.

Pickering, A. 1995. *The Mangle of Practice: Time, Agency, and Science.* Chicago: University of Chicago Press.

Pickering, J. 1997. "Agents and Artefacts." *Social Analysis* 41 (1): 46–63.

Pinch, T. J. and W. E. Bijker. 1987. "The Social Construction of Facts and Artifacts: Or How the Sociology of Science and the Sociology of Technology Might Benefit Each Other." In W. E. Bijker, T. P. Hughes, and T. J. Pinch, eds., *The Social Construction of Technological Systems.* Cambridge, Mass.: MIT Press, 17–50.

Ponge, F. 1977. *L'atelier contemporain.* Paris: Gallimard.

Potter, S. 2002. "Mind over Metal." *New Scientist* 27 (February 2002): 27–29.

Poursat, J.-C. 1992. *Guide de Malia—Quartier Mu.* Paris: École Française d'Athènes, Sites et Monuments VIII.

———. 1996. *Artisans minoens: Les maisons-ateliers du Quartier Mu. Fouilles executées à Malia: Le Quartier Mu III.* Etudes Crétoises 32. Paris: École Française d'Athènes.

Poursat, J.-C. and C. Knappett. In press. *Le Quartier Mu IV. La poterie du Minoen Moyen II: Production et utilisation.* Etudes Crétoises 33. Paris: École Française d'Athènes.

Powell, C. 1995. "The Nature and Use of Ancient Egyptian Potter's Wheels." In B. J. Kemp, ed., *Amarna Reports* VI. London: Egypt Exploration Society, 309–335.

Preda, A. 2000. "Order with Things? Humans, Artifacts, and the Sociological Problem of Rule-Following." *Journal for the Theory of Social Behaviour* 30 (3): 269–98.

Preucel, R. W. and A. A. Bauer. 2001. "Archaeological Pragmatics." *Norwegian Archaeological Review* 34 (2): 85–96.

Prigogine, I. 1967. "Dissipative Structures in Chemical Systems." In S. Claessons, ed., *Fast Reactions and Primary Processes in Chemical Kinetics*. New York: Interscience.

Prigogine, I. and I. Stengers. 1984. *Order Out of Chaos: Man's New Dialogue with Nature*. New York: Bantam.

Rauschecker, J. P. and R. V. Shannon. 2002. "Sending Sound to the Brain." *Science* 295: 1025–29.

Rayner, A. D. M. 1997. *Degrees of Freedom: Living in Dynamic Boundaries*. London: Imperial College Press.

Reed, E. S. 1988a. "The Affordances of the Animate Environment: Social Science from the Ecological Point of View." In T. Ingold, ed., *What Is an Animal?* London: Unwin Hyman, 110–26.

———. 1988b. *James J. Gibson and the Psychology of Perception*. New Haven, Conn.: Yale University Press.

———. 1991. "James Gibson's Ecological Approach to Cognition." In A. Still and A. Costall, eds., *Against Cognitivism: Alternative Foundations for Cognitive Psychology*. London: Harvester Wheatsheaf, 171–197.

Renfrew, C. 1993. "Cognitive Archaeology: Some Thoughts on the Archaeology of Thought." In C. Renfrew, G. Lucas, A. Alexandri, V. Buchli, J. Last, J. Carman, and M. Shanks et al., "Viewpoint: What Is Cognitive Archaeology." *Cambridge Archaeological Journal* 3: 247–70.

———. 1994. "Towards a Cognitive Archaeology." In C. Renfrew and E. Zubrow, eds., *The Ancient Mind: Elements of Cognitive Archaeology*. Cambridge: Cambridge University Press, 3–12.

———. 1998. "Mind and Matter: Cognitive Archaeology and External Symbolic Storage." In C. Renfrew and C. Scarre, eds., *Cognition and Material Culture: The Archaeology of Symbolic Storage*. Cambridge: McDonald Institute Monographs, 1–6.

———. 2001. "From Social to Cognitive Archaeology: An Interview with Colin Renfrew." *Journal of Social Archaeology* 1 (1): 13–34.

Riggins, S. H. 1994a. "Introduction." In S. H. Riggins, ed., *The Socialness of Things: Essays on the Socio-Semiotics of Objects*. Berlin: Mouton de Gruyter, 1–6.

———. 1994b. "Fieldwork in the Living Room: An Autoethnographic Essay." In S. H. Riggins, ed., *The Socialness of Things: Essays on the Socio-Semiotics of Objects*. Berlin: Mouton de Gruyter, 101–47.

Roux, V. and M.-A. Courty. 1998. "Identification of Wheel-fashioning Methods: Technological Analysis of 4th–3rd Millennium BC Oriental Ceramics." *Journal of Archaeological Science* 25: 747–63.

Schlanger, N. 1994. "Mindful Technology: Unleashing the *chaîne opératoire* for an Archaeology of Mind." In C. Renfrew and E. Zubrow, eds., *The Ancient Mind: Elements of Cognitive Archaeology*. Cambridge: Cambridge University Press, 143–151.

Searle, J. R. 1983. *Intentionality. An Essay in the Philosophy of Mind*. Cambridge: Cambridge University Press.

Segalen, M. and C. Bromberger. 1996. "L'objet moderne: De la production sérielle à la diversité des usages." *Ethnologie Française* 26 (1): 5–16.

Semprini, A. 1995. *L'objet comme procès et comme action: De la nature et de l'usage des objets dans la vie quotidienne.* Paris: L'Harmattan.

Sherratt, S., ed. 2000. *The Wall Paintings of Thera: Proceedings of the First International Symposium.* 2 vols. Athens: Thera Foundation.

Sillar, B. 1996. "The Dead and the Drying: Techniques for Transforming People and Things in the Andes." *Journal of Material Culture* 1 (3): 259–89.

Simondon, G. 1958. *Du mode d'existence des objets techniques.* Paris: Aubier.

Sonesson, G. 1989. *Pictorial Concepts: Inquiries into the Semiotic Heritage and Its Relevance for the Analysis of the Visual World.* Lund: Lund University Press.

———. 1998. "Index, Indexicality." In P. Bouissac, ed., *Encyclopedia of Semiotics.* Oxford: Oxford University Press, 306–11.

Spitzer, M. 1999. *The Mind Within the Net: Models of Learning, Thinking, and Acting.* Cambridge, Mass.: MIT Press.

Spring, C. 1997. "Slipping the Net. Comments on Gell (1996)." *Journal of Material Culture* 2 (1): 125–31.

Stallings, W. 1999. *Data and Computer Communications.* 6th ed. Englewood Cliffs, N.J.: Prentice-Hall.

Standage, T. 2002. *The Mechanical Turk: The True Story of the Chess-Playing Machine That Fooled the World.* London: Penguin.

Stock, G. 2002. *Redesigning Humans: Choosing Our Children's Genes.* London: Profile Books.

Stout, D. 2002. "Skill and Cognition in Stone Tool Production: An Ethnographic Case Study from Irian Jaya." *Current Anthropology* 43 (5): 693–722.

Strain, A. J. and J. M. Neuberger. 2002. "A Bioartificial Liver: State of the Art." *Science* 295: 1005–9.

Strathern, M. 1988. *The Gender of the Gift: Problems with Women and Problems with Society in Melanesia.* Berkeley: University of California Press.

Strauss, C. and N. Quinn. 1997. *A Cognitive Theory of Cultural Meaning.* Cambridge: Cambridge University Press.

Strogatz, S. H. 2001. "Exploring Complex Networks." *Nature* 410: 268–76.

Suchman, L. A. 1987. *Plans and Situated Actions: The Problem of Human-Machine Communication.* Cambridge: Cambridge University Press.

———. 2000. "Human/Machine Reconsidered." Draft published by the Department of Sociology, Lancaster University, at: http://www.comp.lancs.ac.uk/sociology/soc040ls.html.

Taylor, C. 1985. "The Person." In M. Carrithers, S. Collins, and S. Lukes, eds., *The Category of the Person: Anthropology, Philosophy, History.* Cambridge: Cambridge University Press, 257–281.

Thomas, J. 1998a. "The Socio-Semiotics of Material Culture." *Journal of Material Culture* 3 (1): 97–108.

———. 1998b. "Some Problems with the Notion of External Symbolic Storage, and the Case of Neolithic Material Culture in Britain." In C. Renfrew and C. Scarre, eds., *Cognition and Material Culture: The Archaeology of Symbolic Storage.* Cambridge: McDonald Institute Monographs, 149–56.

————. 2000a. "Reconfiguring the Social, Reconfiguring the Material." In M. B. Schiffer, ed., *Social Theory in Archaeology*. Salt Lake City: University of Utah Press, 143–55.

————. 2000b. "Death, Identity and the Body in Neolithic Britain." *Journal of the Royal Anthropological Institute* 6 (4): 653–668.

Thomas, N. 2001. "Introduction." In C. Pinney and N. Thomas, eds., *Beyond Aesthetics: Art and the Technologies of Enchantment*. London: Berg, 1–12.

Tilley, C. Y. 1999. *Metaphor and Material Culture*. Oxford: Blackwell.

Tisseron, S. 1999. *Comment l'esprit vient aux objets*. Paris: Aubier.

Tolkien, J. R. R. 1991. *The Lord of the Rings: Fellowship of the Ring*. London: Harper-Collins.

Tomasello, M. 1999. *The Cultural Origins of Human Cognition*. Cambridge, Mass.: Harvard University Press.

Turner, J. S. 2000. *The Extended Organism: The Physiology of Animal-Built Structures*. Cambridge, Mass.: Harvard University Press.

Ullman, S. 1964. *Language and Style*. Oxford: Blackwell.

Van Gelder, T. and R. F. Port. 1995. "It's About Time: An Overview of the Dynamical Approach to Cognition." In R. F. Port and T. van Gelder, eds., *Mind as Motion: Explorations in the Dynamics of Cognition*. Cambridge, Mass.: MIT Press.

Vivieros de Castro, E. 1998. "Cosmological Deixis and Amerindian Perspectivism." *Journal of the Royal Anthropological Institute* n.s. 4: 469–88.

Wagner, R. 1991. "The Fractal Person." In M. Godelier and M. Strathern, eds., *Big Men and Great Men: Personifications of Power in Melanesia*. Cambridge: Cambridge University Press, 159–73.

Warnier, J.-P. 1999a. *Construire la culture matérielle: L'homme qui pensait avec ses doigts*. Paris: Presses Universitaires de France.

————. 1999b. "Conclusion: Le sujet comme 'roue d'engrenage'." In M.-P. Julien and J.-P. Warnier, eds., *Approches de la culture matérielle: corps à corps avec l'objet*. Paris: L'Harmattan, 135–142.

————. 2001. "A Praxeological Approach to Subjectivation in a Material World." *Journal of Material Culture* 6 (1): 5–24.

Warren, P. M. 1969. *Minoan Stone Vases*. Cambridge: Cambridge University Press.

Warwick, K. 2002. *I, Cyborg*. London: Century.

Wattenmaker, P. 1998. *Household and State in Upper Mesopotamia: Specialized Economy and the Social Uses of Goods in an Early Complex Society*. Washington, D.C.: Smithsonian Institution Press.

Watts, D. J. 1999. *Small Worlds: The Dynamics of Networks Between Order and Randomness*. Princeton, N.J.: Princeton University Press.

Watts, D. J. and S. H. Strogatz. 1998. "Collective Dynamics of 'Small-World' Networks." *Nature* 393: 440–42.

Wertsch, J.V. 1998. "Mediated Action." In W. Bechtel and G. Graham, eds., *A Companion to Cognitive Science*. Oxford: Blackwell, 518–25.

Westen, D. 2001. "Beyond the Binary Opposition in Psychological Anthropology: Integrating Contemporary Psychoanalysis and Cognitive Science." In C. C.

Moore and H. F. Mathews, eds., *The Psychology of Cultural Experience*. Cambridge: Cambridge University Press, 21–47.

Whitelaw, T. M., P. M. Day, E. Kiriatzi, V. Kilikoglou, and D. E. Wilson. 1997. "Ceramic Traditions at EM IIB Myrtos Fournou Korifi." In R. Laffineur and P. P. Betancourt, eds., *TEXNH: Craftsmen, Craftswomen and Craftsmanship in the Aegean Bronze Age*. Liège: Aegaeum 16, 265–274.

Wiessner, P. 1983. "Style and Social Information in Kalahari San Projectile Points." *American Antiquity* 48 (2): 253–276.

Williams, E. and A. Costall. 2000. "Taking Things More Seriously: Psychological Theories of Autism and the Material-Social Divide." In P. M. Graves-Brown, ed., *Matter, Materiality and Modern Culture*. London: Routledge, 97–111.

Wilson, D. E. and P.M. Day. 2000. "EM I Chronology and Social Practice: Pottery from the Early Palace Tests at Knossos." *Annual of the British School at Athens* 95: 21–63.

Wobst, M. 1977. "Stylistic Behaviour and Information Exchange." In C. E. Cleland, ed., *For the Director: Research Essays in Honor of James B. Griffin*. Anthropological Papers 61. Ann Arbor: University of Michigan Museum of Anthropology, 317–42.

Wood, G. 2002. *Living Dolls: A Magical History of the Quest for Mechanical Life*. London: Faber and Faber.

Zrenner, E. 2002. "Will Retinal Implants Restore Vision?" *Science* 295: 1022–25.

Index

action: repertoires, 49, 54; pragmatic, 42–43; epistemic, 42–43
Actor Network Theory, 74–76
Aegean prehistory, 135
aesthetic, 126, 180; effect versus intention, 127
aestheticism, 123
affordances, 45–57, 111–12, 175; and associations, 62, 867; canonical, 47; and constraints, 52, 112–13, 140–42; and meaning, 50; relationality of, 4; transparency of, 49–50
Africa, sub-Saharan, 158–60
agency, 11, 22, 75; artifactual, 26; distributed, 64; psychological, 19; social, 23; and structure, 75
agent, 11; technologized human, 25
aggregation, 69
anaesthesia, 24
animacy, 11, 16; biological, 19; corporeal, 24
ant colonies, 69–70
arborescence, 74, 78
Aristotelian, 12
art: and agency, 127; and magic, 128; Minoan, 135–36
artifacts: and artworks, 122–28; humanized, 24–25; as pivots, 55
associations, 85–86, 89
Automatic Turk, 26–28
autopoiesis, 13–14

Barabási, A.-L. and R. Albert, 80–81
Berliner key, 55–56, 122
bicycle technology, 74–75
Bijker, Wiebe, 74–76
bioartificial, 19
bioengineering, 19
biographies, 29
bio-psycho-social dimensions, 11
blind man's cane, 17, 24
Bonnot, Thierry, 118–23

cafetière, 56–57
Carelman, Jacques, 56–57
Cartesian dualism, 3, 168
causality, 91, 122, 155, 161
ceremonial feasting, 136
chaîne opératoire, 5, 6
Childe, V. G., 3–4
Clark, Andy, 40–41
cognition, 35–44; distributed, 41; embodied, 40; and metaphor, 102–4; and perception, 35; situated, 41
cognitive archaeology, 2–3, 5, 7, 137, 170
cognitive-processual approach, 6
cognitive psychology, 102
cognitive science, 3, 35, 168
coil-building of pottery, 159–60
communication, 8–9
connaissance, 5–6, 137
connectionism, 36
contiguity, 91, 94, 100, 115, 122, 147–54
coral, hermatypic, 14
Crete, Minoan, 135
Culler, Jonathan, 100–101
cup: carinated, 140–41, 147; coffee, 111–17; conical, 136; Kamares, 139, 163; Minoan, 136–66
cybernetics, 13
cyborg, 19

Danto, Arthur, 124–25
Day, P. M. and D. E. Wilson, 139–40
Deleuze, G. and F. Guattari, 77–78
design, 58
dividual and individual, 29
drinking vessels, 134–66
Duchamp, Marcel, 97–99, 123, 127
Dynamical Systems Theory, 40

earthworms, 16
Eco, Umberto, 96–97